Contents

Memorable Plays and Memorable Moments (3rd Edition)

Information in this book was derived from numerous news services and college media guides available on the internet, including, but not limited to, Wikipedia, Associated Press, Baltimore Sun, BCSFootball.com, Cotton Bowl Classic website, Orange Bowl Classic website, New York Times, Los Angeles Times, Washington Post, Lansing State Journal, SBNation.com, IndyStar, Columbia Spectator, Lincoln Star, "Sugar Bowl Classic: A history by Marty Mulé", Tiptop25.com, Bentley Historical Library, Notre Dame Football Review, Loyal Sons, Sun Bowl Classic website.

The following Colleges and Universities media guides and/or websites including, but not limited to: Alabama, Auburn, Auburn247Sports.com, Georgia, Florida, Florida State, FloridaGators.com, HuskerMax.com, Nebraska, HawgTales.com, Miami-Florida, Michigan State, MSUSpartans.com, Mississippi, SoonerStats.com, Tennessee, ND.edu.com, USC.

ISBN 9-781393805-34-2

Other Paperback Books available from Steve's Football Bible LLC

"Glorious Games of the Past"

"Trophy Games"

"Rivalry Games"

Bowl Games - 20th Century

Bowl Games – 21st Century   Bowl Games – 21st Century

www.stevesfootballbible.com

Introduction

My love of College Football began in 1966. As a 7 year old kid I remember watching the Notre Dame-Michigan State "Game of the Century". Next, I remember the 1967 USC-UCLA game and O.J. Simpson weaving through the UCLA defense for the winning touchdown with 6 minutes left in the game. I remember the 1968 Rose Bowl, Indiana vs USC. Who was this Indiana team that went to the Rose Bowl over my beloved Minnesota Golden Gopher's?   I attended my first college football game in 1971. Michigan vs Minnesota at Memorial Stadium on the Campus of the University of Minnesota. My Aunt Roberta took me. I was hooked after that. The Golden Gophers were defeated that day 35-7 by the Wolverines. George Honza of the Golden Gophers scored the only touchdown that day on a pass from Craig Curry. Ironically, I met Mr. Honza in January of 2017 while officiating a basketball game. Growing up in a rural farming town (Alden) in southern Minnesota, as a youth I spent a lot of my Saturday's in the fall watching ABC Sports College game of the week.

This book is for all the College Football fans, casual or diehard, historians or those who just plain love the College game. I hope everyone enjoys.

Steve Fulton

Chapter One {1869-1949}

What makes a truly memorable play or memorable moment? The dictionary defines it as worth remembering or easily remembered, especially because of being special or unusual. Is could be a play that turns the tide of a game, or results in a huge upset. Maybe it highlights a tremendous comeback or demonstrates remarkable toughness or athleticism. Is the fact it occurs in a big game, rivalry game or bowl game reason enough to call it a memorable play or moment? Does it matter if it's between FBS teams, FCS, Division II or Division III teams? I think not.

In this book I write about the many memorable plays and memorable moments throughout the history of College Football. There have been many as I have over 200 games that have stood the test of time as being memorable in their own special way. I have included games from all levels of College Football, but most of these involve the big schools (FBS). For many of you it will be a walk down memory lane as you remember listening or watching these games. For the younger generation, it will be a great learning experience about the great game(s) of college football past.

1869 – "The FIRST College Football game"

Princeton vs Rutgers - College Field - New Brunswick, New Jersey {Rutgers 6 Princeton 4}

The 1869 New Jersey vs. Rutgers football game was between the College of New Jersey (now the Princeton Tigers) and the Rutgers Queensmen played on November 6, 1869. The game's rules were based on the London Football Association's early set of rules, which had recently become the most popular set of rules for the game of football at the time. The game, along with the schism between the FA's rules and the rules of the Rugby Football Union, set in motion the events which would lead to the development of modern American football during the following decades.

Painting by Arnold Friberg

The game is considered to have been the first American football game ever played. The game was played in front of approximately 100 spectators. Rutgers won the game 6–4. The game took place at College Field (now the site of the College Avenue Gymnasium at Rutgers University) in New Brunswick, New Jersey. In what might be considered a beginning to college football rivalries, immediately after Rutgers won this game, Princeton's players were literally run out of town by the winning Rutgers students. The Princeton students reportedly jumped in their carriages and quickly made the 20-mile trip back to their campus.

1893 - "First Helmet"

Army vs Navy - Worden Field - Annapolis, Maryland {Navy 6 Army 4}

First documented use of a football helmet by a player in a game. Midshipman Joseph M. Reeves had a crude leather helmet made by a local shoemaker/blacksmith and wore it in this game after being warned by doctors that he risked death if he continued to play football after suffering a kick to the head in an earlier game.

1903 - Trick or Treat

Carlisle at Harvard - Harvard Stadium - Cambridge, Massachusetts {Harvard 12 Carlisle 11}

In 1903, an Indian team coached by the legendary Pop Warner first employed its infamous "hidden-ball play" against heavily favored Harvard. Warner, as coach at Cornell, had already used it against Penn State in 1897, but it had not achieved much notice. Carlisle led Harvard at halftime, and hoping to keep the game's momentum, Warner elected to try the play on the ensuing kickoff. Harvard

Chapter One {1869-1949}

What makes a truly memorable play or memorable moment? The dictionary defines it as worth remembering or easily remembered, especially because of being special or unusual. Is could be a play that turns the tide of a game, or results in a huge upset. Maybe it highlights a tremendous comeback or demonstrates remarkable toughness or athleticism. Is the fact it occurs in a big game, rivalry game or bowl game reason enough to call it a memorable play or moment? Does it matter if it's between FBS teams, FCS, Division II or Division III teams? I think not.

In this book I write about the many memorable plays and memorable moments throughout the history of College Football. There have been many as I have over 200 games that have stood the test of time as being memorable in their own special way. I have included games from all levels of College Football, but most of these involve the big schools (FBS). For many of you it will be a walk down memory lane as you remember listening or watching these games. For the younger generation, it will be a great learning experience about the great game(s) of college football past.

1869 – "The FIRST College Football game"
Princeton vs Rutgers - College Field - New Brunswick, New Jersey {Rutgers 6 Princeton 4}

The 1869 New Jersey vs. Rutgers football game was between the College of New Jersey (now the Princeton Tigers) and the Rutgers Queensmen played on November 6, 1869. The game's rules were based on the London Football Association's early set of rules, which had recently become the most popular set of rules for the game of football at the time. The game, along with the schism between the FA's rules and the rules of the Rugby Football Union, set in motion the events which would lead to the development of modern American football during the following decades.

Painting by Arnold Friberg

The game is considered to have been the first American football game ever played. The game was played in front of approximately 100 spectators. Rutgers won the game 6–4. The game took place at College Field (now the site of the College Avenue Gymnasium at Rutgers University) in New Brunswick, New Jersey. In what might be considered a beginning to college football rivalries, immediately after Rutgers won this game, Princeton's players were literally run out of town by the winning Rutgers students. The Princeton students reportedly jumped in their carriages and quickly made the 20-mile trip back to their campus.

1893 - "First Helmet"
Army vs Navy - Worden Field - Annapolis, Maryland {Navy 6 Army 4}

First documented use of a football helmet by a player in a game. Midshipman Joseph M. Reeves had a crude leather helmet made by a local shoemaker/blacksmith and wore it in this game after being warned by doctors that he risked death if he continued to play football after suffering a kick to the head in an earlier game.

1903 - Trick or Treat
Carlisle at Harvard - Harvard Stadium - Cambridge, Massachusetts {Harvard 12 Carlisle 11}

In 1903, an Indian team coached by the legendary Pop Warner first employed its infamous "hidden-ball play" against heavily favored Harvard. Warner, as coach at Cornell, had already used it against Penn State in 1897, but it had not achieved much notice. Carlisle led Harvard at halftime, and hoping to keep the game's momentum, Warner elected to try the play on the ensuing kickoff. Harvard executed the kick, and the Indians formed a circle around the returner. With the aid of a specially altered jersey, the ball was placed up the back of the returner. The Indians broke the huddle and quarterback Jimmy Johnson shoved the ball in the back of guard Charlie Dillon, then spread out in different directions. Each player feigned carrying the ball, except Dillon, the man with the ball up the back of his jersey. The ruse confused the Crimson players, and they scrambled to find the ball carrier. Dillon, empty arms swinging, sprinted the length of the field ignored by the Crimson, raced into the end zone. Referee Mike Thompson, forewarned by Warner, ruled it a touchdown. With the score, Carlisle extended its lead to 11–0, but Harvard came back and eventually won 12–11. Nevertheless, the close match, and trick play, resulted in national attention. Warner had learned the trick from John Heisman while facing Auburn in 1895 during his tenure as coach of the Georgia Bulldogs. In 1911, the NCAA changed its rules, condemning the hidden-ball play to backyards forever.

1905 - Down and Out
Michigan at Chicago - Marshall Field - Chicago, Illinois {Chicago 2 Michigan 0}

The game, dubbed "The First Greatest Game of the Century," broke Michigan's 56-game unbeaten streak and ended in controversy in the final game of 1905 and marked the end of the "Point-a-Minute" years. The 1905 Michigan team had outscored opponents 495-0 in its first 12 games. The game was lost in the final ten minutes of play when Denny Clark was tackled for a safety as he attempted to return a punt from behind the goal line. Clark caught a Chicago punt in the end zone, crossed the goal line and cried, "Down!" But the official didn't hear him, and when Mark Catlin tackled Clark back into the end zone, Amos Alonzo Stagg's Chicago squad scored the only two points of the game. Newspapers described Clark's play as "the wretched blunder" and a "lapse of brain work."

Marshall Field - 1903

Clark transferred to M.I.T. the following year and was haunted by the play for the rest of his life. In 1932, he shot himself, leaving a suicide note that reportedly expressed hope that his "final play" would atone for his error at Marshall Field in 1905. It took proponents 11 years, citing Michigan's loss all the while, to change the rule.

1911 - "First Homecoming Game"
Kansas at Missouri - Rollins Field - Columbia, Missouri {Missouri 3 Kansas 3}

This game is widely considered, although contested, to be the first college football homecoming game ever played. More than 1,000 people gathered in downtown Lawrence, Kansas to watch a mechanical reproduction of the game while it was being played.

First Homecoming game at Rollins Field in Columbia, Missouri

A Western Union telegraph wire was set up direct from Columbia, with information "broadcast" to Lawrence. A group of people then would announce the results of the previous play and used a large model of a football playing field to show the results. Those in attendance would cheer as though they were watching the game live, including the school's *Rock Chalk, Jayhawk* cheer.

1911- The Dobie "Bunk Play"
Washington at Oregon - Multnomah Field - Portland, Oregon {Washington 29 Oregon 3}

Gilmour Dobie was a legendary coach for the University of Washington football team. The team has been called Huskies ever since 1922, but in the Dobie era it did not have an official name or mascot. In his nine seasons at UW (1908-1916), Dobie never lost a game, and his remarkable record of 58-0-3 has never been surpassed. He is honored in the College Football, Husky, University of Minnesota, University of North Dakota, Naval Academy, Cornell, and Boston College Halls of Fame.

Dobie managed to infuriate the University of Oregon in 1911. He came up with his devious play (legal by rules of the day) forever known as the "Bunk Play." Over and over they practiced it. Said Wee Coyle, "For thirty minutes each night we practiced this play, and the eleven starters were the only ones in on the secret. Dobie had us try it out finally on the second team in a scrimmage. It worked so well and I remember that the coach burst out laughing, the only occasion he did that in my four years under him." Washington wins 29-3 in Portland, using a trick play orchestrated by Wee Coyle, who pretends his leather helmet is the football. All of Oregon's defensive players chase the helmet-lugging Coyle, while on the opposite side of the field, a lonesome Wayne Sutton carries the real pigskin over the goal line. The play stupefied spectators and many left the stands after the game unable to fathom the workings of the fake." Recalled Coyle years later with a laugh, "It was great! Nobody knew what the hell happened and here was Sutton with a touchdown." Washington used it one other time, before it was declared illegal. The University of Oregon led the protest.

1921 - "First Radio Broadcast"
West Virginia at Pittsburgh - Forbes Field - Pittsburgh, Pennsylvania {Pittsburgh 21 West Virginia 13}

This game isn't known for a significant play, but for its historical significance, being the first radio broadcast of a college football game. The game was broadcast live by KDKA Radio, the first college football game to do so. The game was played at Forbes Field in Pittsburgh, Pennsylvania. Pittsburgh won the game 21–13, after West Virginia's George Hill returned a kickoff for a touchdown on the final play of the game. It was the 17th meeting of the Backyard Brawl, a rivalry game between the two programs.

1922 - "Rise of the South begins"
Alabama at Pennsylvania - Franklin Field - Philadelphia, Pennsylvania {Alabama 9 Pennsylvania 7}

Beating one of the "big 4" Ivy League institutions in a major upset, it is considered one of the most important wins in Alabama football history, giving the team some of its first national recognition. One writer called the game the hardest fought battle on Penn's field in seven years. John Heisman's Penn team was highly favored. Noted sports columnist Grantland Rice predicted a 21–0 Quaker victory. Alabama quarterback Charles Bartlett set up the winning touchdown with a dash from the 35-yard line to the 6. College Football Hall of Fame inductee Pooley Hubert was a freshman at fullback. After the game, when the news reached Tuscaloosa, "they started burning red fires and celebrating in a manner that Tuscaloosa had never seen before in its history."

Action in the 1922 Alabama-Pennsylvania game

It was a well-known "fact" around the football world that the West coast was the power and the East was a close second with the South being a distant third but Alabama travelled 2,500 miles up to Pennsylvania and stunned all the critics with their 9-7 victory. Penn's game against Navy the afternoon before game the coaching staff a chance to see the squad in person before the game which gave Alabama a tactical advantage. Alabama got going early in the game when Bull Wesley kicked a long field goal to but the Tide up by 3. Later in the quarter Penn came back to take the lead but Bama was not about to go home on the losing end. Alabama came back strong in the second quarter on the back of leader Charles Bartlett. Bartlett drove the team down the field on most notably a 22 yard run from the 27 that put the ball on the Penn 4 yard line. Pooley Hubert went in the rest of the way but fumbled the ball in the end zone. Shorty Propst recovered the ball and gave Alabama the 9-7 lead that they would never give up. Penn threatened again very late in the fourth quarter but faced a fourth and long play. Alabama covered the receivers downfield and threw the quarterback for a loss and the game went the way of Alabama and also in some ways the entire south.

1922 - "First National Radio Broadcast"
Princeton at Chicago - Stagg Field - Chicago, Illinois {Princeton 21 Chicago 18}

Once again, this game isn't known for a significant play, but for its historical significance. The 1922 Princeton vs. Chicago football game, was the first college football game to feature an intersectional audience on radio. The game was broadcast from KYW, a Westinghouse radio station in Chicago, to WEAF, an American Telephone & Telegraph station in New York City, and from there to the rest of the country. The "hotly contested" match-up was the first game to be broadcast nationwide on radio. Princeton's team won, 21–18. It was to be the national champion of 1922, and in this game received its nickname, "Team of Destiny", from Grantland Rice.

Action in the 1922 Princeton-Chicago game

Fullback John Webster Thomas scored Chicago's three touchdowns, one in each of the first three quarters, but the team failed to score an extra point for any of them. Walter Camp wrote in picking Thomas first-team All-American: "It is safe to say he did far more against the Princeton line in effective scoring than did any backs of the East who met the Tigers". The Tigers had scored a single touchdown in the second quarter, and also the extra point for a total of seven; they then scored two additional touchdowns for 14 points in the final quarter to win the game, while holding Chicago scoreless. With 12 minutes to play and Chicago nursing an 18–7 lead, Howdy Gray of Princeton picked up a Jimmy Pyott fumble and ran it 40 yards for the touchdown. Gray's father, the president of the Union Pacific Railroad, reacted by waving his program in the air, striking a woman in the shoulder. After an additional Princeton touchdown was scored, Chicago responded with a fierce drive ending in a goal line stand with Thomas falling short of the goal. Halfback Harry "Maud" Crum scored Princeton's other touchdowns.

1924 - "Galloping Ghost is born"
Michigan at Illinois - Memorial Stadium - Champaign, Illinois {Illinois 39 Michigan 14}

A flashing, red-haired youngster, running and dodging with the speed of a deer, gave 67,000 jammed into the new $1,700,000 Illinois Memorial Stadium the thrill of their lives today, when Illinois vanquished Michigan, 39 to 14. Harold (Red) Grange, Illinois phenomenon, All- America halfback, who attained gridiron honors of the nation last season, was the dynamo that furnished the thrills. Grange doubled and redoubled his football glory in the most remarkable exhibition of running, dodging and passing seen on any gridiron in years-an exhibition that set the dumbfounded spectators screaming with excitement. Individually, Grange scored five of Illinois' six touchdowns in a manner that left no doubt as to his ability to break through the most perfect defense. He furnished one thrill after another.

Red Grange "The Galloping Ghost"

On the very first kickoff Grange scooped up the ball on the Illinois five-yard line and raced 95 yards through the Michigan eleven for a touchdown in less than ten seconds after the starting whistle blew. Before the Michigan team could recover from its shock, Grange had scored three more touchdowns in rapid succession, running 66, 55 and 40 yards, respectively, for his next three scores. Coach Bob Zuppke took him out of the line-up before the first quarter ended. He returned later to heave several successful passes and score a fifth touchdown in the last half. Grange surpassed all his former exploits in every department. He handled the ball 21 times, gained 402 yards and scored 5 touchdowns.

On the second kickoff, Grange received the ball and raced 10 yards. Illinois lost the ball on downs but recovered by the same method on its 33-yard line. Then Grange tore off 66 yards for a second touchdown around right end. A moment later, on the same play, he ran 55 yards for a touchdown and shortly after scored his fourth of the quarter from Michigan's 40-yard line.

1926 Rose Bowl - "South rises again"
Alabama vs Washington - The Rose Bowl Stadium - Pasadena, California {Alabama 20 Washington 19}

The 1926 Rose Bowl Game was held on January 1, 1926 in Pasadena, California. The game is commonly referred to as **"the game that changed the south."** The game featured the Alabama Crimson Tide, making their first bowl appearance, and the Washington Huskies. Alabama were victorious 20–19, as they scored all twenty points in the third quarter. With the victory, the Crimson Tide were awarded with their first National Championship. The game made its radio broadcast debut, with Charles Paddock, a sportswriter and former Olympian track star, at the microphone. Coach Wade was later inducted into the Rose Bowl Hall of Fame in 1990. Wallace Wade's Alabama (9-0) launches the "Age of Dixie" by edging Washington (10-0-1) in a 20-19 thriller despite the heroics of the Huskies' great running back George Wilson. In the 38 minutes Wilson can play, Washington scores three times and gains 300 yards, but in the 22 minutes he is out with an injury, his team gains only 17 yards and is outscored three touchdowns to none. Wilson has 134 yards in 15 carries and completed five passes. Johnny Mack Brown and "Pooley" Hubert lead Alabama rally after trailing 12-0 with three third-quarter touchdowns. Bill Buckler's two of three conversions makes the victory difference.

Johnny Mack Brown of Alabama

The play that made the difference in the game was a 30 yard touchdown pass from Pooley Hubert to Johnny Mack Brown. A fumble gave Alabama another chance at the Washington 30. On first down Hubert told Brown to run as fast as he could for the goal. "When I reached the three, I looked around," said Brown. "Sure enough, the ball was coming down over my shoulder. I took it in stride, used my stiff arm on one man and went over carrying somebody. The place was really in an uproar."

1928 - "Win one for the Gipper"
Army vs Notre Dame - Yankee Stadium - Bronx, New York {Notre Dame 12 Army 6}

Notre Dame had its worst season under Knute Rockne, going 5-4. It's the only time in 13 seasons that he lost more than two games. Despite the struggles of the Fighting Irish, they came from behind to win one for the Gipper and end Army's unbeaten run at Yankee Stadium. There was no score after two quarters, when Rockne supposedly gave the most famous motivational speech in sports history, telling his team about a dying request of former Notre Dame star George Gipp, who died in 1920 at age 25, encouraging Rockne at his hospital bedside to use his story as motivation one day, to tell his team to dig deep and "win just one for the Gipper."

Action in the 1928 Army-Notre Dame game

On the field, Notre Dame then fell behind 6-0 in the second half before mounting a comeback. The Irish scored one TD to even the score, and Johnny O'Brien came off the bench in the fourth quarter to catch the go-ahead 35-yard TD from Johnny Niemiec late in the game. Army went on a drive to try to tie or win, but the final whistle blew with the Cadets just shy of the goal line, and Notre Dame's upset win would go on to be immortalized.

1929 Rose Bowl - "Wrong way Riegels"
Georgia Tech vs California - The Rose Bowl Stadium - Pasadena, California {Georgia Tech 8 California 7}

The 1929 Rose Bowl was the 15th annual Rose Bowl Game. The Georgia Tech Yellow Jackets defeated the California Golden Bears by a score of 8–7. The game was notable for a play by California All-American Roy Riegels in which he scooped up a Georgia Tech fumble and ran towards his own goal line. The two-point safety on the ensuing punt proved to be the margin of victory.

Roy Riegels of California

California teammates consoling Riegels

The margin of victory for Tech was provided in the second quarter. With the score tied 0-0, Tech's Stumpy Thomason was hit by the Golden Bears' Benny Lom and fumbled around the Tech 35-yard line. California center Roy Riegels scooped up the ball and raced for the end zone. But in the confusion, Riegels got turned around and was heading toward the wrong end zone. He ran 64 yards, reaching the California one-yard line before he was tackled by his own teammate, Lom. On the next play, Tech's Vance Maree broke through the line and blocked Lom's punt for a safety. The Golden Tornado of Georgia Tech completed a perfect 10-0 season by stunning California, 8-7, in one of the strangest Rose Bowl games ever played.

1934 - "Columbia's greatest win"

1934 Rose Bowl - Rose Bowl Stadium - Pasadena, California {Columbia 7 Stanford 0}

Winning the 1934 Rose Bowl has, to date, been the greatest accomplishment in Columbia football history. For the three days before the game, torrential rains soaked the field. The Pasadena fire department pumped out the stadium. Game day itself, though, was also uncharacteristically rainy for Southern California, and the muddy field rendered the game scoreless going into the second quarter.

Al Barabas runs around left end for the game's only touchdown

At that time, and with the ball on the Stanford 17-yard line, Columbia quarterback Cliff Montgomery executed a trick play called KF-79. During the play, he spun and slipped the ball to Al Barabas, then faked a handoff to Ed Brominski, who ran in the opposite direction. While the Indians went for Montgomery and Brominski, Barabas successfully ran around the defense to score for the Lions. Columbia ended up winning the game, 7-0, capping one of the biggest upsets in Rose Bowl history. The win also cemented Lou Little's reputation at Columbia as the Lions' greatest coach thus far.

1934 - "Jock Jam"

Minnesota at Pittsburgh - Pitt Stadium - Pittsburgh, Pennsylvania {Minnesota 13 Pittsburgh 7}

National powers Minnesota and Pittsburgh are tied, 7-7, in the fourth quarter. The Gophers are stalled, fourth-and-goal at the Panthers' 4. Glenn Seidel hands off to Stan Kostka, who runs into the line, turns and laterals to Pug Lund, who passes to Bob Tenner for the touchdown. Tenner had also caught the touchdown pass that beat Pitt 7-3 in 1933. Pittsburgh coach Jock Sutherland would call the 13-7 loss "the greatest game between the two greatest teams that ever played on the same field."

Pitt had gone 8-1 in 1933, losing 7-3 at Minnesota, and talk heading into the 1934 rematch was that the winner would go on to take the mythical national championship. The week before the game, Pitt hosted tormentor Southern Cal, who had beaten them 47-14 and 35-0 in Rose Bowls following the 1929 and 1932 seasons, and Pitt got their revenge 20-6. That had everyone abuzz about Pitt, though USC ended up having a bad season (4-6-1). Minnesota, meanwhile, had more than 2 weeks to prepare for Pitt. Their previous game had been a 20-0 win over 6-3 Nebraska. This was the furthest East Minnesota had ever ventured, and many Eastern writers would be seeing them for the first time. Pug Lund and ends Butch Larson and Bob Tenner played all 60 minutes for Minnesota. Pittsburgh was held to just 2 of 14 passing, and they threw 3 interceptions. Pitt won out, routing 6-3 Notre Dame 19-0, 6-3 Nebraska 25-6, and 8-1 Navy 31-7, and they ended up ranked #3. Minnesota would win their remaining 5 games and finish the season 8-0 on the way to being crowned National Champions, outscoring all opponents 280-38, including 4 shutouts (Nebraska, Michigan, Indiana and Wisconsin).

1935 - "Maroons shock Cadets"

Mississippi State at Army - Michie Stadium - West Point, New York {Mississippi State 13 Army 7}

The game was arranged by Coach Major Ralph Sasse, a WWI veteran and regarded as an armored warfare genius by no less of an authority than George Patton. He'd been a good coach at Army too, before a player's death broke him emotionally. Sasse was lured back into football thanks to a chance meeting with State's president, and accounts are he inherited a good club recruited by the campus secretary. Army doesn't seem to have taken their guests, the 'Farm Boys from Mississippi' as media labeled them, lightly either.

1935 Mississippi State vs Army game

Bobby Thames scored the day's first touchdown; Army tied it in the second quarter and were driving in the third before Ike Pickle picked off a pass at the State ten-yard line. Minutes into the final period Pee Wee Armstrong and Fred Walters hooked up for a 35-yard touchdown pass. That lead held and all 'Farm Boys' fans who'd paid the $37 round trip fee to watch the game went back to their fields well-rewarded.

1939 - "Trojans ruin Blue Devils perfect season"

Rose Bowl - Duke vs USC - Rose Bowl Stadium - Pasadena, California {USC 7 Duke 3}

The 1939 Rose Bowl featured the USC Trojans (8–2) against the Duke Blue Devils (9–0), with USC as the pre-game favorite. Duke was undefeated and unscored upon during the 1938 season. Scoreless after three quarters, Duke gained the lead with a 23-yard field goal by Tony Ruffa early in the fourth. However, backup quarterback Doyle Nave of the Trojans completed four straight passes to "Antelope" Al Krueger, who outmaneuvered Eric "The Red" Tipton and scored the winning touchdown with one minute remaining. Krueger's touchdown marked the first points scored against Duke during the season.

Al "Antelope" Krueger game winning catch in 1939 Rose Bowl

The Blue Devils' famed "Iron Dukes", with co-captains Dan Hill and Eric Tipton leading the way, entered the Rose Bowl having completed the regular season unbeaten, untied and unscored upon, but Southern Cal ruined that perfect season in the final minute of Duke's first bowl appearance. The game itself rocked back and forth for three quarters, mostly a punting duel between Granny Lansdell and Mickey Anderson of the Trojans and Tipton of the Blue Devils. Late in the third quarter, Lansdell booted one to George McAfee who returned it 26 yards to the Trojan 49, and two plays later, McAfee took a pass from Tipton and went to the USC 25. After Roger Robinson, Tipton and Bob O'Mara had picked up nine yards in three rushes, Tony Ruffa booted a field goal and Duke led, 3-0, with just a minute played in the fourth quarter. With seven minutes remaining in the game, a Duke fumble gave the Trojans the ball on the Blue Devil 10-yard line, but three plays later they were back at the 15-yard line and then missed a 24-yard field goal attempt. It looked like Duke had it, but with two minutes to go and the Trojans on the Duke 35, Coach Howard Jones sent in Doyle Nave, their number four quarterback. He simply completed three straight passes to Al Krueger, their number two left end, with the clincher coming from the 16-yard line. But the game was not over. On the very last play, Tipton threw a forward pass to McAfee who went 17 yards to the Trojan 40-yard line where the final Trojan caught him. USC's winning touchdown ended Duke's defensive domination after the Blue Devils had held opponents scoreless in the previous nine games.

1939 - "When punts rained from the sky"

Texas Tech at Centenary - Centenary College Stadium - Shreveport, Louisiana {Centenary 0 Texas Tech 0}

This game isn't so much for one memorable play as it is for how many times each team punted the ball. The 1939 Texas Tech vs. Centenary football game was played between the Texas Tech Red Raiders and Centenary Gentlemen on November 11, 1939, at Centenary College Stadium in Shreveport, Louisiana. In "one of the weirdest games in NCAA History," torrential downpour and muddy field conditions prevented either Texas Tech or Centenary from advancing the ball either running or passing. To cope with the conditions, both teams resorted to repetitive and immediate punting. Both teams combined to punt 77 times. With each punt, both teams hoped to recover a fumble at the other end of the field. 6 of 14 fumbles were lost, but none of the turnovers led to a score. 42 punts were returned, 19 went out of bounds, 10 were downed, 1 went into the end zone for a touchback, 4 were blocked, and 1 was fair caught. 67 punts (34 by Texas Tech, 33 by Centenary) occurred on first down, including 22 consecutively in the third and fourth quarters. The game ended in a 0–0 tie with Centenary owning a statistical edge with 31 yards of total offense compared with a one-yard loss for Texas Tech.

The 1939 Texas Tech vs Centenary game is referenced in the 2013 edition of the NCAA Football Records Book 14 times. More NCAA single-game records (13 total) were set in the 1939 Texas Tech vs Centenary game than any other game played in NCAA history. Steve Boda, a former associate director of NCAA statistics, researched the record in 1987. Stunned by the brief wire-service report of the game, he used a play-by-play account to confirm the details. All NCAA records set during the game have remained unbroken.

1939 - "First Televised Football Game"

Waynesburg at Fordham - Triborough Stadium - New York, New York {Fordham 34 Waynesburg 7}

Broadcast by NBC, the contest was the first American football game ever televised. NBC broadcast the game on station W2XBS with one camera and Bill Stern was the sole announcer. Estimates are that the broadcast reached approximately 1,000 television sets.

Bill Stern announcing from the sideline

Fordham entered the game a preseason pick for the national championship, but the first score was completed by Waynesburg when Bobby Brooks completed a 63-yard run for a touchdown on the third play of the game. Waynesburg only scored in the first quarter but managed to keep Fordham within reach during the early part of the game. Fordham scored in every quarter leaving the final score at 34–7. Fordham's offense managed 16 first downs and 337 yards, while Waynesburg managed only five first downs for a total of 157 yards. Fordham blocked a punt in both the first and second halves of the game and recorded an interception in the fourth quarter that the offense was able to turn into a touchdown.

1940 - "Fifth Down Game"

Cornell at Dartmouth - Memorial Field - Hanover, New Hampshire {Dartmouth 3 Cornell 0}

Cornell entered the contest with 18 straight victories over a two-year period. Dartmouth would manage to hold off Cornell's offense for nearly the entire low-scoring game. Dartmouth scored first, achieving a field goal for three points in the fourth quarter. Finally, with less than a minute left in the game, Cornell got the ball on Dartmouth's six-yard line. Cornell expected to have four chances to win the game. On its first down, fullback Mort Landsberg gained three yards. On its second down, Cornell halfback Walt Scholl managed to run the ball to the one-yard line. On the third down, Mort Landsberg tried to run up the middle but did not gain more than a few inches. On the fourth down, Cornell was penalized for delay of game, and Referee Red Friesell spotted the ball just over the 5-yard line in order to replay the fourth down. With nine seconds left on the clock, quarterback "Pop" Scholl threw an incomplete pass into the end zone. Normally, the ball would have gone to Dartmouth, which would have used up the remaining seconds and won the game, 3–0. But following the fourth down, Linesman Joe McKenny signaled that it was first down and that the ball should go to Dartmouth at the 20 yard line. Referee Friesell did not agree and gave the ball to Cornell and placed it on the six-yard line on fourth down when in actuality it was "fifth" down. Making the most of the unexpected opportunity, quarterback Scholl threw a touchdown pass to William Murphy, and following the extra-point kick, Cornell won the game 7–3.

Referee Red Friesell in white pants and shirt

It wasn't that No. 2 Cornell scored on a fifth-down, 6-yard pass in the final minute to defeat Dartmouth 7-3 in 1940 that made referee Red Friesell's blunder so memorable. It was that, after seeing the films, Cornell president Dr. Edmund Ezra Day directed his team to forfeit the game. Cornell lost its 18-game unbeaten streak but gained stature for playing with honor, instead of merely by the rules. Officials discovered their error after reviewing the game films. Cornell's players, Coach Carl Snavely, acting athletic director Bob Kane, and President Edmund Ezra Day, a Dartmouth alumnus, agreed that Cornell should send a telegram to Dartmouth offering to forfeit the game. Dartmouth accepted. Although there is some doubt whether the 1940 Cornell forfeit was "official" according to NCAA rules, the game is regarded as a 3–0 Dartmouth victory, instead of a 7–3 triumph by Cornell. This is described as the only time in the history of football that a game was decided off the field.

1940 - "Probably the greatest game in football history"
Georgetown at Boston College - Fenway Park - Boston, Massachusetts {Boston College 19 Georgetown 18}

The following is an excerpt from one of the most famous sports writers of the 20th century. This is a game recap from Grantland Rice.
Grantland Rice | Syndicated Columnist November 17, 1940

Forty thousand spectators saw an American football classic at Fenway Park yesterday afternoon as Boston College stopped Georgetown's three-year unbeaten mark by the score of 19 to 18. In many ways it was probably the greatest football game ever played by colleges or by pros. When you look back over the dizzy panorama of this cold, gray afternoon it was something more than the battle of the mastodon and the mammoth. The mastodons and mammoths were on hand in droves. But so were the Eagles and the Gazelles. There was not only crashing power along the ground as giants frames collided. There was also a dazzling battle through the chilly November air. There was every type of play that football has yet seen. There were double and triple passes. There were double reverses. There were spreads and shifts and fakes and feints that kept the packed stands not only thrilled but completely bewildered.

It was the greatest all-around exhibition of power, skill, deception and flaming spirit that I have ever seen on a football field for over 40 years. Especially the spirit shown. Boston College won by a single point, winding up Georgetown's unbeaten sweep of 23 victories. But as they finished in the dark on an unlighted field, it was Georgetown storming at the gates of victory as Charlie O'Rourke, B.C.'s brilliant captain, accepted a safety with only 65 seconds left. Here were the two teams that averaged over 200 pounds, where both teams were fast and smart. And yet both teams offered the finest open play in the way of laterals, passes and ball handling that any football crowd ever saw in action. This may seem to be over praise. It isn't and through all this swirl of deceptive action, you saw blocking and tackling that frequently left two or three men at a time flat on their broad backs and completely out. You didn't have to see this blocking and tackling. You could hear it 20 miles away. That's the way they were hitting. It was Georgetown who got the jump by scoring 10 points in the first part of the first period through Lio's 42-yard field goal and blocked a kick that gave Koshlap his chance to drive across the line on a touchdown play. Georgetown was now on the march, and the Georgetown section was a riot in the way of vocal cataclysm.

The Eagle had wounded wings at this point, but the Eagle was still flying as Charlie O'Rourke struck back. Georgetown held the lead through the first period at 10 to 6. Then Boston College swing back to set the pace in the second period at 13 to 10 as Holovak raced across the line. You got the idea that almost everyone on B.C. was handling the ball. Back and forth -- to and fro. The first half ended with Boston College leading 13 to 10. Then Georgetown ended a 65-yard march as Joe McFadden on a double reverse scored for the Hoyas to take the lead at 16 to 13. Once more Boston College was trailing with the Eagle in trouble. But once again O'Rourke, Maznicki and others swing back to work as O'Rourke again whipped a pass to Maznicki that picked up 32 yard and a touchdown. Now Boston College was leading 19 to 16. By this time the big crowd was as dizzy as the players. I think every once in the stands realized they were looking on the great game of the year -- one of the greatest ever played. Goodreault, the star end for the Eagles, had been carried off the field with a badly sprained knee after exceptional play while he was around on the job. Others were dazed and stunned by the swift impact of so much fast flesh. At the end, Boston College was fighting desperately to protect its three-point lead. Georgetown was scrapping with equal destruction to break through. To break through and win. Georgetown threw away a safe chance for a tie game on fourth down only 20 yards away from the goal posts with a field goal shot. Georgetown gambled to win -- not to tie. The pass was knocked down. This was the spirit in which this game was played. As darkness settled over the cold and soggy scene, Georgetown drove the Eagle almost out of his eyrie. The Hoyas forced their rivals back to the eight-yard line where O'Rourke, one of the day's brilliants, a really great back, decided to take a safety and win by a point. The last few plays were made in almost total dusk. But you could still hear the crash and crack of mammoths meeting mastodons -- of bones that either had to bend or break. It will be a long, long time before any football crowd will ever see a game like this one -- a game that carried all the ingredients of manpower, speed, skill, deception, blocking and tackling -- almost every detail that belongs to football. It took a great football team to beat Georgetown today -- and Boston College was a great football team. So was Georgetown. I doubt that any other team in the country could have beaten either.

1941 - "First Penalty Flag used"

Oklahoma City at Youngstown State - Rayen Stadium - Youngstown, Ohio {Youngstown State 48 Oklahoma City 7}

Prior to the use of flags, officials used horns and whistles to signal a penalty. The Oklahoma City-Youngstown State game marks the first use of the penalty flag in American football. Game official Jack McPhee said, "Through the use of the signal flag, everyone in the stadium knows that something is wrong. It's been a big help." Officials generally agreed that the game play was better with the use of the penalty flag instead of the previous methods of blowing a whistle to mark a penalty. The four game officials Hugh McPhee, Jack McPhee, Bill Renner, and Carl Rebele all agreed to use the flag. McPhee went on to use the penalty flag in other games including the Rose Bowl. In 1969, the original penalty flag was turned over to the College Football Hall of Fame.

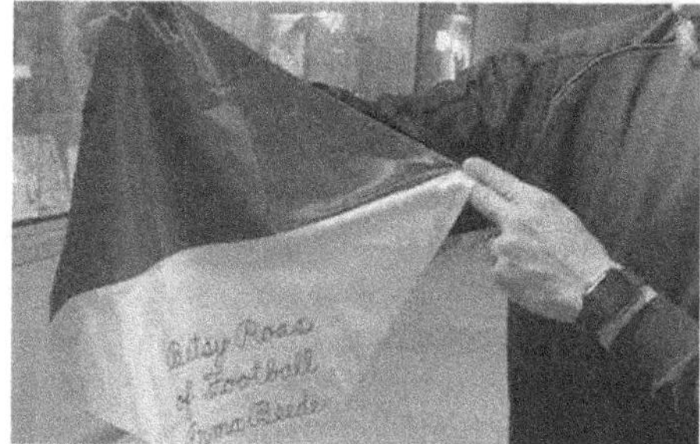

The first Penalty Flag used in College Football

1941 - "Dreams Crushed"
TCU at Texas - Texas Memorial Stadium - Austin, Texas {TCU 14 Texas 7}

The Longhorns were ranked No. 2, but hopes for the school's first national title were ended on November 15. The game was tied 7-7 in the fourth quarter. But on a very risky call, Texas failed to convert a fourth and one on its own 27-yard-line. The Horned Frogs then threw a touchdown pass with 19 seconds on the clock to win, 14-7. The loss was especially disappointing for Texas, considering that just over a week later the Longhorns were able to spoil then-No. 2 Texas A&M's national championship hopes with a 23-0 crushing in College Station.

1942 - "Safety First"
1942 Sugar Bowl - Tulane Stadium - New Orleans, Louisiana {Fordham 2 Missouri 0}

The 1942 edition to the Sugar Bowl featured the Missouri Tigers and the Fordham Rams. Those who watched the game were concerned by the attack on Pearl Harbor, which had occurred less than four weeks previously. Despite the entry of the United States into World War II, the bowl game was played on schedule. New Year's Day, 1942, saw a cold, driving rainstorm in New Orleans. During the first quarter, a blocked Tigers punt, turned back by Fordham tackle Alex Santilli, led to a two-point safety being scored by defensive end Stanley Ritinski. As the rain continued and no further points were scored, the final tally was Fordham 2, Missouri 0, which is the lowest possible combined point total for an untied American football game and stands as a bowl game record for an untied game (there have been four 0–0 ties). Fordham had won the game without completing a single forward pass; their total game yardage was 137 yards, all of it on the ground. Missouri finished with 169 total yards, 148 yards rushing and 21 yards passing. Missouri completed 2 of the 5 passes they attempted.

1946 - "Midshipmen run out of time"
Army vs Navy - Municipal Stadium - Philadelphia, Pennsylvania {Army 21 Navy 18}

The biggest game of the 1946 season -- one of the most highly anticipated in sports history -- was No. 1 Army vs. No. 2 Notre Dame at Yankee Stadium on Nov. 9. Three weeks later, Army played what proved to actually be the best and most consequential game of the season against Navy. The Cadets and Fighting Irish tied, 0-0, leaving Army still atop the AP poll when it met 1-7 Navy in the final game in the college careers of Mr. Inside and Mr. Outside, legendary Heisman winners Doc Blanchard and Glenn Davis. Army had not lost in 28 games -- not since the Navy game in 1943 -- entering the rivalry clash in front of 102,000 fans at Philadelphia's Municipal Stadium. Army was a 28-point favorite, according to the Philadelphia Inquirer.

Doc Blanchard (#35) carries the ball for Army

With President Harry S. Truman in attendance, the Cadets dominated the first half, building a 21-6 lead on TDs by Blanchard and Davis. With three TDs but no PATs, Navy cut the lead to 21-18 and converted a fourth down all the way to the Army three-yard line with a minute and a half left. After being stopped twice, Navy was penalized for delay of game. Pete Williams carried the ball back to the four-yard line near the sideline. Navy thought Williams got out of bounds. The officials didn't stop the clock. Time ran out before Navy could run one last play, and Army avoided the upset. Merely avoiding the upset wasn't enough, though. Army's close call combined with Notre Dame's 20-point win over USC prompted AP voters to vault the Fighting Irish to No. 1 and the national title.

1947 "Offsides, Offsides, Offsides"
Northwestern at Ohio State - Ohio Stadium - Columbus, Ohio {Ohio State 7 Northwestern 6}

With 1:47 to go, Northwestern was leading, 6-0, on Frank Aschenbrenner's touchdown in the first minute of the fourth quarter, and had stopped the Buckeyes on the Wildcat one-yard line. Jim Farrar, on the first play after the ball changed hands, sneaked to the five. Northwestern was put back to the one-yard line for taking too much time, then Ohio State was penalized five for offside. On the next play Northwestern was offside and back went the ball to the one-yard line. There were 55 seconds left when the Wildcats were offside once more, but this time the penalty was declined. That cost Northwestern a down. Farrar, on another quarterback sneak, went to the eight-yard line where, with fourth down and 43 second to go, Ohio State called time. When play was resumed Tom Worthington punted to Bob Demmel on the Wildcat 24. A pass, Pandel Savic to Demmel, was complete on the 13. Savic passed again and Worthington intercepted. At this point the band marched onto the field, thinking the game was over. But no! A Northwestern player, being replaced by a substitute, had not reached the sideline before the ball was snapped, so Northwestern had too many players on the field. That called for a five yard penalty. Thirteen seconds remained and the ball was on the eight-yard line. Ollie Cline was stopped on a plunge but again Northwestern was offside and the ball was placed three yards from the goal. Then Savic passed to Jim Clark in the end zone for a touchdown and a 6-6 tie. Ohio State's place-kicking specialist, Emil Moldea, was called from the bench and, with Savic holding, swung his foot. Northwestern's defensive end Don Stonesifer, blocked the kick, but for the umpteenth time Northwestern was offside and Moldea got a chance to try again. This time his kick was perfect. Ohio State had won, 7-6.

Chapter Two {1950-1999}

1951 - "Rejected Touchdown"

Central Missouri State at Southwestern (KS) - Sooner Stadium - Winfield, Kansas {Central Missouri State 6 Southwestern (KS) 6}

     The game is known for Southwestern (KS) rejecting a touchdown awarded by the game officials. Central Missouri's head coach Tate C. Page called it "the finest act of sportsmanship" that he ever saw. In the third quarter, Southwestern halfback Arthur Johnson completed a long run down the sidelines nearest Southwestern's bench. The referee signaled a touchdown and the crowd of 2,000 went wild with enthusiasm. Southwestern's head coach Harold Hunt ran out on the field to shout, "Southwestern rejects the touchdown!" He then informed the officials that Johnson had stepped out of bounds, nullifying the touchdown. Not a single one of the referees had been in a position to see him do so, but they agreed to nullify the touchdown and returned the ball to the point where Coach Hunt said Johnson had stepped out. Referee W. P. Astle noted that there had been only three officials at the game instead of the regulation four. He later said, "If the fourth official had been present to cover what was impossible for me to cover ... I would never have discovered the 'biggest' man I ever met." Southwestern's Coach Hunt was nominated for "Football's Man of the Year" by This Week magazine because of this display of sportsmanship.

1951 - "Racism rears its ugly head"

Drake at Oklahoma A&M - Lewis Field - Stillwater, Oklahoma {Oklahoma A&M 27 Drake 14}

     Then-unbeaten Drake was led by quarterback Johnny Bright, who was leading the nation in total offense at the time and had been touted as a Heisman Trophy candidate. Two years earlier, he had been the first black player to appear in a game at A&M's home field, without incident. The same could not be said about this game.

Wilbanks Smith elbow to Johnny Bright

     Bright was forced to leave the game in the first quarter after suffering three concussions and a broken jaw as the result of a racially motivated attack by white A&M player Wilbanks Smith, and A&M ultimately won 27–14. The attack was immortalized in a photo sequence in the Des Moines Register that won the photographers a Pulitzer Prize. It was an open secret that Oklahoma A&M players were targeting Bright. Both Oklahoma A&M's student newspaper, The Daily O'Collegian, and the local newspaper, The News Press, reported that Bright was a marked man, and several A&M students were openly claiming that Bright "would not be around at the end of the game." Although Oklahoma A&M had integrated in 1949, the Jim Crow spirit was still very much alive on campus. A six photograph sequence of the incident captured by Des Moines Register cameramen John Robinson and Don Ultang clearly showed Smith's jaw-breaking blow was thrown well after Bright had handed the ball off to Drake fullback Gene Macomber, and was well behind the play.

1952 - "First Nationally Televised College Football Game"
Rose Bowl - Illinois vs Stanford - Rose Bowl Stadium - Pasadena, California {Illinois 40 Stanford 7}

The **1952 Rose Bowl** was the first nationally televised college football game. Stanford led Illinois 7 to 6 on a Harry Hugasian touchdown until late in the third quarter. Illinois then scored 34 consecutive points including 27 points in the 4th quarter to defeat Stanford 40 to 7. Illinois running back Bill Tate rushed for 150 yards and 2 touchdowns. Leading Illinois to 434 yards of total offense. All-American Johnny Karras rushed for 58 yards and a touchdown for Illinois. It was the second Rose Bowl win for Illinois coach Ray Eliot. Stanford coach Chuck Taylor became the first man to ever be both a player and coach in the Rose Bowl, having played as one of Stanford's undefeated Wow Boys in the 1941 Rose Bowl

1953 - "Fainting Irish"
Iowa at Notre Dame - Notre Dame Stadium - South Bend, Indiana {Iowa 14 Notre Dame 14}

Once again, this game isn't memorable for one play, but numerous memorable plays where Notre Dame Players fell to the ground faking injury, to conserve time on the clock, at the end of the first half as well as the end of the game. The ruse worked to the "Fainting Irish" favor, as they were able to avoid an upset at the hands of the Iowa Hawkeyes.

The Irish were 13-point favorites, and it's easy to see why. They were led by senior halfback Johnny Lattner, who would go on to claim the 1953 Heisman Trophy. Junior quarterback Ralph Guglielmi, a future College Football Hall of Famer, would finish fourth in the Heisman Trophy voting in 1954. In all, twenty players from that 1953 Notre Dame team would go on to play professional football. Clearly, Notre Dame was ranked #1 in the nation for a reason. But the 1953 Irish were about to get the challenge of a lifetime

From the opening whistle, Iowa took control of the game. The Steubenville Trio – Cal Jones at guard, Frank Gilliam at end, and Eddie Vincent at halfback – all started the game and stood out against their opponents. The Hawkeyes held a 7-0 lead late in the first half when the first controversy struck. Notre Dame drove into Iowa territory with seconds remaining in the half. Notre Dame had no timeouts remaining, though, so they would need to be careful. The Irish had the ball at Iowa's seven-yard line when Guglielmi dropped back for a pass attempt. But he was tackled for no gain before he was able to get the pass away, so the clock continued to run. The Irish had a plan – fake an injury to stop the clock. Unfortunately, the man assigned to the task, lineman Frank Varrichione, didn't get the memo. "Normally, I'd be blocking somebody, and there would be a big pileup at the end of the play, so I'd just lay there and pretend to be injured," Varrichione revealed to Craig Chval. But Varrichione initially thought that the Guglielmi sack was an incomplete pass, which would have stopped the clock anyway. "I had made my block and I saw the ball bouncing out of bounds. I thought the official had stopped the clock," Varrichione admitted. When he got back to the huddle, he realized his error. "We were walking back after the play and Ralph [Guglielmi] said to me, 'Why didn't you fake an injury?'" The Irish huddled up, but they knew they wouldn't have any time to get another play away. Varrichione now knew he had made a mistake, and he needed to compensate quickly. "We were trying to call a play and I saw the clock ticking down so I knew I had to stop the clock so I just dropped at the line of scrimmage. Just like I had dead out fainted," Varrichione recalled. That's right...he walked all the way back to the middle of the field, saw the time about to expire on the half, and fell down right in the middle of the Notre Dame huddle. Chval describes it thusly: Irish left tackle Frank Varrichione let out a blood-curdling scream and collapsed to the turf, seemingly suffering a very sudden and mortal injury. Under existing college football rules, the officials were obligated to stop the clock and allow Varrichione to be helped off the field. The Irish offense took advantage of the stoppage in play to line up, and on the final play of the half, Ralph Guglielmi threw a 12-yard touchdown pass to Dan Shannon, tying the score. Evashevski was furious. Varrichione's antics stopped the clock with two seconds remaining. After escorting him off the field, the Irish broke their huddle and the officials signaled for the clock to start. Yet Notre Dame was somehow able to set down the lines, call signals, and snap the ball, all in two seconds before time expired on the half, which made Guglielmi's touchdown toss possible. Evy was actually more upset at the time that the clock operator didn't start the clock on the official's signal and that Notre Dame was able to cram their pre-snap activities into two seconds than he was over Varrichione's fake injury.

Varrichione managed to recover from his near-fatal wounds to play the majority of the second half. His antics didn't faze the Hawks, who bounced back from the incident to take back control of the game. With 2:06 remaining in the game, Bob Stearnes threw a touchdown pass to Frank Gilliam to put the Hawks back on top. Notre Dame now trailed, 14-7, and Hawkeye fans could sense an upset victory over the top-ranked team in the nation. Notre Dame had one last chance to come back. As Tom Kirkendall recalled, "Notre Dame had the ball, but again had no time outs and no way to stop the clock. In the final two minutes, Notre Dame moved sixty yards in eight plays, and after each play, one or more Notre Dame Players faked an injury to stop the clock." With the benefit of these repeated injuries, the Irish were able to advance the ball down to Iowa's nine-yard line, but the clock continued to run and dipped under ten seconds. Since the Irish were again out of timeouts, right tackle Art Hunter was scheduled to fake Notre Dame's next injury. But with time running down and the game slipping away, end Don Penza couldn't wait. He didn't want to risk another near-miss like what happened at the end of the first half, when Varrichione didn't realize it was his turn. So Penza fell to the ground to stop the clock.

What Penza didn't realize was that Hunter had been paying attention and knew it was his time to fake an injury. As a result, Penza and Hunter fell to the ground simultaneously, each apparently unaware of the other. The officials stopped the clock with six seconds remaining, and both players left the field unassisted. Guglielmi had time for one more play, and he tossed a touchdown pass to Shannon in the end zone to salvage a 14-14 tie on the extra play granted by the officials. Evy was livid at Notre Dame coach Frank Leahy. "I thought Forest Evashevski was going to come across the field and kill Leahy," Lattner recalled. The NCAA reprimanded Coach Frank Leahy and outlawed fake injuries. Worse, the voters dropped the No. 1 "Fainting Irish" to No. 2 and kept them there.

1954 - "12th Man Tackle"
Cotton Bowl Classic – Alabama vs Rice - Cotton Bowl Stadium - Dallas, Texas {Rice 28 Alabama 6}

Rice won the game 28–6, but its victory was overshadowed by Alabama's Tommy Lewis and his "12th man tackle" of Rice running back Dicky Moegle in the second quarter. Midway through the second, Moegle was awarded a touchdown on one of the more infamous plays in college football history. After taking the handoff from quarterback LeRoy Fenstemaker, Moegle broke free for what was to be a deemed 95-yard touchdown run. In what was dubbed the "12th man tackle," Alabama running back Tommy Lewis left the Alabama bench, entered the field of play and tackled Moegle at the Alabama 42-yard line, apparently believing that even if the 5-yard penalty for illegal participation were enforced, his illegal move would have still stopped the score. However, referee Cliff Shaw instead awarded Moegle a 95-yard touchdown on the play under the palpably unfair act rule, which accounts for situations when a flagrant rule violation prevents a player from scoring by awarding the score anyway. The incident became the first in bowl game history where a man on the bench tackled a runner, and also the first where a runner received credit for a touchdown while flat on his back 38 yards from the goal line.

Dicky Moegle of Rice being tackled by Tommy Lewis, who left the Alabama bench.

The celebrated bench tackle by Alabama's Tommy Lewis overshadowed the awesome performance of Rice's Dicky Moegle, who set all-time bowl records with 265 yards rushing and touchdown runs of 79, 95, and 34 yards. For the day, Moegle averaged an unbelievable 24.1 yards per play on just 11 carries.

1956 - "Desegregation of the South"

Sugar Bowl - Pittsburgh vs Georgia Tech - Tulane Stadium - New Orleans, Louisiana {Georgia Tech 7 Pittsburgh 0}

In December 1955, Gov. Marvin Griffin of Georgia, a segregationist, demanded that Georgia Tech not play in the Sugar Bowl against Pittsburgh because the Panthers' team included a black player, Grier. "The South stands at Armageddon," Griffin said in a telegram to Georgia's Board of Regents, detailing his request that teams in the state's university system not participate in events in which races were mixed on the field or in the stands. "The battle is joined. We cannot make the slightest concession to the enemy in this dark and lamentable hour of struggle." A black football player had never played in the Sugar Bowl. Black players had participated in other bowl games, like the Cotton Bowl in Dallas, but Grier was credited as being the first black player to participate in a bowl game in the Deep South. Grier's participation in the 1956 Sugar Bowl resonated as one of the "last gasps of segregation in the South."

Bobby Grier of Pittsburgh

The game was a high caliber defensive game. The two teams gave up a combined 7 points, on 453 combined yards. The only score of the game came on a 1-yard touchdown run by quarterback Wade Mitchell. Georgia Tech was held without any points the remaining three quarters of the game, and ended up winning by a 7-0 margin. Pittsburgh, despite dominating the game in terms of yardage (311-142) lost because of 2 lost fumbles, and 72 penalty yards. Grier played offense and defense in the game and had the games longest run -- a 28-yarder. The margin of victory mostly resulted from a disputed first quarter pass interference penalty which was called on Grier by a Southeastern Conference official. A pass interference call against Grier on the goal line moved the ball from the 33-yard line to the 1. Grier said that Ellis pushed him, and a photograph from the game shows Grier flat on the ground and Ellis leaping for the ball, which grazed his fingertips and fell incomplete.

1957 - "Bob White's Run for the Roses"
Iowa at Ohio State - Ohio Stadium - Columbus, Ohio {Ohio State 17 Iowa 13}

There was 7:51 left in the game and 68 yards stood between the Buckeyes and a trip to Pasadena. Bob White plowed over right tackle for 4, then dragged several Iowa tacklers with him on a 9-yard romp, giving OSU a first down at their own 45. Kremblas sent White over left guard and he broke out for 29 yards and a first down at the Hawkeye 26. Ohio Stadium was going absolutely bananas as Dick LeBeau gave White a breather and hit the same hole at left guard for 3 yards. Bob White picked up 5 more and for the first time on the drive the Buckeyes faced a third down. It didn't take a genius to figure out what to do- White drove for 10, giving the Bucks a 1st-and-goal at the 8. Once more White got the call and blasted for 5. Legend has it that in the huddle Frank Kremblas asked White, "Got anything left, Bob?" to which the big redhead simply nodded. Kremblas handed to White who hammered in for the go ahead score, the fourth time the lead had changed hands in the ballgame. Don Sutherin converted and the Buckeyes lead 17-13 with 3:53 left as the record crowd shook the 'Shoe to its foundation.

It was now up to the defense as Iowa took over at their 25. Iowa QB Randy Duncan hit Don Norton for 16 and Jim Gibbons for 12 to put Iowa at the OSU 47. On the next play, Duncan went on top again but Bill Jobko, intercepted the pass while falling backward at the Buckeye 33. After his heroics at fullback, Bob White actually moved back to center and led Kremblas on three straight quarterback sneaks. With the clock down to 36 seconds, Kremblas punted to Iowa's 31. Three Duncan aerials fell incomplete and the Buckeyes were Big Ten champions and had punched their ticket to the Rose Bowl. The fans stormed the field, tearing down both goalposts and carrying Bob White off the field. White finished the day with 157 yards on 22 carries, two more than Iowa's entire rushing total for the game. Vice-President Richard Nixon had watched Ohio State's 1957 win over Iowa from Senator John Bricker's box in section 17A. That evening he and Woody Hayes had dinner together at Bricker's home, sparking a lifelong friendship between the two.

1957 - "The Streak ends"
Notre Dame at Oklahoma - Owen Field - Norman, Oklahoma {Notre Dame 7 Oklahoma 0}

This game is not so much for a memorable play, but more for a memorable drive that ended the longest winning streak in College Football history. Notre Dame, fresh off back-to-back double-digit losses, visited Oklahoma on Nov. 16, 1957, the Sooners -- actually ranked No. 2 in the AP poll -- had not lost a game since Sept. 26, 1953, a season-opening defeat at the Fighting Irish. Oklahoma tied Pitt the next week, then began the greatest streak in college football history. The Sooners went undefeated three straight seasons, with no ties. They brought a 47-game winning streak into the '57 game against Notre Dame. The Sports Illustrated cover that week read, "Why Oklahoma Is Unbeatable." All streaks end, though, and Bud Wilkinson's Sooners finally met their match.

Dick Lynch of Notre Dame scoring winning touchdown vs Oklahoma

It was a game of missed opportunities for both teams, with defenses bending but not breaking, and it remained scoreless into the fourth quarter, when Notre Dame got the ball at its own 20. The Irish proceeded on a 20-play, 80-yard drive that took most of the final period. Facing fourth-and-goal at the three, Dick Lynch took a pitch from Bob Williams and crossed the goal line for the touchdown with 3:50 left. The streak ended with a final Notre Dame interception in the end zone.

1959 - "Billy Cannon's Halloween Run"
Mississippi at LSU - Tiger Stadium - Baton Rouge, Louisiana {LSU 7 Mississippi 3}

During the 1959 LSU vs Mississippi game on Halloween night in 1959, Billy Cannon of LSU returned a punt 89 yards for a touchdown against the Ole Miss Rebels. The return occurred late in the fourth quarter and provided the only touchdown scored in the game, as the Tigers won 7–3. Featuring several broken tackles, it was a signature play of Cannon's Heisman Trophy-winning season and a notable moment in the LSU–Ole Miss football rivalry.

Tiger Stadium was filled to capacity with 68,000 fans packing the stands. As expected, the game was a defensive struggle. The Rebels scored a field goal in the first quarter, and spent the rest of the game relying on defense and trying to pin the Tigers deep in their own territory. With LSU still trailing 3–0 late in the fourth quarter, on fourth-and-17 from the Ole Miss 42 yard line, Gibbs punted the ball 47 yards to the LSU 11-yard line. He intended to kick it out of bounds, as instructed by Vaught. Cannon picked up the ball after a bounce, defying coach Paul Dietzel's orders not to field punts that close to the end zone. Dietzel described his reaction to Cannon fielding the punt as "'Billy, no-no-no...' to 'Billy, go-go-go!'" He eluded and bounced off seven would-be tacklers down the east sideline, then raced the last 60 yards untouched to the end zone to give LSU a 7–3 lead.

Billy Cannon of LSU

Billy Cannon reflected on his run: "After I caught the ball, the first person looking me in the eye was Larry Grantham. I knew how good he was. I wanted to go to the left toward the open field, but there he was, so I cut back to the right, and he missed the tackle. I started down field, following the sideline, picking up a few blocks, and some guys missed their tackles. Finally, I broke into the open, and there was nobody left but me and Jake Gibbs. Gibbs thought I was going to the wide side of the field, so I gave him a little head fake. Now I've got to give Jake credit on this: That was the only tackle he had missed in his entire career to that point. Of course, with the team he had around him, that was the only tackle he tried to make in four years. After I had the clear sailing to the goal line, it was a question of was I going to make it, was the referee going to beat me there, or was the cameraman gaining on both of us going to outrun the whole bunch."

1961 - "Great Rose Bowl Hoax"
1961 Rose Bowl - Rose Bowl Stadium - Pasadena, California {Washington 17 Minnesota 7}

The Great Rose Bowl Hoax occurred during halftime. As seen by an estimated 30 million television viewers, students from nearby Caltech altered the plans for the Washington card stunts, which spelled "CALTECH" instead of "HUSKIES" and showed the Caltech Beaver mascot instead of the Washington Husky. The Minnesota marching band performed first, followed by UW band, when the card stunts began. The Washington card section was on the east side of the Rose Bowl stadium, facing the press box and television cameras. The NBC national television broadcast was trained on the band and card stunts. The 14th card stunt design displayed "CALTECH" instead of "HUSKIES" in big block letters on a white background. The announcers and the stadium fell silent for several moments before breaking into laughter.

"Great Rose Bowl Hoax"

Washington wore their home purple jerseys, gold pants and gold helmets. Minnesota wore white away jerseys with maroon and gold shoulder stripes and white helmets. The ceremonial pregame coin toss to determine first possession employed a souvenir gold dollar minted for Alaska's statehood in 1959.

George Fleming of Washington

The Huskies dominated the first half, scoring all 17 points. Minnesota lead in all the final statistics, but the most telling one was its passing game: Gopher quarterback Sandy Stephens completed only 2 of 10 passes for 21 yards and was intercepted three times. MVP Bob Schloredt completed only 2 of 4 passes for 16 yards (no interceptions), but was the game's leading rusher with 68 yards on five carries.

1961 - "Fifth Down Play (or was it)"
Syracuse at Notre Dame - Notre Dame Stadium - South Bend, Indiana {Notre Dame 17 Syracuse 15}

On Nov. 18, 1961 Syracuse and Notre Dame played in one of the most controversial games in college football history. Trailing 15-14 with only a few seconds left on the clock, Notre Dame sent in kicker Joe Perkowski to attempt a 56-yard field goal. He missed the kick as time expired, but there were flags on the field as Syracuse player Walt Sweeney was called for roughing the kicker. The penalty normally carries 15 yards, but the clock had expired and Syracuse fans had already started to rush the field to celebrate their victory. Making a decision on the spot, the referees decided to enforce the standard penalty for roughing the kicker. Even though time had expired, Perkowski was given 15 yards and a second attempt. He made the second chance, giving Notre Dame the 17-15 win with a 41-yard field goal with no time on the clock.

The Big 10 and Eastern College Athletic Conferences, who supplied the officials for the game, and the NCAA rules chairman General Bob Neyland reviewed the play but it was determined the officials on the field had final say and Notre Dame was granted the controversial win. As a result of the play, a rule was put into place that states a half cannot end on an accepted defensive foul. The rules were changed in 1962 to prevent any future confusion should a similar circumstance arise. At the White House the next week, President Kennedy asks Notre Dame President Ted Hesburgh if the Irish will forfeit the win. Hesbergh says, "No. We won."

1962 – "First Televised College Football Game in Color"
Rose Bowl - Minnesota vs UCLA - Rose Bowl Stadium - Pasadena, California {Minnesota 21 UCLA 3}

The 1962 Rose Bowl was broadcast on the NBC television network and was the first national color television broadcast of a college football game.

Sandy Stephens (#15) of Minnesota

The weather was sunny, and Minnesota wore their home maroon jerseys, with white helmets and white pants, while UCLA also wore their home powder blue uniforms with gold pants. Using the single wing offense, UCLA struggled against the Gophers, netting only one field goal to open the scoring in the first quarter. Minnesota had 21 first downs to UCLA's 8, and the Gophers held the Bruins to 107 total yards, while gaining 297 yards on 66 plays. Stephens rushed for 46 yards on 12 carries, including two rushing touchdowns, and was 7 for 11 in passing for 75 yards. Minnesota quarterback Sandy Stephens was named the Rose Bowl Player of The Game and became the first African American to get the award.

1963 - "Sayers goes 99"

Kansas at Nebraska - Memorial Stadium - Lincoln, Nebraska {Nebraska 23 Kansas 9}

On the third play of the final quarter, Nebraska punted the ball dead on the Kansas one yard line, and Husker fans breathed easy — the Jayhawks were really bottled up. But on the next play, All America halfback Gale Sayers cut around left end, sidestepped one tackler, sprinted away from two others and tore down the west sidelines to score — a Big 8 record: 99-yard TD run.

1963 - "Birth of Instant Replay"

Army vs Navy - Philadelphia Stadium - Philadelphia, Pennsylvania {Navy 21 Army 15}

Instant replay, a staple of TV broadcasts of sporting events for decades, made its debut at the 1963 Army-Navy game. Replay was the brainchild of CBS' college football director, 29-year old Tony Verna. One reason for choosing the annual service clash to unveil the new toy was the Midshipmen's star junior QB, Roger Staubach, who had led Navy to a 8-1 record and #2 ranking entering the annual finale. Viewers could see his TD runs and passes again.

Game action in the 1963 Army-Navy game

The 1963 Army-Navy game was postponed a week following the assassination of President John F. Kennedy in Dallas. The game itself featured a starring performance by Navy's Pat Donnelly in a 21-15 victory. A halfback, Donnelly scored three touchdowns to give the Midshipmen a 21-7 lead with four minutes gone in the fourth quarter. However, the Cadets made it interesting, going 52 yards (all on running plays), culminating with a 1-yard touchdown and then successful two-point conversion run by quarterback Rollie Stichweh. Stichweh then recovered the onside kick at the Navy 40. He led Army all the way to the Midshipmen 4 when time ran out.

1964 - "Hatfield breaks free"
Arkansas at Texas - Texas Memorial Stadium - Austin, Texas {Arkansas 14 Texas 13}

In the 1964 season, Ken Hatfield was a senior and had been moved to defensive safety where he would lead the nation in punt returns. When the Texas game finally came around, both teams were 5-0 and the Longhorns were once again in the #1 spot.

With the game now underway, it soon turned into a punting battle between Texas' Ernie Koy and the Hog's Bobby Nix. Midway through the second quarter Koy got off a 47 yard punt that was brought in by Hatfield at the 19. In a play that has become famous, Ken Hatfield followed his blockers and found his way to the alley along the sideline to scamper 81 yards for the TD. Hatfield's punt return in the second quarter had set the tone for the win that was to come.

Ken Hatfield of Arkansas

After the game, Texas Coach Darrell Royal commented on Hatfield's punt return by saying "That's their game, and he's the one. He's done that for them for three years now." During his career from 1962-64, Hatfield averaged 16.01 yards per punt return (in 1964 his average was 16.71 yards per return). In a game against Rice in 1964, Hatfield set the school record of most punt returns in a game at 9, and had the season and career most punt return yardage record at 518 and 1153, respectively.

1964 - "We wuz robbed"
Kansas at Oklahoma State - Lewis Field - Stillwater, Oklahoma {Kansas 14 Oklahoma State 13}

The Cowboys held Kansas' star running back Gayle Sayers to 67 yards rushing. The Cowboy faithful claim that the officials did what Kansas couldn't do all day, beat them. A mistake in explaining the options on a punt penalty led to a 38 yard shift in field position, and a six minute delay as Oklahoma State coach Phil Cutching and Kansas coach Jack Mitchell argued with the officials. Kansas led 14-7 late in the game when they tried a field goal, which was blocked by Jerry Gill of Oklahoma State and returned 60 yards for a touchdown. Cutching chose to go for 2 points and the win. Quarterback Baxter threw to Tony Sellari, who made a leaping catch at the goal line and was sandwiched by two Jayhawk defenders as he came down. The official signaled that Sellari didn't cross the plane of the end zone. A photo in the local paper next day showed Sellari straddling the goal line. Kansas wins 14-13.

1964 – "Nittany Lions ain't no breather"
Penn State at Ohio State – Ohio Stadium – Columbus, Ohio {Penn State 27 Ohio State 0}

The Nittany Lions brought a record of 3-4 into that '64 game while the home team had crushed all six of its opponents, yielding a total of only 39 points and earning a No. 2 ranking in the country. Even though Penn State had upset Ohio State, 10-7, in 1963, and the 1964 team had begun to gel with consecutive wins over West Virginia and Maryland, the Lions got no respect. The Chicago Sun-Times summarized the prevailing attitude with this statement: "The Buckeyes have a breather in Penn State this week."

Actually, the Ohio State players had trouble breathing at all after being hit in the gut by linemen like Glenn Ressler, a future Baltimore Colt, who recorded 15 tackles. For the first half, the Buckeyes achieved 0 first downs while totaling 0 yards passing and -14 yards in rushing. Indeed, the stunned Bucks did not record their initial first down of the game until midway through the third quarter, and that resulted from a Penn State penalty. The final score was 27-0 and the final stats reflected total domination:

Penn State gained 194 net yards in rushing to Ohio State's 30; Penn State passed 12-for-22 and 147 yards while Ohio State threw 3-for-14 and 30 yards; Penn State achieved 22 first downs and Ohio State had five.

Rip Engle, the Lions' head coach from 1950 to 1966, offered this comment some years later. "A football team has never played a perfect game, but at Ohio State in 1964 our team came as close to it as I ever saw."

Penn State had throttled the nation's second-ranked team, and the Lions had done it before 84,279 spectators — the largest crowd in their football history, home or away. (Back then, Beaver Stadium had a seating capacity of less than 50,000.) Said losing Coach Woody Hayes, "It was the soundest trouncing we ever had. We didn't seem to be able to establish anything. They were a great team today."

1964 - "First indoor College Football Game"

1964 Liberty Bowl - Atlantic City Convention Hall - Atlantic City, New Jersey – {Utah 32 West Virginia 6}

The 1964 Liberty Bowl was the first major college football bowl game ever played indoors, the first broadcast nationwide in the United States and the only one ever played in Atlantic City, New Jersey. It was played indoors at a temperature of 60 °F (16 °C) on December 19 before 6,059 at the Atlantic City Convention Hall. The venue had been shifted to Atlantic City after the bowl was played for its initial five years outdoors in Philadelphia Stadium, often in temperatures below freezing. In the 1964 postseason, the Liberty Bowl was one of just eight major bowl games. The American Broadcasting Company agreed to broadcast the game nationally, and brought Paul Christman, Curt Gowdy and Jim McKay to announce the game, paying $95,000 for the rights to broadcast the first nationwide telecast of an indoor football game.

1964 Liberty Bowl - Atlantic City Convention Hall

West Virginia featured running back Dick Leftridge and Utah's offense featured All-American Roy Jefferson. Utah used their speed, and dominated West Virginia from start to finish and won 32–6. Utah Halfback Ron Coleman gained 154 yards on 15 carries, scoring a touchdown on a 53-yard run. Utah quarterback (and safety) Pokey Allen was named the game's outstanding player. The 1964 Liberty Bowl was the last edition played in the Northeast; the game was moved to Memphis, Tennessee in 1965 and has continued to play in Memphis since then.

1965 - "Longhorns goal line stand"

1965 Orange Bowl - Orange Bowl Stadium - Miami, Florida {Texas 21 Alabama 17}

Texas upset No. 1 Alabama 21-17 in the first night game in Orange Bowl history. The Longhorns stopped Alabama quarterback Joe Namath inches short of the goal line on a crucial fourth-down play late in the game that would have given the Crimson Tide the lead. The defeat overshadowed a heroic performance by Namath, who didn't start the game because of a knee injury. He completed 18-of-37 passes for 255 yards and two touchdowns and was named the game's Most Outstanding Player. The Longhorns' Ernie Koy ran for a 79-yard touchdown on Texas' first possession. Texas went up 14-0 after quarterback Jim Hudson hit George Sauer for a 69-yard score.

Alabama head coach Bear Bryant then sent in Namath to replace starter Steve Sloan. He completed 10 passes on an 87-yard touchdown drive. Koy gave Texas a 21-7 lead with 27 seconds remaining in the first half. Namath came out firing in the second half, hitting Ray Perkins with a 20-yard pass to close the gap to 21-14. When Texas' Marvin Kristynik fumbled late in the fourth quarter, Namath was at the controls once again. Three plays later at the one-yard line, Namath tried a quarterback sneak and Longhorn left tackle Frank Bedrick and All-American linebacker Tommy Nobis stopped him short of the goal line.

1965 - "Dawg and Lateral"
Alabama at Georgia - Sanford Stadium - Athens, Georgia {Georgia 18 Alabama 17}

The 1965 Georgia Bulldogs opened the season against reigning national champion Alabama. Few gave the 1965 Georgia team any better chance against the winningest college football program of the 1960s. Still, Georgia's resurgence and Alabama's fame led NBC to make the 1965 season opener in Athens the game of the week, the only televised game of the day from coast to coast. The game began with both defenses playing well. After watching the first team offense do nothing, Vince Dooley inserted the entire second-string offense. Back-up quarterback Kirby Moore set the Bulldogs up for a field goal and a 3 – 0 lead with a nifty 15-yard sweep. Georgia Patton then claimed a mid-air fumble recovery and romped fifty yards. With Georgia leading 10 – 0, the Bulldog faithful became delirious and legendary former Oklahoma coach-turned-TV color man Bud Wilkinson began openly cheering for the upstart Bulldogs. Alabama showed its championship mettle in the second half. The Tide took a 17 – 10 lead with just over three minutes remaining in the game on quarterback Steve Sloan's short run. It appeared the hapless Georgia football program would become just another victim of Alabama football supremacy. Three minutes and fourteen seconds show on the scoreboard clock. Alabama 17 Georgia 10. Georgia owns the ball at its own 27 yard line. The Bulldogs scored only three offensive touchdowns in their last four games. Georgia starting quarterback Preston Ridlehuber is out with pulled muscles. Backup rookie quarterback, Kirby Moore, is at the helm. The Georgia football team desperately needed something good to happen. It did.

Was the Knee down?

Georgia QB Kirby Moore dropped back to pass and threw to Pat Hodgson at the 35 yard line. Hodgson then lateraled the ball to Bob Taylor who took the ball down the sideline untouched for a 73 yard touchdown. Georgia chose to go for two to win the game and Kirby Moore passed again to Pat Hodgson for the conversion and winning points.

1965 - "The Turning Point"
Texas Western at Utah - Ute Stadium - Salt Lake City, Utah {Texas Western 20 Utah 19}

On November 13, 1965 Texas Western took on the Utah Utes in Salt Lake City. A year earlier in El Paso the Utes and run around, over and through the Miners on their way to a 41-0 win. The Miners were battling a three game losing streak as they took the field in '65. Bob Wallace was a flyer, allegedly with 9.7 speed in the 100. When he first arrived in El Paso, Stevens didn't anticipate Wallace's speed. He under-threw Wallace consistently in practice until one day he finally let one fly seemingly out of reach of his transfer receiver and watched Wallace turn on his jets, glide under it and make the catch. From that point Stevens and Wallace became one of the best big play duos in college football. That came in handy in Salt Lake City.

Wallace actually started the scoring with an 89 yard punt return for a touchdown that gave the Miners a 7-0 lead. Utah used three second half Miners turnovers and the running of Ben Woodson to take a 19-7 lead. Stevens took the Miners 76 yards in the fourth quarter including three long completions to Wallace to set up a touchdown that made it a one score game, 19-13. Then the magic happened. First Utah drove the ball all the way down to the Miner eight yard line but with just 24 seconds remaining, rather than kicking a field goal to salt the game away, the Utes went for it on fourth down and the Miner defense held. Stevens then had sixteen seconds and 92 yards to make something happen. Stevens dropped back into his own end zone looking for Hughes, but the Utes had him bracketed, as Stevens went through his progression when saw the 6'2" Wallace and lofted a ball to him. Wallace ran under it at the 48 and streaked down the left sideline in front of a stunned 8,000 Ute fans as time expired.

"Turning Point" painting by Tom Lea

Joe Cook knocked the point after through and Texas Western had an improbable, season defining moment. Wallace's 92 yard catch is still the longest play in UTEP history and was part of his four catch 164 yard day.

1966 – "Judgement Day in the Bowls I"

The day started with #2 Arkansas playing rival LSU in the Cotton Bowl. LSU knocked off the Razorbacks 14-7. Next up, the Rose Bowl between #1 Michigan State and #5 UCLA. In a bruising affair, the Bruins knocked off the Spartans 14-12, to open up the door for the Orange Bowl, between #3 Nebraska playing #4 Alabama. What a day for College Football Bowl games. Alabama ended up the big winner, with a convincing 39-28 win over Nebraska. Read on...

1966 Cotton Bowl – LSU vs Arkansas – Cotton Bowl Stadium – Dallas, Texas {LSU 14 Arkansas 7}

The 1966 Cotton Bowl Classic was played with national championship implications between the Southwest Conference champion Arkansas Razorbacks and the LSU Tigers. Arkansas and LSU's rivalry had been discontinued since 1956, and Arkansas had not beaten the Bayou Bengals since 1929. This was the second Cotton Bowl Classic meeting, after the Hogs and Tigers met in the 1947 Cotton Bowl Classic. The game, sometimes referred to as the Ice Bowl, ended a tie in the bitter cold, 0–0. For the second time in four years, the Bengal Tigers presented Coach Charles McClendon with a perfect Cotton Bowl game. Unranked LSU (7-3-0) sprang one of the Classic's biggest upsets, downing No. 2 Arkansas, 14-7 in front of 76,200 spectators, and ended college football's longest winning streak at 22. The Hogs (10-0-0) last defeat came by the same score, on the same Cotton Bowl turf, to SMU in the ninth game of 1963. That also was the last time the Hogs had been blanked in the final two quarters until the Bengals turned the trick today.

But, things were different now. The Razorbacks were the heavy favorites, and the unexpected happened. Prone to turnovers and injuries throughout the season, LSU did not yield a fumble or an interception to the Hogs while Quarterback Pat Screen handled the mixture of short passing and the inside power game to perfection.

But it didn't start out that way. On its second possession, Arkansas rolled 87 yards on 11 brilliantly executed plays en route to its only score. Harry Jones dazzled the Tigers with power sweeps and Bobby Burnett pounded the middle. Quarterback Jon Brittenum was in total control, and whipped a 19-yard aerial to Bobby Crockett for the touchdown. The drive consumed just 1:27 and the Razorbacks were on the scoreboard, 7-0. The Tigers roared back two possessions later for an 80 yard march of their own. Tailbacks Jim Dousay and Joe Labruzzo pounded the middle of the Hogs' defense repeatedly with short but effective gains that led to the Arkansas end zone. The LSU drive consisted of 16 plays, and by the time Labruzzo carried over from the three, a full 8:17 had elapsed. Doug Moreau's kick tied it at 7-7.

Three plays after the LSU touchdown, Brittenum was forced to the sideline with a shoulder injury. His replacement, Ronny South, fumbled on the very next play at the Arkansas 34. LSU seized the momentum. Labruzzo again hammered for short yardage, carrying on five consecutive plays, the last one took him over for the score with 18 seconds left in the half and LSU led for the first time. Brittenum returned to duty for the Hogs in the third quarter and twice moved Arkansas inside LSU territory, only to come up empty each time. LSU couldn't move the ball at all and failed to gain a first down the entire period. However, as the fourth quarter rolled around, momentum had shifted again. LSU began a march that would take them all the way to the Arkansas two before the Hog defense forced the Tigers to go for three. But, the kick sailed wide and the Hogs had escaped. Twice in the closing minutes, Brittenum took his Hogs on long drives, only to be intercepted at the LSU 20 to kill the first one, and time simply ran out on them at the end with the ball on the Tiger 24. LSU had done it again. Next up, the Rose Bowl...

1966 Rose Bowl - Michigan State vs UCLA - Rose Bowl Stadium - Pasadena, California {UCLA 14 Michigan State 12}

The game was a rematch of the season opener in East Lansing, Michigan, that Michigan State won, 13–3. Unknown UCLA quarterback Gary Beban had a long touchdown pass play nullified by a penalty in that game. As it turned out, UCLA gave MSU one of its toughest games of the season in its home opener, a fact that was forgotten when the 14-point odds came out favoring MSU for the Rose Bowl re-match. The two previous meetings also were won by Michigan State, the 1954 Rose Bowl and 1956 Rose Bowl.

UCLA's Bob Stiles after delivering the "Knockout Punch"

Michigan State trailed 14-6 late in the fourth quarter, when they got the ball back at the UCLA 49 after Bubba Smith partly blocked a punt by UCLA punter Larry Cox. The Spartans began to march down field in the waning moments, switching on this drive to a two-quarterback system. They alternated Juday and Raye with Daugherty sending in the plays. Three times in this final drive the Spartans went for it on fourth down and picked up the first down. A pass to fullback Eddie Cotton brought the ball to the one-yard line. With thirty-one seconds to play, Juday scored on a quarterback sneak. Trailing 14–12, Daugherty had the Spartans line up on the left hash mark for a two-point conversion attempt. On a play called "option pitch", Raye tossed the football to the sophomore Bob Apisa who ran to the right, and as he turned the corner, it appeared he would fall into the end zone to tie the game. But Apisa was forced by Jim Colletto to run parallel to the goal line. Then Apisa was slowed down by Dallas Grider. Finally, Bob Stiles ran full speed and threw himself into Apisa. Although Apisa knocked Stiles unconscious, Stiles' sacrifice kept Apisa out of the end zone. Next up, the Orange Bowl...

1966 Orange Bowl – Alabama vs Nebraska – Orange Bowl Stadium – {Alabama 39 Nebraska 28}

The 1966 Orange Bowl of the Orange Bowl featured the third ranked Nebraska Cornhuskers and the fourth ranked Alabama Crimson Tide. With the losses of #1 Michigan State in the Rose Bowl and #2 Arkansas in the Cotton Bowl earlier in the day, the game had turned into a de facto national championship game, as the AP would be taking a post-bowl vote for the first time ever. Alabama coach Bear Bryant gave Quarterback Steve Sloan the green light to throw on any down, and Sloan set Orange Bowl passing records in leading the Tide to a 39-28 victory over powerhouse Nebraska. Sloan completed 20-of-28 passes for 296 yards and two touchdowns. A fine three-touchdown performance by Nebraska Quarterback Bob Churchich was not enough to overcome four Nebraska fumbles and a 24-7 halftime deficit.

Steve Sloan of Alabama in 1966 Orange Bowl

Alabama scored first on a 32-yard touchdown pass from Steve Sloan to Ray Perkins as Alabama took a 7–0 lead. In the second quarter, Nebraska's Bob Churchich threw a 33-yard touchdown pass to Tony Jeter to tie the game at 7. Alabama's Les Kelly scored on a 4-yard touchdown run as the Crimson Tide led 14–7. Sloan and Perkins connected for the second time of the game, as Alabama led 21-7. An 18-yard field goal before halftime gave Alabama a 24–7 lead. In the third quarter, Churchich threw a 49-yard touchdown pass to Ben Gregory as Nebraska narrowed the deficit to 24-13. Steve Bowman scored on a 1-yard touchdown run giving Alabama a 32–13 lead. In the fourth quarter, Churchich scored on a 1-yard run making it 32–20. Bowman scored on a 3-yard run as Alabama led 39–20. Churchich threw a 14-yard touchdown pass to Tony Jeter as the final score was Alabama 39, Nebraska 28.

1966 - "Spur of the Moment"

Auburn at Florida - Ben Hill Griffin Stadium - Gainesville, Florida {Florida 30 Auburn 27}

There was a record crowd of 60,511 present on October 29 at Ben Hill Griffin Stadium. The game was bizarre and unusual, with Florida totaling 442 yards of offense compared to Auburn's 18 yards of total offense. Auburn scored on an 89 yard kickoff return by Larry Ellis and a 91 yard fumble return by Gusty Yearout.

Late in the fourth quarter, Florida started a 10 play drive from its own 26 yard line. A penalty against Florida set up a 4th and 14 from the Auburn 24 yard line. The score was tied, 27-27. Florida Quarterback Steve Spurrier lined up to kick a field goal, the Tigers didn't bother to rush. Who thought he would kick? Spurrier knuckled one over the crossbar, the Gators won, and a legend was cemented. Spurrier said after the game, "What was scary was the snap came back and Larry Rentz, the holder, had to put it down with the laced pointed right at me, I just tried to concentrate on hitting them square and managed to get the ball over the post." When the Heisman Trophy ballots went out a week later, it was no contest.

Steve Spurrier kicking game winning 41 yard field goal vs Auburn

1966 - "Bounce Pass Play"

Wyoming at Colorado State - Colorado Field - Fort Collins, Colorado {Colorado State 12 Wyoming 10}

On October 29th, 1966, the #10 ranked Wyoming Cowboys traveled to Fort Collins, Colorado to play their rival, the Colorado State Rams. Colorado Field was a packed house at 14,900. Many fans that were there that day said it was closer to 20,000. The night before, some Wyoming people had burned letters into the grass of Colorado Field, enough to upset the players and fans of CSU. It was a bright and sunny day, perfect for a football game, with Wyoming the heavy favorite. Wyoming had won 10 straight vs Colorado State.

The Cowboys struck with a touchdown early in the first quarter and it appeared they would run away with the game. The Rams defense dug in strong and held Wyoming to that lone touchdown to end the first half 7-0 in Wyoming's favor. The Rams exploded in the third quarter when Oscar Reed rushed 45 yards on one play to the Wyoming 34-yard line. After a series of plays took the Rams to the 15, Al Lavan kicked a field goal and CSU trailed by just four points. The Rams' defense continued to contain Wyoming's potent offense, and with 2:30 left in the third quarter, CSU took over at its own 11-yard line. The Rams drove to the Wyoming 35-yard line when Mike Lude decided to pull out a trick play he had worked on for three weeks. Based on a play first done by Texas Tech several years earlier, Lude utilized his backup tailback, Larry Jackson, to mount the play known as the Bounce Pass. The Bounce Pass was supposed to be executed on third down at the Wyoming 35-yard line, but quarterback Bob Wolfe accidentally threw it directly into Larry Jackson's arms, allowing him to be tackled right away, losing a yard. On the next play, Coach Mike Lude decided to give the Bounce Pass one more try, even though it was fourth down. Wolfe once again threw to Jackson, but this time bounced the ball into Jackson's hands to make it appear the quarterback had flubbed another pass. The lateral throw actually was considered a live ball. Larry Jackson then yelled, "Bobby what the heck's wrong with you? Can't you throw the ball right?"

This scripted action fooled everyone in Larimer County to think the ball was dead as the offense and defense both stopped play. Without a whistle to blow the play dead, Jackson then threw the ball down the field to Tom Pack, who waited all alone. Pack easily scored a touchdown and after Lavan missed the extra point, CSU took the lead 9-7 against the No. 10 team in the country. Both teams traded field goals, with Colorado State's Al Lavan kicking a 26 yard field goal late in the game to give Colorado State a 12-10 victory.

1966 - "Racial barriers broken"

1966 Tangerine Bowl - Tangerine Bowl Stadium - Orlando, Florida {Morgan State 14 West Chester 6}

The 21st annual Tangerine Bowl was played on December 10th, 1966. The Morgan State Bears finished unbeaten with a 9-0 record and was led by future NFL Linebacker and Hall of Famer, Willie Lanier. The West Chester Rams finished the season 8-3.

1966 Morgan State Bears

The Morgan State Bears were breaking a major racial barrier in central Florida, where the Tangerine Bowl had never before invited a historically black college team to participate, and the city of Orlando had never before played host to an integrated high school or college football game. The Bears were one of the winningest college programs in the country under Coach Earl Banks and were in the midst of a 31-game winning streak when they were invited to Orlando. Morgan State defeated West Chester 14-6. The victory in the Tangerine Bowl was the 18th win in that streak, which would stretch into 1968.

1967 - "The Snake's 47 yards to glory"

Alabama vs Auburn - Legion Field - Birmingham, Alabama {Alabama 7 Auburn 3}

The first night game in Iron Bowl history was met with a massive rainstorm that turned the Legion Field turf into a quagmire. Alabama quarterback Ken Stabler didn't care. Trailing 3-0 after his defense posted two critical goal-line stands to the Tigers, Stabler took off on a 47-yard touchdown run early in the fourth quarter, weaving through defenders and then outrunning the Tigers secondary in the mud to post the game-winning score.

1967 - "Blast off"

USC vs UCLA - Los Angeles Memorial Coliseum - Los Angeles, California {USC 21 UCLA 20}

{Game of the Century} On November 18, 1967, The UCLA Bruins, 7–0–1 and ranked No. 1, with senior quarterback Gary Beban as a Heisman Trophy candidate, played the USC Trojans, 8–1 and ranked No. 4, with junior running back O. J. Simpson also as a Heisman candidate. This game is widely regarded as the signature game in the UCLA-USC rivalry as well as one of the 20th century Games of the Century. The 64 yard run by O. J. Simpson for the winning touchdown is regarded as one of the greatest run plays in college football.

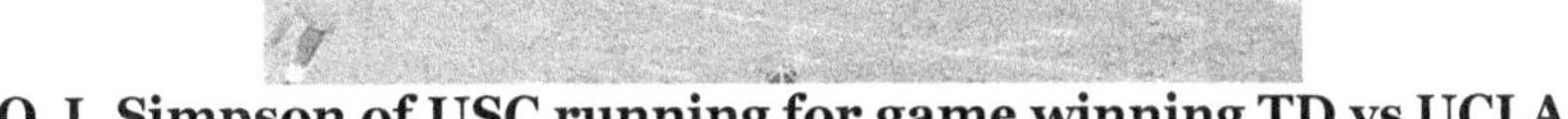

O.J. Simpson of USC running for game winning TD vs UCLA

UCLA led USC 20-14 in the fourth quarter in 1967 when junior O.J. Simpson made the most famous run in Trojan history. USC quarterback Toby Page audibled to 23-Blast. Simpson, behind guard Steve Lehmer and tackle Mike Taylor, started left, moved to the middle, stumbled, righted himself and sped away 64 yards for the winning score. The Trojans won the national title. Simpson waited a year to win his Heisman.

1968 - "Student beats the teacher"

1968 Cotton Bowl - Cotton Bowl Stadium - Dallas, Texas {Texas A&M 20 Alabama 16}

Alabama opened the game with a ten-play, 80-yard drive with Ken Stabler scoring on an eight-yard run to give the Crimson Tide a 7–0 lead. The Aggies responded with a 13-yard Edd Hargett touchdown pass to Larry Stegent to tie the game at 7–7 at the end of the first quarter. After Steve Davis hit a 36-yard field goal on the first play of the second quarter for Alabama, A&M responded late in the quarter with a 7-yard Tommy Maxwell touchdown reception from Hargett. After the ensuing extra point failed, the Aggies took a 13–10 lead at the half. A&M extended their lead to 20–10 early in the third after Wendell Housley scored on a 20-yard touchdown run. The final points of the game came later in the third when Stabler scored his second touchdown of the game, and with a failed two-point conversion attempt and a scoreless fourth, the Aggies won 20–16.

Bear Bryant of Alabama with Gene Stallings of Texas A&M

For his performance, Texas A&M quarterback Edd Hargett was named the Most Valuable Player of the game. As A&M coach Stallings was both a former player and assistant coach under him, Bryant carried him off the field to celebrate the victory.

1968 - "First College Football Game televised in Prime Time"
Alabama at Miami - Orange Bowl Stadium - Miami, Florida {Alabama 14 Miami 6}

This game is noted for being the first college football game to be telecast nationally on prime time television. The game was broadcast on ABC TV. After their victory over LSU, Alabama reentered the AP Poll at the No. 16 position prior to their game at Miami. On homecoming at the Orange Bowl, Alabama defeated the Hurricanes 14–6 behind a long touchdown reception and interception return. The Crimson Tide took a 7–0 lead in the first quarter when Scott Hunter threw a 73-yard touchdown pass to Donnie Sutton. Alabama remained up by a touchdown through the fourth quarter when Mike Dean intercepted a Lew Pytel pass and returned it 69-yards for a touchdown and a 14–0 lead. The Hurricanes responded late with a two-yard Bobby Best touchdown run that made the final score 14–6.

1968 - "Vols win 17-17"
Georgia at Tennessee - Neyland Stadium - Knoxville, Tennessee {Tennessee 17 Georgia 17}

The 1968 game was the first time the two schools had played each other in 31 years. Lastly, in front of a national television audience, the two teams played a memorable football game that ended in a tie in pre-overtime days. The game, which was the 1968 opener for both teams in the days when the first game usually was not played until mid-September, had taken on its unusual flavor back in the summer, when Georgia surprisingly learned that Tennessee was installing an artificial Tartan surface. Once the late afternoon game began, Tennessee – a slight favorite -- went ahead 7-0 in the second quarter, when Mike Jones scored following a fumble recovery by Captain Dick Williams deep in Georgia territory.

In the third quarter, Georgia finally scored, when Jim McCullough kicked a 40-yard field goal after a fourth-down penalty against Tennessee put the Bulldogs within kicking range. Later in the third quarter, Georgia safety Jake Scott caught a Herman Weaver punt at the Georgia 10-yard line, eluded three Vol tacklers and sprinted down the sideline for a 90-yard touchdown to put Georgia up 10-7. Tennessee linebacker Steve Kiner quickly tackled Georgia quarterback Donnie Hampton in the end zone to give the Vols a safety late in the third quarter. The score was now 10-9 in favor of Georgia. In the fourth quarter, Georgia again appeared as if it would be the winning team. Running back Bruce Kemp went through the line, shook off a Vol tackler and sprinted 80 yards for a Georgia touchdown. The score was now 17-9 in favor of Georgia. After Tennessee was forced to punt after three downs, the Bulldogs were able to eat up precious time before having to punt. Tennessee went to work in its own territory.

Bubba Wyche of Tennessee

Only 2:41 remained in the game and Tennessee quarterback Bubba Wyche had completed only seven of 22 passes. The outlook seemed bleak for the Big Orange. Slowly, however, Wyche began moving the Vols down the field. With the help of a 14-yard pass to the pioneering McClain, Tennessee had the ball on the Georgia 9. The game was getting very late. Two Georgia sacks in three plays put the ball back at the 21. Time existed for only one more play, which was a fourth down anyway. For Tennessee, two miracles took place. Gary Kreis caught the touchdown pass from Wyche as time expired, and then Wyche hit Ken DeLong for the successful two-point conversion.

1968 - "Harvard beats Yale 29-29"
1968 Yale at Harvard - Harvard Stadium - Cambridge, Massachusetts {Harvard 29 Yale 29}

The game played November 23, 1968 was highlighted by the Crimson scoring 16 points in the final 42 seconds to tie a highly touted Bulldog squad. Harvard head Coach John Yovicsin substituted twice quarterback Frank Champi -- number 27 - the man of the moment who earned one varsity H at Harvard-- for George Lalich to reignite the Crimson's nearly-extinguished offense. Champi singed the Yale defense at the close of the first half with a touchdown drive (however, Yovicsin returned Champi to the bench at the start of the second half), then Champi, again substituting for the lackluster Lalich, immolated the Yale defense in the closing minutes of the contest. Yale lost six fumbles, an all-time record, adding logs to the fire. Poor officiating and poor timekeeping contributed to the outcome, Yale partisans and players have suggested; nonetheless, Pete Varney, who would later play MLB, ran a slant route, caught the pass right in front of a Yale defensive back Ed Franklin, and Harvard had its 29th point. Yale had a 16-game winning streak. Both teams were 8–0. For the first time since 1909 both adversaries were undefeated and untied for the contest. Yale was ranked at the lower end of a few top national college football polls. Calvin Hill, soon to be the first ever and only Ivy League football athlete selected in the First Round of the NFL draft, and Tommy Lee Jones were in uniform. The Yale roster included two future Rhodes Scholars, Kurt Schmoke and Tom Neville, who would later captain a Yale football squad. The Harvard roster included one future Rhodes Scholar, Paul Saba.

Pete Varney of Harvard 2 point conversion catch

The outcome inspired The Harvard Crimson to print the logically impossible "Harvard Beats Yale, 29–29" headline.

This headline was later used as the title for a 2008 documentary about this Game, directed by Kevin Rafferty. Yale Daily News editors headlined "Johns Stage Dramatic Rally Tie Elis for Title, 29 - All" at top right half of front page of its November 25, 1968 issue. John T. Downey, a Yale football letter winner before joining the CIA, was a prisoner-of-war in 1968. His Chinese captors allowed correspondences from home while he endured solitary confinement. Downey received from a friend a postcard announcing Yale had won, 29 - 13. Months later he learned of the "loss".

1969 Orange Bowl - "Twelve is too much"
Kansas vs Penn State - Miami Orange Bowl - Miami, Florida {Penn State 15 Kansas 14}

Mike Reeves gave Kansas a 7-0 lead on his touchdown run, but Penn State tied the game before halftime on Charlie Pittman's touchdown run. John Riggins gave the Jayhawks a 14-7 lead on his touchdown plunge in the fourth quarter. Later in the game, Kansas had another chance to score with the ball at Penn State's 14 on fourth down with one yard to go. Instead of kicking the field goal, they went for the first down, but Riggins was stuffed for no gain.

Action in the 1969 Orange Bowl - Kansas vs Penn State

With 1:16 to go in the game, a blocked punt gave the ball back to Penn State at the 50. Bob Campbell caught a pass from Chuck Burkhart and was tacked at the 3 yard line. Campbell scored on a touchdown plunge to make it 14-13, pending the conversion attempt. Penn State's conversion attempt fell short, but they were given another chance due to Kansas having 12 men on the field. Given a second try due to a Kansas penalty, Penn State scored on a late two-point conversion to beat the Jayhawks, 15-14, in the 35th Orange Bowl. Kansas held on the previous attempt, but referee Foster Grose noticed 12 men on the field and awarded a second try to the Nittany Lions. Bob Campbell swept over the left side of the line for the win. The final three plays of the game, Kansas had 12 men on the field, but went unnoticed by the officials. It wasn't until Penn State's failed 2-pt conversion attempt that the officials noticed that Kansas had 12 men on the field, and gave Penn State another try which they cashed in on.

1969 - "Shoestring Play"
North Carolina at Duke - Wallace Wade Stadium - Durham, North Carolina {Duke 17 North Carolina 13}

Late in the third quarter, 3rd and 9 on the 47, without a huddle, Duke quarterback Leo Hart bent over to tie his shoe, but the rest of his teammates lined up for a snap. Receiver Marcel Courtillet took the ball and connected with Wes Chesson (who is now in his 33rd year as an analyst on Duke's radio broadcasts) for a 53-yard touchdown. The UNC players, still in defensive huddle, were taken by surprise and Chesson went untouched into the end zone. The **"shoestring play"** snapped a 7-7 tie late in the third quarter and sent Duke onto a victory.

1970 - "Game that changed the Jim Crow South"
USC at Alabama - Legion Field - Birmingham, Alabama {USC 42 Alabama 21}

Through the 1970 season, all college football teams in the south were lily white, no black players were on any teams. The "Jim Crow South" was coming to an end. Teams from the south rarely scheduled teams that had black players on the rosters. The only time they met were in Bowl games, and there are many documented stories of southern teams resisting having to play teams from the North or West that had black players. There are many instances of Bowl games held in the south trying to pressure teams with black players to leave those players home if they wanted to play in the Bowl game. One game changed all this and it took the "Dean" of southern coaches, Paul "Bear" Bryant to realize things had to change. Getting drilled 42-21 by USC in the 1970 season opener, opened his eyes. Paul "Bear" Bryant did as much or more than anyone to integrate the south. Once ol' Bear started playing black players, everyone else followed suit.

The 1970 USC-Alabama game has become well-documented legend. Bear Bryant's all-white Alabama Crimson Tide hosted the Trojans in the opening game of the season, a showdown of two of the best and yet two of the most different teams of the previous decade. USC featured a black starting quarterback, fullback and tailback along with a host of other African-American players, and would be the first fully integrated team to play in the state of Alabama.

Sam "Bam" Cunningham of USC

The outcome would change everything about SEC football in the years to come. Sam Cunningham was somewhat of an unlikely hero to play a shaping role in integrating college football in the South. Despite what urban legend claims, Cunningham was not grandly introduced to the Alabama locker room after the game, but he did receive a polite and earnest congratulations from one of the winningest coaches in college football history. Bear Bryant met Cunningham, Jimmy Jones and Clarence Davis, USC's all-black backfield, outside the locker room to complement each on a game well-played, and the team set off back home to California. College football in Alabama--and in the South--was never the same. As former Bryant assistant coach Jerry Claiborne noted, "Sam Cunningham did more to integrate Alabama in 60 minutes that night than Martin Luther King had accomplished in 20 years."

1970 - "Mr. Clutch"

UCLA at Texas - Texas Memorial Stadium - Austin, Texas {Texas 20 UCLA 17}

Texas would enter the game #2 in both the AP and UPI polls. UCLA took a 3–0 record into Austin to play defending national champ and #2 ranked Texas. Trailing 13–3 at the half, UCLA rallied and had a 17–13 lead in the final minute. But with 12 seconds left, Texas completed a long pass when Cotton Speyrer caught the ball between two UCLA defenders, who then collided, allowing Speyrer to score.

Action in the UCLA vs Texas game

On the second play of the game, Texas halfback Billy Dale was blasted by a UCLA linebacker just as QB Eddie Phillips pitched him the ball on the option. UCLA recovered the fumble and the fight was on. UCLA coach Tommy Prothro was the first coach to attack the Wishbone with a "mirror" defense, essentially playing man-to-man on every member of the offensive backfield. He would disguise where the man was coming from and Royal admitted after the game that he and his staff were caught completely off guard by the maneuver. Texas survived the initial turnover, giving up only a field goal, and the 'Bone worked well enough to produce a 13-3 halftime lead for Texas. That lead didn't last long after halftime, since among the people Prothro brought with him to Austin was Dennis Dummit, a QB with a cannon for a right arm. He completed 19-30 passes for 340 yards and two touchdowns. The Bruins owned the 3rd quarter with two drives of 90 and 95 yards for those scores. UCLA led 17-13 going into the 4th quarter. Late in the 4th quarter, UCLA took over on downs with a little over 2 minutes to go. The air went out of the stadium, and there was only 52 second left when Texas got the ball back, with no timeouts. Facing 3rd and 19, Royal called "86 pass, Ted crossing, Sam post." Jim Bertlesen broke the 'bone and ran a short hook to help clear the middle. Tight End Tommy Woodard (Ted) ran a deep middle route, while Cotton Speyrer (Sam) ran the post. The ball barely went over Woodard's head and as it reached Speyrer the UCLA defender, playing in the prevent defense, tried for the interception while another UCLA defender nearby was caught leaning the wrong way. Just another "Clutch" catch in Cotton Speyrer's career at Texas.

1971 - "Judgement Day in the Bowls II"

The day started with #1 Texas playing #6 Notre Dame in the Cotton Bowl. The Fighting Irish knocked of Texas, opening the door for #2 Ohio State. The Rose Bowl followed with #2 Ohio State playing #12 Stanford. The Indians scored 14 unanswered points in the 4th quarter to upset Ohio State, opening the door for #3 Nebraska. The night closed with #3 Nebraska playing #5 LSU in the Orange Bowl. The Cornhuskers needed a win to claim the National Championship. What a day!

1971 Cotton Bowl - Cotton Bowl Stadium - Dallas, Texas {#6 Notre Dame 24 #1 Texas 11}

Notre Dame scored 21 straight points after Texas' initial field goal before Texas scored in the second quarter to make it 21-11 before Notre Dame added a field goal before halftime, making it 24-11. Parseghian's wishbone defense held the Longhorns in check the rest of the game as neither team scored again, as Texas committed six turnovers (five fumbles and an interception) while Notre Dame had only two turnovers. Notre Dame's win ended the Longhorns 30-game winning streak. The loss by #1 Texas opened the door for #2 Ohio State to claim the National Championship in the Rose Bowl later that day. Stay tuned.....

1971 Rose Bowl - Rose Bowl Stadium - Pasadena, California {#12 Stanford 27 #2 Ohio State 17}

Stanford stunned the college football world with a convincing 27-17 upset over previously unbeaten Ohio State. Ohio State had a chance to claim the National Championship with a victory, as #1 Texas had lost to Notre Dame in the Cotton Bowl earlier in the day. Heisman Trophy winner Jim Plunkett completed 20 of 30 passes for 265 yards and one touchdown, while the Stanford defense, led by defensive tackle Dave Tipton and Linebacker Jeff Seimon, limited the Buckeyes to just three points in the second half as the Indians erased a 14-10 halftime deficit. Stanford trailed 17-13 after three quarters, but Plunkett engineered an 80 yard, 13 play scoring drive culminated by a one yard touchdown run by Jackie Brown. On the Buckeyes next possession, Stanford's Jack Schultz intercepted a Rex Kern pass, giving the Indians the ball on the Ohio State 25 yard line. Four plays later, Plunkett connected with Randy Vataha for a 10-yard touchdown to give Stanford a 27-17 lead with just over eight minutes left to play. Stanford held on for the win, thus leaving the door open for #3 Nebraska......

Jackie Brown of Stanford scoring one of his two touchdowns

1971 Orange Bowl - Orange Bowl Stadium - Miami, Florida {#3 Nebraska 17 #5 LSU 12}

Now it was #3 Nebraska's turn. The 1971 Orange Bowl featured the third-ranked Nebraska Cornhuskers, champions of the Big Eight Conference, and the fifth-ranked LSU Tigers, champions of the Southeastern Conference. Earlier on New Year's Day, the two top-ranked teams lost their bowl games: #1 Texas in the Cotton Bowl and #2 Ohio State in the Rose Bowl. The Huskers were aware when they took the field that night that they could claim the top ranking in the AP Writers poll with a victory. An LSU victory would likely have given Notre Dame the national title.

Paul Rogers kicked a 25-yard field goal for Nebraska to take an early 3–0 lead. Joe Orduna scored on a 3-yard touchdown run, as Nebraska extended its lead to 10–0. In the second quarter, LSU got a 36-yard field goal to cut the lead to 10–3, the score at halftime. In the third quarter, the Tigers added a 25-yard field goal to make it 10–6. On the final play of the third quarter, Buddy Lee threw a 31-yard touchdown pass to Al Coffee to put LSU ahead 12–10. Husker quarterback Jerry Tagge scored from a yard out with 8:50 remaining; it was the game's last scoring play and gave Nebraska the 17–12 win.

Jerry Tagge scoring the winning touchdown

This was the first Orange Bowl played on artificial turf, on Poly-Turf, a competitor to AstroTurf. Airing in primetime on the East Coast, the 1971 Orange Bowl thus became the last televised sporting event to carry cigarette ads, the final one (for Winston) airing at 10:54 p.m. (The very last tobacco advertisement, for Virginia Slims, was shown at 11:59 p.m. during a break on The Tonight Show).

1971 - "We are...Marshall"

Xavier at Marshall - Fairfield Stadium - Huntington, West Virginia {Marshall 15 Xavier 13}

It was the first home game after a 1970 plane crash that killed 36 players, the coaches and other members of the Marshall Football family. The two teams traded field goals, with Xavier going up 6-3 midway through third quarter. Oliver scored on a quarterback sneak with 11:58 to go in the fourth to put Marshall back up 9-6. With 5:18 left, however, an Esbaugh punt was returned by the X-men for a touchdown and Marshall was down 13-9. The two teams traded punts and it appeared Marshall was down to its last chance with 1:18 to play, at the Thundering Herd 48-yard line

Terry Gardner scoring winning touchdown for Marshall

History was in the making. Marshall drove down to the Xavier 13 yard line with time winding down on the game clock. Red Dawson sent down the play and it was signaled into Oliver, a 213 bootleg screen. Oliver called the play, broke the huddle and snapped the ball just before the clock ticked to 0:00. Thundering Herd quarterback Reggie Oliver threw a 13-yard screen to Terry Gardner for a touchdown on the game's final play. Marshall stunned Xavier, 15-13.

1971 - "My first game"

Michigan at Minnesota - Memorial Stadium - Minneapolis, Minnesota {Michigan 35 Minnesota 7}

This one is memorable for me. This if the first college football game I attended. I was 12 years old. My Aunt Roberta took me. I remember after the game, walking behind the band from the stadium to whatever building the band went to. They played the whole way. I thought that was so cool. To this day, watching a band take the field at any college football game sends shivers down my spine.

On October 23, 1971, in the annual Little Brown Jug game, Michigan defeated Minnesota, 35–7, in front of 44,176 spectators in Minneapolis. Billy Taylor rushed for 166 and two touchdowns on 33 carries. He also surpassed Ron Johnson's career total of 2,524 rushing yards to become Michigan's all-time career rushing leader. Michigan rushed for 391 yards in all, including 96 yards for Ed Shuttlesworth, 62 yards and a touchdown for Glenn Doughty, and 25 yards and a touchdown to Fritz Seyferth. Michigan's passing game never got on track, as Tom Slade completed only one of seven passes for 13 yards.

George Honza of Minnesota

Coming into the game in the second half, Larry Cipa threw a five-yard touchdown pass to Larry Gustafson. Dana Coin converted all five point after touchdown kicks for Michigan. Minnesota's lone touchdown came on a 73 yard pass from Craig Curry to George Honza, to tie the game at 7-7. It was all Michigan after that.

1971 - "The Pick"
Ohio State at Michigan - Michigan Stadium - Ann Arbor, Michigan {Michigan 10 Ohio State 7}

Michigan's indomitable Wolverines rallied in the fourth quarter to defeat valiant Ohio State, 10-7, in one of the wildest finishes in the 68-year history of this great football series. Bill Taylor rambled 21 yards on a sweep around right end with 2:07 left in the game for the winning points to climax an uphill battle and send the stadium into bedlam. An all-time NCAA record throng of 104,016 came to see Michigan bury Ohio State and celebrate the Wolves' first perfect season since 1948, but someone forgot to tell the Buckeyes, who played with intense dedication and ferocity. The Wolverines marched 72 yards in 11 plays to preserve their perfect record, overcoming Ohio's 7-3 lead fashioned on an electrifying 85-yard punt return by Tom Campana, gutty Buckeye safetyman, in the third period.

Woody Hayes is irate at Referee Jerry Markbreit's call

This game is known for two memorable moments. Michigan's Tom Darden intercepted a pass by Ohio State quarterback Don Lamka. Darden climbed the back of Split End Dick Wakefield and no interference penalty was called. Ohio State coach Woody Hayes thought interference should have been called. Hayes then put on a disgraceful performance in the closing seconds of the game. First, he raced on the field to protest a pass interference call which he thought should have been called on Michigan. He argued long and hard with the referee, who marched off two consecutive 15-yard penalties. But Hayes was still raving mad. He grabbed the down marker which is used on the sidelines by the chain gang and ripped it to shreds. He flung its pieces onto the playing field. Then Hayes went for another pole, grabbing it from the official's hands and throwing it to the ground.

1971 - "Jolly Rodgers"
Nebraska at Oklahoma - Owen Field - Norman, Oklahoma {Nebraska 35 Oklahoma 31}

{Game of the Century} The 1971 Nebraska vs. Oklahoma football game was the 51st edition of the rivalry, another game dubbed the "Game of the Century." The top-ranked Nebraska Cornhuskers, defending national champions with a 20-game winning streak (and 29 without a loss), traveled south to play the second-ranked Oklahoma Sooners. The game was played at Owen Field in Norman on Thanksgiving Day. Not only at stake was the Big Eight title, but also the #1 national ranking in the polls. However, the bowl trips had already been determined before the game, with Nebraska going to the Orange in Miami and Oklahoma headed for the Sugar in New Orleans. Two days after Thanksgiving, #5 Auburn (9–0) with Heisman Trophy winner Pat Sullivan at quarterback, hosted #3 Alabama (10–0) for the SEC title, the two opponents that Oklahoma and Nebraska would play. Given the magnitude of the game, Devaney had even had his players' food flown in from Lincoln, in case gamblers attempted to induce a hotel chef to give the Huskers food poisoning. The NU-OU game went back and forth, with three lead changes in the second half. The Cornhuskers struck first, with Rodgers shocking the Sooners with a

72-yard punt return for a touchdown after the Sooners' first possession was stopped. Although over 45 years ago, the punt return remains one of college football's signature moments.

Johnny Rodgers of Nebraska

The first modern **Game of the Century** lived up to its billing: No. 1 Nebraska edged No. 2 Oklahoma, 35-31, in a game that came down to the final seconds. But all anyone remembers is the first score of the game: the Huskers' Johnny Rodgers' skittering 72-yard punt return. To this day, whether Rodgers scored because of an uncalled clip depends on your favorite shade of red: Sooner crimson or Husker scarlet. After the game, Dave Kindred of the Louisville Journal wrote, "They can quit playing now, they have played the perfect game."

1972 – "Fifth Down and 24 to go"

Tulane at Miami – Orange Bowl Stadium – Miami, Florida {Miami 24 Tulane 21}

Trailing 21-17 late in the fourth quarter, Miami had first and ten at the Tulane 18. The following sequence of plays then occurred. Chuck Foreman gains two yards. Second-and-eight at the 16. Ed Carney's pass to Foreman is incomplete. Third-and-eight at the 16. Carney complete to Foreman but Miami penalized for illegal procedure. Third-and-13 at the 21. Carney sacked for an 11-yard loss. Fourth-and-24 at the 32. Carney incomplete pass to Phil Corrigan. Fifth-and-24 at the 32. Carney throws TD pass to Witt Beckman with 1:05 to play. Miami thus won the game 24-21 because the officials lost track of the downs. Tulane president Dr. Herbert Longnecker stated: "Had Tulane won a game under these conditions, the alleged victory would have been rescinded by our own actions and the game's outcome would have been reversed ..." However, the Miami coach, Fran Curci, kept the win. Thirteen years later, Tulane would get its revenge against Fran Curci in the "Miracle of all Saints day". {Page 65}

1972 - "When time stood still"

Mississippi at LSU - Tiger Stadium - Baton Rouge, Louisiana {LSU 17 Mississippi 16}

"Entering Louisiana," read a sign put up on the Louisiana-Mississippi state line after this game. "Set your watch back four seconds." Bert Jones somehow got off two passes in the final four seconds, the second to Brad Davis for a 10-yard TD as time expired. Rusty Jackson's PAT left the Rebels singing the "One Second Blues."

LSU winning touchdown vs Ole Miss as time expires

On November 4, 1972, a record 70,502 fans packed Tiger Stadium to witness the Tigers take on the Rebels of Ole Miss. The Fighting Tigers were undefeated at 6-0, and looking to bounce back from a loss to the Rebels in the previous season. The Tigers and Rebels battled neck-and-neck in front of an electric crowd the entire night. In the fourth quarter, the immense Tiger Stadium crowd was temporarily silenced as Ole Miss nailed a 40-yard field goal to take a 16-10 lead. In the following possessions, LSU struggled to put points on the scoreboard. However, the Tigers were granted one last opportunity on their own 20-yard line with 3:02 left to play. Jones lined up under center 80 yards away from conquering his aspiration. The Ruston Rifle would not disappoint. Jones led the Tigers to the Ole Miss 10-yard line on a drive that included two fourth-down conversions. With four seconds remaining, the Tigers appeared to be down to their final chance to win. Jones dropped back 10 yards away from the end zone and threw a pass intended for Jimmy LeDoux that fell incomplete. It appeared that the Tigers had suffered their first loss of the 1972 season. With one second miraculously remaining in the game, LSU was granted one final opportunity. The Rebels used their final timeout of the game. The Tigers gathered around LSU Head Coach Charles McClendon, hoping to scheme a way to get the ball across the goal line. The Tigers took the field with three receivers lined up on the left-hand side, including Davis in the slot. As Jones received the snap, Davis ran an out route toward the left pylon. As time expired, Jones spotted Davis near the pylon and threw the ball in his direction. Davis bobbled the football, but maintained his concentration and made the catch. He then dived into the end zone, tying the game at 16-16. Rusty Jackson tacked on the game-winning extra point, propelling LSU to 7-0 on the season.

1972 - "Punt Bama Punt"

Alabama vs Auburn - Legion Field - Birmingham, Alabama {Auburn 20 Alabama 17}

There have been many memorable games as well as plays in the "Iron Bowl" rivalry. None is more remembered than this one. The game was played on December 2, 1972 at Legion Field in Birmingham, Alabama. The 2nd-ranked and undefeated (10–0) Alabama team led by head coach Bear Bryant came into the game as a 14-point favorite over the Ralph Jordan-coached Tigers, who entered the game 8–1. For the first three and a half quarters the Tide seemed to have the game well in hand. Alabama led 16–0 with ten minutes left in the game. With less than 10 minutes left, an Auburn drive stalled and managed only a field goal, which made it 16–3. Jordan later joked that his decision was derided by all the faithful in attendance: Auburn fans booed for the appearance of giving up, while Alabama fans joined in because the field goal ruined the point spread. On the ensuing possession Alabama was forced to punt. Auburn's Bill Newton blocked Greg Gantt's punt and his teammate David Langner ran the ball back 25 yards for an Auburn touchdown, narrowing the score to 16–10.

First blocked punt

Second blocked punt

Several minutes later, Alabama was forced to punt again. Like last time, Newton blocked the punt and Langner returned it for a touchdown. Gardner Jett kicked the extra point to give Auburn a 17–16 lead.

With the clock winding down, Langner intercepted an Alabama pass to stop their attempted comeback. When Langner reached the sideline, he found Coach Jordan upset. Langner reportedly said, "But coach, I intercepted the pass", to which Coach Jordan said, "Yeah, but our plan was to make them punt."

1973 - "Artful Dodger"
Tennessee at Georgia Tech - Bobby Dodd Stadium - Atlanta, Georgia {Tennessee 20 Georgia Tech 14}

Tennessee visited Bobby Dodd Stadium on October 13, 1973, to play Georgia Tech. They had beat the "Wrambling Wreck" six straight times. Condredge Holloway was a quarterback who was way ahead of his time. While his scrambling ability and athleticism is something that is common among today's QBs, it was a sight to behold in the early 70s. There are countless examples on film of his ability to extend plays and make unbelievable runs, and the greatest of these has to be his touchdown scramble versus Georgia Tech in 1973.

Holloway rolled out looking for an open receiver, but decided to take off after being unable to find the open man. He immediately avoided one would-be tackler behind the line of scrimmage, and then dragged another for five yards before losing him. He then managed to escape three Yellow Jackets at once and then broke the tackle attempts of two more defenders before waltzing into the end-zone for the score. This play was instrumental in the Vols' 20-14 win over the Yellow Jackets and is remembered as one of Holloway's most unforgettable displays of athletic prowess.

1973 Sugar Bowl - "Rockin Robin"
Alabama vs Notre Dame - Tulane Stadium - New Orleans, Louisiana {Notre Dame 24 Alabama 23}

Notre Dame opened the scoring with a Wayne Bullock 6-yard touchdown run, and after a missed extra point took an early 6–0 lead. In the second quarter, Alabama took the lead on a 6-yard Randy Billingsley touchdown run, only to see the Irish go up 14–7 on the following play. On the ensuing kickoff, was returned 93-yards for a touchdown by Al Hunter. The Tide cut the lead to 14–10 late in the quarter on a 39-yard Bill Davis field goal. In the third quarter, the teams traded touchdowns with Alabama scoring first on a 5-yard Wilbur Jackson touchdown run and Notre Dame on a 12-yard Eric Penick touchdown run to make the score 21–17 entering the final period. After Quarterback Richard Todd made a 25-yard touchdown reception from Mike Stock on a beautiful trick play, Davis missed the extra point to only put Alabama up 23–21. The Irish responded with a 19-yard field goal by Bob Thomas.

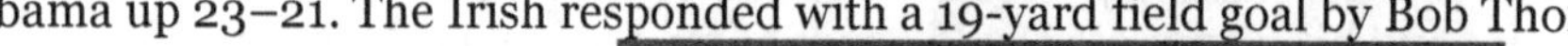

Tom Clements pass to Robin Weber in 1973 Sugar Bowl

Notre Dame led Alabama, 24-23, with 2:00 left when Tide coach Bear Bryant elected to punt the ball. Smart play: The 69-yard kick pinned the Irish at their goal line. Two plays gained only 2 yards. On third down, however, quarterback Tom Clements found backup tight end Robin Weber at the sideline for a 35-yard gain that gave the Irish a first down and allowed them to run out the clock. Why was he open? It was his second catch of the season. With their victory, the Associated Press awarded the Irish the national championship in ranking them #1 in their final poll.

1974 - "Who won the damn game"
Ohio State at Michigan State - Spartan Stadium - East Lansing, Michigan {Michigan State 16 Ohio State 13}

Michigan State manages a considerable upset at home, topping then #1 Ohio State, 16-13. Fullback Levi Jackson scores the final points of the game on an 88-yard TD run, followed by a Hans Neilsen point after touchdown. In a tumultuous finish, Ohio State fails to convert at the Spartans' 1-yard line as time expires. Big Ten Commissioner Wayne Duke went to referee Gene Calhoun and the team of officials to confirm that the Buckeyes had not attempted their second-down play before the clock ran out.

Michigan State players jumped for joy as the scoreboard light bulbs flashed to zero. Moments later, Ohio State's guys were doing the same. One referee signaled a touchdown. Another waved his arms, determining the game had ended. Woody Hayes' volatile temper boiled over as he backhanded an MSU fan who had rushed the field. All Pat McClowry knew was he and the rest of the Spartans' defense had stopped Harold "Champ" Henson at the goal line when it mattered most. And in the process, they had just pulled off perhaps the greatest upset in school history.

Levi Jackson of Michigan State scoring winning TD

Controversial goal line stand by Michigan State

As the clock was ticking down, Ohio State QB Cornelius Greene stepped under center again, with Archie Griffin, Champ Henson and Brian Baschnagel behind him. He handed the ball to Henson, who darted for the line. He was met with a crash. Pat McClowry's helmet slammed into Henson's first. Then Jim Taubert and Kim Rowekamp met him low. Then Terry McClowry joined his brother and others in hitting Henson high. Officials didn't signal a touchdown. The ball was marked down at the half-yard line and the clock kept going. OSU players — after an extended un-piling from the Spartans, who were taking their time getting up — looked around confused, trying to hurry to the line for one final play. The ball got snapped with players moving, bounced off Greene's hands and right to Baschnagel. He landed on it in the end zone. One referee signaled touchdown. Two others said time had expired. Away the officials darted off into the wilderness, as Spartan Stadium's floor became a jungle of fans.

What happens next is legendary. Big Ten Commissioner Duke had been in the press box and ordered the teams to stick around as he looked for the officials, attempting to figure out what happened in those final frantic seconds in an era before replay. A stadium announcement told fans to stay in their seats. Duke wanted to talk to the officials. Coach Hayes ranted and raved and made his players wait in the tunnel, certain they would go back onto the field for one final play. After they entered the locker room, Duke eventually came and told Hayes that, indeed, MSU had won. Hayes went berserk. He immediately went after the commissioner verbally and told him that the Buckeyes got hosed. Baschnagel admits that he never thought his recovery in the end zone would be ruled a touchdown. "The reality is, we didn't get the play off in time and we were in motion anyway. As far as that play is concerned, it wouldn't have been a legal play anyway," he said. "The real question was, should the officials should have stopped the clock and let us get set, because the Michigan State players had been holding us down."

1975 Rose Bowl - "Diggs this win"

USC vs Ohio State - Rose Bowl Stadium - Pasadena, California {USC 18 Ohio State 17}

The 1975 Rose Bowl was game played on January 1, 1975. It was the 61st Rose Bowl Game. Fifth ranked USC Trojans defeated third ranked Ohio State Buckeyes 18-17 in one of the most exciting games in the history of the Rose Bowl. USC quarterback Pat Haden passed to Shelton Diggs for the two-point conversion that gave the Trojans the Rose Bowl victory and the UPI's college football national title.

Shelton Diggs winning 2 point conversion catch for USC in 1975 Rose Bowl

Despite two field goals by Chris Limahelu and a Jim O'bradovich touchdown catch of a Pat Haden pass, USC trails 17-10 because of touchdowns by Buckeyes Champ Henson and Cornelius Greene and a Tom Klaban field goal. USC wins it in spectacular fashion with 2:03 left on the clock. Sub Allen Carter (75 yards) carries on for injured Anthony Davis and spearheads the winning drive before Haden fires a 36-yard touchdown pass to McKay's son, J.K., and a two-point conversion pass to Shelton Diggs. Johnny McKay ends his Rose Bowl career with a 5-3 record, tying Howard Jones for victories.

1975 - "End of an Ara"

1975 Orange Bowl - Orange Bowl Stadium - Miami, Florida {Notre Dame 13 Alabama 11}

The contest was also notable as being Ara Parseghian's final game as Notre Dame Head coach as he announced his resignation from the position December 15. Notre Dame players sent coach Ara Parseghian out with a win, upsetting number one-ranked Alabama 13-11, in an exciting Orange Bowl contest that went down to the wire. With less than two minutes remaining, Alabama needed just a field goal for the win. Facing a second-and-two situation on the Notre Dame 38, Alabama quarterback Richard Todd was intercepted by Reggie Barnett. Underdog Notre Dame led quickly in this contest, 13-0, on a pair of touchdown runs by Wayne Bullock and Mark McLane. Alabama cut it to 13-3 at the half on a 21-yard field goal by Danny Ridgeway. In the fourth quarter, Todd hit Russ Schamun on a 48-yard scoring strike and followed it up with a two-point conversion pitch to George Pugh to narrow the gap to 13-11. A few more yards and the Tide would be in field goal range, but Barnett stepped in front of intended receiver, intercepted the Alabama pass and sealed the victory for Notre Dame.

1975 - "Heart stopping, Literally"

Pittsburgh at West Virginia - Old Mountaineer Field - Morgantown, West Virginia {West Virginia 17 Pittsburgh 14}

The 1975 Backyard Brawl was tied at 14 with less than 20 seconds left in the game. The Panthers were buried deep in their own territory and getting ready to punt. Johnny Majors noticed his punt team was one man short, and Pitt was out of timeouts, so he ran onto the field to draw the penalty so Pitt could get another player on the field. The Mountaineers fair-caught the punt and fumbled out of bounds to stop the clock. West Virginia's Bill McKenzie kicked a 38-yard field goal to win the game over Tony Dorsett and the Panthers.

Fans storming the field after Mountaineers win vs Pitt

Two fans in the stands had heart attacks. Heart-stopping indeed! The victory led to one of the longest post-game celebrations ever at old Mountaineer Field.

1975 - "Sun Devils shock the world"

1975 Fiesta Bowl - Sun Devil Stadium - Tempe, Arizona {Arizona State 17 Nebraska 14}

The 1975 Fiesta Bowl matched the #7 Arizona State Sun Devils and the #6 Nebraska Cornhuskers. Ultimately, it was Danny Kush who started and ultimately ended the scoring in this game that arguably put the Fiesta Bowl game and Arizona State on the map. He gave ASU an early lead in the first quarter, but Monte Anthony gave Nebraska the lead on his touchdown run. With less than a minute remaining in the half, the Sun Devils would drive down the field and narrow the lead to 1 with another Kush field goal. Anthony added in another touchdown run in the third quarter to make Nebraska's lead 14-6. Trailing once again, John Jefferson would catch a touchdown pass from Fred Mortensen, who had taken over at QB after Sproul was briefly hurt on a sneak earlier in the game. Wanting to tie the game, Larry Mucker caught a pass from Mortensen to convert the conversion and make it 14-14.

Danny Kush of Arizona State

After Nebraska failed to make a successful drive, ASU was given the ball back. Dennis Sproul, ready to QB for ASU after a brief injury, drove his team down the field and Kush kicked a 29 yard field goal with 4:50 remaining to give Arizona State the lead as the Sun Devils held Nebraska scoreless the rest of the game as ASU won their fourth Fiesta Bowl. John Jefferson was named Offensive MVP after catching

8 passes for 115 yards. Despite out gaining ASU on rushing, ASU outgained them in passing and total yards and had less turnovers (2 to Nebraska's 3) while only needing one touchdown the whole game.

1976 - "Woods to the rescue"
Missouri at Ohio State - Ohio Stadium - Columbus, Ohio {Missouri 22 Ohio State 21}

Mizzou's late-September 1976 win in Columbus has to be considered one of the greatest in Mizzou's history. Ohio State was ranked 2nd in the country. Mustachioed backup Pete Woods would see his first career start in front of the third-largest crowd in Ohio Stadium history (87,936), against a team that had won 25 straight homes games. Early in the game, Buckeye LB Nick Buonamici tipped and intercepted a Woods pass, setting up a Pete Johnson touchdown that gave OSU a comfortable 21-7 halftime lead. Johnson ran for 103 yards and three touchdowns in the first half, and it looked like Ohio State would win easily.

Mizzu scoring game winning TD vs Ohio State

But then the Mizzou defense stiffened. OSU would gather just 82 yards of offense in the second half (Johnson had just 19). Chris Garlich intercepted a pass near midfield early in the third quarter, Mizzou's Curtis Brown scored from four yards out to cut the lead to 21-14. From there, it became a battle of punting units; Woody Hayes was as conservative as they come, and in assuming that eventually his players would execute well enough to win, he took few chances. On the other sideline, Al Onofrio was not interested in handing the game to Ohio State either. Tiger DE Blaine Henningsen sacked OSU QB Rod Gerald with about five minutes left in the game, OSU was forced to punt. A previously boisterous crowd was starting to get anxious. Milking the clock and attempting just two passes, the Tigers moved down the field, benefitting from a timely Ohio State holding penalty and moving into Buckeye territory. On third-and-6 from the OSU 40, Brown burst through the line for 31 yards. On third-and-goal with 16 seconds left, Woods took a quick, three-step drop and threw a lob to Leo Lewis near the left corner of the end zone. Lewis barely got a foot down and barely held on long enough, but the officials ruled the play a touchdown, and it was 21-20. Without hesitation, Onofrio decided to go for the win. Under pressure while rolling right, Woods threw incomplete, but there was a flag on the play: defensive holding. On the second attempt, Woods evaded two tacklers and sneaked into the end zone. After getting dominated for most of the first half, Mizzou had straight-up stolen a 1-point win in Columbus.

1976 - "79 yards to Glory"
Duke at North Carolina - Kenan Memorial Stadium - Chapel Hill, North Carolina {North Carolina 39 Duke 38}

Needing a victory to secure a 9-2 regular season, seal a bid to the Peach Bowl and deny Duke a winning season, North Carolina got everything it could have wanted in thrilling fashion. Down 38-31 with 2:53 to play, the Tar Heels engineered a 79-yard drive capped with quarterback Matt Kupec's touchdown pass to fullback Billy Johnson with 37 seconds to play. Carolina went for two, and tailback Mike Voight locked up the win after taking an option pitch. It was a perfect cap to a career for Voight, who rushed for 261 yards (which ranks sixth in Carolina history) on a whopping 47 carries to lock up his second consecutive ACC player of the year award. It also turned out to be his final college game; he would miss the Peach Bowl with an ankle injury suffered in practice.

1977 - "The Kick"
Oklahoma at Ohio State - Ohio Stadium - Columbus, Ohio {Oklahoma 29 Ohio State 28}

The Kick refers to Uve Von Schamann's last second field goal on September 24, 1977 in a college football game between the Oklahoma Sooners and Ohio State Buckeyes at Ohio Stadium in Columbus,

Ohio. Make or miss, his field goal attempt would have been the last play of the game. This kick turned out to be the only last-second Oklahoma win in Barry Switzer's coaching career at Oklahoma. The kick eventually went down in Sooners' lore as one of the most memorable plays in Oklahoma history.

This was the first ever meeting between Ohio State and Oklahoma. Within the first four minutes of the game, Oklahoma jumped out to a 14–0 lead. Oklahoma led 17–0 after the first quarter. Uwe von Schamann made a field goal early in the second quarter to put the Sooners ahead 20–0. However, at that point, Oklahoma star running back Billy Sims had a nagging ankle injury and the team's starting quarterback hurt his hamstring. All of a sudden, Oklahoma couldn't move the ball, and the Buckeyes began to capitalize. Ohio State scored a pair of touchdowns to cut the Oklahoma lead to 20–14 by halftime. Ohio State would then score a pair of touchdowns in the third quarter to take a 28–20 lead. Oklahoma would score a touchdown late in the game, but they would miss the game-tying two-point conversion, and thus, they would trail 28–26. It appeared at that point that Oklahoma was going to lose, but however, Oklahoma recovered Schamann's onside kick with just enough time to set up the potential game-winning field goal. After a pass got the Sooners in von Schamann's range, Switzer called back-to-back running plays to set up the ball at midfield. As the clock ticked down, Switzer called a timeout with just six seconds left.

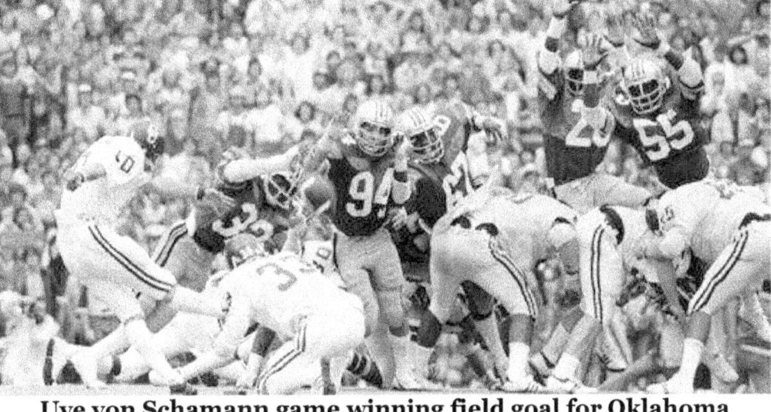

Uve von Schamann game winning field goal for Oklahoma

The kick, made or missed, would be the final play of the game. Woody Hayes called timeout to ice the kicker. However, rather than icing him, it invigorated him. After hearing fans scream "block that kick" during the timeout, von Schamann did the unthinkable. He turned to the crowd and started cheering with them. He raised his arms up and down, imploring them to be louder. He would then hit the 41-yd field goal to win it for Oklahoma 29–28.

1977 - "The Catch"

Clemson at South Carolina - Williams-Brice Stadium - Columbia, South Carolina {Clemson 31 South Carolina 27}

The Gamecocks were still smarting from the previous year's loss in Clemson when the Tigers, despite winning just two games prior to it, pounded USC, 28-9, knocking it out of contention for a possible Peach Bowl bid. The roles were reversed this time around. The Gamecocks were sitting at 5-5 and knew their season was over regardless of the outcome, but Clemson (7-2-1) was in the running for a Gator Bowl invitation and needed a victory over their archrival to secure the bid and go bowling for the first time since 1959. During the first two-and-half quarters, everything was pretty much going according to plan. The Tigers had a veteran team that was hungry and had a head coach that got them believing in themselves. The Gamecocks were young and unsure of what they could accomplish. The Tigers jumped out to a 17-0 lead by halftime, thanks to a Warren Ratchford touchdown, a 30-yard field goal by Obed Ariri and a Lester Brown touchdown from the one. When fullback Ken Callicutt rumbled 52 yards midway through the third quarter, Clemson found itself up 24-0 and well on its way to victory. "Dwight Clark and I did the unpardonable; we started talking about how great we had played," quarterback Steve Fuller said to The (Columbia) State Newspaper back in November of 2002. It was about that time when South Carolina's Spencer Clark raced untouched for a 77-yard touchdown to cut the lead to 24-7. Over the next eight minutes, the Tigers could do nothing right and USC could do no wrong. On Clemson's next three possessions, it fumbled the ball, went three-and-out and then shanked a punt 10 yards. USC took advantage of each mistake to crawl back in the game with two Steve Dorsey touchdowns to make the score 24-20.

Jerry Butler of Clemson making "The Catch"

With 7:02 to play, South Carolina again gained possession of the football and had a chance to take the lead for the first time all night as they moved the ball to the Clemson 40. When Logan curled, quarterback Ron Bass delivered a strike. It was fourth-and-10 at the Clemson 40, and USC seemed desperate to make one last play to at least extend the drive. What Logan did not expect was to be so wide open. "I expected to be hit, but nobody was there," he said. "I cut across the field, got some blocks and I was never touched." Logan's 40-yard touchdown gave the Gamecocks a 27-24 lead with one minute and 48 seconds to play. Logan and his teammates were so confident the game was over. Logan was seen lifting his jersey to the crowd revealing a garnet t-shirt underneath with white letters which read "No Cigars Today." It appeared to motivate the entire Clemson offense. Facing a third down-and-seven, from the Clemson 36 yard line, Fuller hit Rick Weddington for 26-yards to the South Carolina 38 yard line and a first down. After an incompletion, Fuller found Clark across the middle for 18 yards, setting Clemson up at the 20. The Tigers quickly rushed to the line to run another play, when Fuller noticed South Carolina's defense was confused and they had trouble getting players onto the field. The play called for Jerry Butler to cut to the corner, but USC got pressure to Fuller and forced him to throw the ball earlier than he would have liked.   Butler made a leaping, twisting catch that no one else could have made in that game, and no one else has made since. Instead, it's a play simply known as **"The Catch"**. The 20-yard pass play gave Clemson the lead and with the extra point Clemson led 31-27, with 49 seconds left. The Tigers held on to defeat the Gamecocks.

1978 Gator Bowl - "Punch Out - End of Woody"

Clemson vs Ohio State - Gator Bowl Stadium - Jacksonville, Florida {Clemson 17 Ohio State 15}

The 1978 Gator Bowl was played between the Ohio State Buckeyes and Clemson Tigers on December 29, 1978. This game proved to be Coach Woody Hayes' last game at OSU as well as his last game as a college football coach.

Woody Hayes of Ohio State being restrained by his players in 1978 Gator Bowl

With just over two minutes left in the game, OSU trailed 17–15. Ohio State quarterback Art Schlichter threw a pass that sailed wide of an Ohio State back and was intercepted by Clemson Middle Guard Charlie Bauman. Bauman ran towards the OSU sideline avoiding tackles and was finally shoved out of bounds, but after he got up coach Hayes punched Bauman through his face mask. The next day Ohio State fired Hayes after 28 seasons as the Buckeyes head coach.

1979 – "Bowl games for the Ages"

January 1st, 1979, a day for watching three classic Bowl games on New Year's Day. First up was the showdown for the national championship between #2 Alabama and #1 Penn State on ABC Sports. Two legendary coaches, Bear Bryant of Alabama and Joe Paterno of Penn State squaring off. Over in Dallas, Texas, #9 Houston was playing #10 Notre Dame in the Cotton Bowl and broadcast on CBS. Later on in the afternoon, #5 Michigan was playing #3 USC in the Rose Bowl and being telecast on NBC. Three Bowl games, three memorable moments in College Football history.

1979 Sugar Bowl - "Goal line Tide"
Alabama vs Penn State - Louisiana Superdome - New Orleans, Louisiana {Alabama 14 Penn State 7}

On January 1, 1979 the planets aligned to pit No. 2 Alabama against No. 1 Penn State in a dogfight to decide the nation's pre-eminent power. The confrontation could not have been sweeter for a Superdome crowd of 76,824 that was not only treated to the top two teams in college football, but also two of its most exalted coaches. Alabama legend Paul "Bear" Bryant was determined to finish the season just as his Crimson Tide had entered it: ranked No. 1. Penn State's legend-to-be, Joe Paterno, hoped to bring Happy Valley its first national championship. The game was a defensive stalemate for the majority of the first half, leaving the contest scoreless until the final eight seconds of the second quarter. Alabama had the ball with just over one minute remaining in the half, and had originally planned to run out the clock. However, the Nittany Lions called two timeouts during the drive in the hopes of taking over possession with enough time to kick a field goal. Nathan scampered 37 yards on two plays to take the Crimson Tide down to the Penn State 30-yard line. From there, 'Bama quarterback Jeff Rutledge hit an open Bruce Bolton for a 30-yard touchdown, sending the Tide into the half with a 7-0 lead.

Scoring didn't come much easier in the second half, but the Nittany Lions finally tied the score at seven with around four-and-a-half minutes remaining in the third quarter. Penn State's Pete Harris intercepted Rutledge on the Alabama 48-yard line setting up the scoring drive that culminated with a 17-yard Chuck Fusina pass to Scott Fitzkee in the end zone. Shortly thereafter, Alabama answered with a 62-yard Lou Ikner punt return to the Lions' 11-yard line. Indeed, they did. Three plays later, it was Major Ogilvie himself, who jaunted eight yards to the goal line to put the Tide back on top 14-7. As time erased invaluable minutes from the clock in the fourth quarter, the Lions were in need of a break. They got one. On a misdirected option play, Penn State linebacker, and future NFL standout, Matt Millen forced a fumble, which was recovered by the Lions at 'Bama's 19-yard line. JoePa's troop managed a first down at the Alabama 8-yard line, giving them four shots at the end zone. The following series would later come to define the contest. First down brought a two-yard gain. From the Crimson Tide's six-yard line on second-and-goal, Fusina found Fitzkee once again just before the goal line, but as he turned toward the end zone, Alabama's Don McNeal materialized, hammering Fitzkee backward and preventing the touchdown.

Matt Suhey of Penn State stonewalled by the Crimson Tide

Matt Guman of Penn State stopped by Alabama at the goal line

On third-and-goal, fullback Matt Suhey readily accepted the hand-off, and lumbered up the middle for what would have been the tying score. But 'Bama's defense enfolded the line, halting him just inches short of the stripe. That left the Nittany Lions one final play to break the standoff. On fourth-and-inches, Joe Paterno called upon tailback Matt Guman to plod up the gut into the heart of the Crimson Tide's defense. But All-America linebacker Barry Krause emerged from the trenches to stunt Guman's progress, making a stop that has gone down as one of the biggest tackles in college football history. It was the first of two consecutive national championships for the Crimson Tide.

1979 Cotton Bowl Classic - "Joe Cool"
Houston vs Notre Dame - Cotton Bowl Stadium - Dallas, Texas {Notre Dame 35 Houston 34}

On New Year's Day 1979, Notre Dame and Houston met in the 43rd Cotton Bowl Classic following a brutal winter storm in Dallas. Though the Fighting Irish jumped out to a 12-0 lead, the Cougars scored the next 20 and held an eight-point lead at halftime. Fighting the flu and struggling to stay warm, quarterback Joe Montana stayed in the locker room when the team returned to the field, while the medical staff covered him with blankets and fed him chicken soup. Houston added two more touchdowns, and the outlook looked bleak for the Fighting Irish.

Kris Haines of Notre Dame game winning touchdown reception

After spotting Houston a 34-12 lead, Montana returned and Notre Dame scored 23 points in the fourth quarter to pull off a 35-34 victory. To this day, it remains one of the greatest comebacks in college football history. Montana led a 23-point fourth-quarter comeback, finishing it with an 8-yard touchdown to Kris Haines in the final seconds. The Montana legend that grew in San Francisco had its birthplace in Fair Park.

1979 Rose Bowl - "Phantom Touchdown"
Michigan vs USC - Rose Bowl Stadium - Pasadena, California {USC 17 Michigan 10}

The 1979 Rose Bowl between the USC Trojans and the Michigan Wolverines was a showdown between two top five teams. Michigan came into the game ranked 5th with a 10−1 record. USC came into the game ranked second in the Coaches' Poll and third in the AP Poll with an 11−1 record. The marquee matchup, however, might best be remembered for a controversial call. In the second quarter, From the Michigan three-yard line during the second quarter, in a dive over the middle towards the goal-line, Charles White fumbled the ball before he entered the end-zone.

The officials for this game were made up of a Pac-10/Big Ten crew. Upon White's fumble, a Pac-10 official immediately and correctly marked the ball around the one-yard line and signaled that there had been a change of possession. Then a Big Ten official came running in raising his hands signaling that White had scored a touchdown. This touchdown has become known as White's "Phantom Touchdown" as he was awarded the score after first fumbling, then entering the end-zone without the ball. This was confirmed by White himself. The score turned out to be the difference in the game as USC went on to win 17-10 and capture their 16th Rose Bowl.

1979 - "Turn on the A.C."
Indiana at Michigan - Michigan Stadium - Ann Arbor, Michigan {Michigan 27 Indiana 21}

It was homecoming weekend for Michigan, as the 5-1 Wolverines faced Indiana on October 27, 1979. The Hoosiers were historically pretty lousy even back then, but under head coach Lee Corso, they had enjoyed a little bit of a resurgence; from 1976-1980, Indiana was over .500. Michigan appeared to be putting this game in hand without much distress. The Wolverines had a 21-7 lead in the fourth quarter, and the game wasn't terribly compelling. But then the Hoosiers scored twice, including a touchdown drive that ended with under a minute to go, and suddenly, Corso and his gang looked like they could walk out of the Big House with a tie, back when that was a major, major accomplishment.

The Wolverines got the ball at their own 22 with 51 seconds left, and they passed midfield before, with six seconds left, running back Lawrence Reid pitched the ball out of bounds at Indiana's 45 to stop the clock. That's now illegal, but it happened, and it gave Michigan one last shot at victory. QB John Wangler took the snap, dropped back, and found Anthony Carter all alone in the Hoosier secondary. Carter eluded two tacklers en route to the end zone with no time left on the clock. The Big House exploded, and Michigan fans stormed the field in wild celebration as the Wolverines snatched victory from the jaws of a tie.

1980 - "Baby Bull"

Georgia vs Tennessee - Neyland Stadium - Knoxville, Tennessee {Georgia 16 Tennessee 15}

The season began with junior Donnie McMickens starting ahead of Herschel Walker at tailback as the Bulldogs faced the University of Tennessee on September 6 in Knoxville. With Tennessee gaining a 9–0 lead early in the 2nd quarter, coach Dooley told his offensive coordinator, "I'm putting Herschel in...Don't be afraid to let him carry the ball.

Bill Bates, meet Herschel Walker. Georgia, who trailed early 15–0, rallied back behind Herschel Walker, who, on his first collegiate touchdown, ran right over Tennessee defender Bill Bates, from 16 yards out. Walker scored again five minutes later on a 9-yard touchdown run. Georgia would go on to win 16–15, their first victory of an undefeated national championship season.

1980 - "Run Lindsay Run"

Florida vs Georgia - Gator Bowl Stadium - Jacksonville, Florida {Georgia 26 Florida 21}

On November 8th, 1980, the #2 Georgia Bulldogs met the #20 Florida Gators at the Gator Bowl Stadium in Jacksonville, Florida. The rivalry was known as "The world's largest outdoor Cocktail Party". Fans were at a fever pitch for this game and lived up to its pre-game billing. It is one of the greatest games in this long standing rivalry between these SEC foes.

With time running out on 3rd-and-11, Trailing the underdog 1980 Florida Gators with their perfect season and their No. 2 ranking in jeopardy, The most important play of Georgia's lone AP national championship season, came with the Dawgs trailing Florida 21-20, the ball on their 7-yard line, third-and-11, 1:03 to play. In other words: hopeless. The call, Left 76, was supposed to pick up a first down. But Buck Belue threw over the middle to Lindsay Scott, who caught the ball and sprinted 93 yards, right into the hearts of Georgia fans forever. The

improbable 93-yard pass play sealed the Bulldogs' 26–21 victory, and kept Georgia's national championship hopes alive. The Bulldogs moved to No. 1 in the next round of polls and would go on to win the 1980 consensus national championship.

1981 - "Mazur to Cornwell"

#2 Oklahoma at #1 USC - L.A. Memorial Coliseum - Los Angeles, California {USC 28 Oklahoma 24}

At the end of an afternoon filled with mistakes by the two highest-ranked college football teams, a game in which it was obvious that the winner would be the team that avoided the last blunder, Fred Cornwell redeemed himself today. Cornwell, a tight end who 10 seconds earlier got in the way of a pass that could have gone for a touchdown, caught a 7-yard pass from John Mazur with two seconds to play to give Southern California a frantic 28-24 victory over second-ranked Oklahoma. The victory should preserve Southern Cal's top ranking for another week, but it is a tenuous position. Oklahoma fumbled 10 times and lost the ball on five of those fumbles. Two lost fumbles abruptly ended drives that could have extended the Sooners' lead in the third quarter. Still, the Trojans were 10 points behind in the fourth quarter. All day long, before a national television audience and a crowd of 85,651, both teams slipped as if banana peels were strewn on the field. Even the two most trustworthy Trojans - Traveler, the white horse who is the mascot, and Marcus Allen, the latest in the line of outstanding tailbacks - could not keep their footing at times. Traveler fell as he raced around the Los Angeles Memorial Coliseum after U.S.C.'s next-to-last touchdown. Allen gained 208 yards to tie a national collegiate record with his third straight game of 200 or more, had touchdowns runs of 27 and 3 yards, and played what Coach John Robinson called "the best game of any tailback we've ever had." But during the final drive, with U.S.C. trailing by 24-21 and facing a third-and-2 situation at the Oklahoma 26-yard line, Allen slipped. Mazur, the sophomore quarterback, had to carry the ball on the broken play. He landed short of the first down, but fell forward on the next play to maintain the drive. Three plays later, on third-and-10, with the Trojans determined not to settle for a tying field goal, Mazur passed to Malcolm Moore for a 15-yard gain to the Sooner 7. The crowd roared for what seemed to be the inevitably heroic Trojan finish. But today nothing could be taken for granted. With 12 seconds to play, on second-and-goal from the 7, the Trojans tried to improvise. And the result was Cornwell's biggest mistake. Robinson changed Cornwell's assignment, so that Cornwell would delay at the line of scrimmage before he ran his pattern. Mazur spotted Allen in the end zone and let go of the ball for what he thought would be a touchdown. He even started to raise his hands in the victory signal. But Cornwell, who had caught only one pass in his college career, thought the pass was intended for him. He reached up and touched the ball, knocking it to the ground. Allen was still waiting. With nine seconds to go, on third down, the Trojans ran the same play. This time Cornwell ran on his regular assignment, but Mazur could not find an open receiver. Time was running out, and Mazur started to run to his left. First, an open path to the goal line disappeared, and two Oklahoma defenders were suddenly closing in. "Then," Mazur said, "all of a sudden here comes Fred with his arms up." So he threw a soft pass to Cornwell, who had eluded Keith Stanberry, a freshman defensive back on the left side, for the winning score.

Fred Cornwell of USC scoring the winning touchdown

Of the Oklahoma fumbles, only two were forced by U.S.C. tackles. Kelly Phelps, the starting quarterback who scored the first touchdown of the game on an 11-yard run, lost one fumble. And Stanley Wilson, the Sooner fullback who scored on the second Sooner touchdown on a 1-yard run in the second quarter, lost two fumbles. Weldon Ledbetter, the backup fullback, also lost one, and a freshman punt returner, Elbert Watts, had a fair catch slip through his hands with 3:05 to go in the first half. U.S.C. recovered Watts's fumble and, after failing to gain a yard in two possessions, the Trojans, trailing by 17-7, had the ball at the Oklahoma 40. Seven plays later, after Mazur's 1-yard pass to a sophomore, John Kamana, they were within 3 points. When the Sooners lost the ball three straight times at the start of the second half, the game seemed to be slipping away from them, despite Darrell Shepard's 7-yard run at the start of the fourth quarter that put them ahead, 24-14. "Two times we could have had touchdowns," said Buster Rhymes, an Oklahoma halfback. "I didn't even know how they were fumbling sometimes. I'd look back and see U.S.C. with the ball and figure, 'wow, what happened?' " But once Cornwell had grabbed the ball, he would not let it go. Long after the second catch of his career, he held the ball in his lap.

1982 Sugar Bowl - "Marino to Brown"
Georgia vs Pittsburgh - Louisiana Superdome - {Pittsburgh 24 Georgia 20}

In an intense battle featuring five lead changes, Pittsburgh quarterback Dan Marino clinched the 1982 Sugar Bowl with a late-game, 33-yard touchdown pass to tight end John Brown. The Panthers (10-1) entered the game in an ornery mood. They topped the Associated Press poll for the last four weeks of the regular season. However, a 48-14 thrashing by Penn State in the last game of the season quelled their dreams of a national championship. According to Brown, he and his teammates saw the trip to New Orleans as a chance for redemption. Pittsburgh had a worthy opponent in Georgia (10-1), who was riding an eight-game winning streak. The Bulldogs had an outside shot at repeating as national champions thanks to sophomore running back Herschel Walker, who had banged out 1,807 yards during the regular season. Georgia took a 13-10 lead into the fourth quarter. Four plays after Pittsburgh recovered a fumble on the Bulldogs' 23, Marino and Brown hooked up for a six-yard touchdown. Georgia answered with an 80-yard touchdown drive and led 20-17 with 8:31 remaining. Still down three with 3:36 left, Pittsburgh started its final drive at its own 20. Thomas' clutch running and a key scramble by Marino helped carry the Panthers to the Georgia 33.

John Brown and Dan Marino of Pittsburgh

Facing a fourth down and five in the final minute, Pittsburgh called a timeout to consider its options. Sherrill called for a play designed to gain the five yards necessary for a first down. However, when Pittsburgh's running backs kept Georgia's blitzing linebackers in check, Marino had ample time to pick out an open man downfield. Brown was that man, catching Marino's bomb in the middle of the end zone with just 35 seconds on the clock. The touchdown gave the Panthers a 24-20 win and a No. 4 ranking in the final AP poll. Georgia followed at No. 6.

1982 - "It only takes Two"
Nebraska at Penn State - Beaver Stadium - State College, Pennsylvania {Penn State 27 Nebraska 24}

Penn State's Kirk Bowman caught two passes all season. Both of them were for touchdowns against Nebraska, propelling the Nittany Lions to a thrilling 27-24 victory over the Cornhuskers. The host Nittany Lions were ranked #8 in the AP Poll in the week leading up to the game with #2 Nebraska. Both teams were undefeated.

Todd Blackledge (#14) of Penn State

After Nebraska took a 24-21 lead late in the fourth quarter, Penn State returned the ensuing kickoff to their own 20 yard line, but Nebraska's David Ridder was flagged for a personal foul. The fifteen yard penalty saw the final drive start from the Penn State 35. Blackledge led Penn State down the field to the Nebraska 28, where the drive appeared to have stalled, but on fourth down and 11, Penn State kept the drive alive when Blackledge completed a pass to Jackson for a first down. The next (and most controversial from Nebraska's point of view) completion, on second down and four yards to go, saw Blackledge hook up with Mike McCloskey for 15 yards to set up first and goal from the Nebraska 2, with nine seconds remaining on the clock. Nebraska defensive players thought McCloskey was out of bounds, but without the benefit of instant replay, Penn State took advantage and Blackledge hooked up with Bowman on the winning touchdown pass with 4 seconds left.

1982 - "The Play"

Stanford at California - Memorial Stadium - Berkeley, California {California 25 Stanford 20}

The Play was a last-second kickoff return during the Stanford Cardinal and California Golden Bears Rivalry game on Saturday, November 20, 1982. Given the circumstances and rivalry, the wild game that preceded it, the very unusual way in which The Play unfolded, and its lingering aftermath on players and fans, it is recognized as one of the most memorable plays in college football history and among the most memorable in American sports. Stanford took a 20–19 lead on a field goal with four seconds left. The Golden Bears used five lateral passes on the ensuing kickoff return to score the winning touchdown and earn a disputed 25–20 victory. Members of the Stanford Band came onto the field midway through the return, believing that the game was over, which added to the confusion and folklore. There remains disagreement over the legality of two of the backward pass attempts, adding to the passion surrounding the traditional rivalry of the annual "Big Game." This was the two teams' 85th Big Game.

With Cal leading 19–17 late in the fourth quarter, quarterback John Elway and the Cardinal overcame a 4th-and-17 on their own 13-yard line with a 29-yard completion, then managed to get the ball within field goal range for placekicker Mark Harmon. Elway called a timeout with 8 seconds left on the clock. Had Elway let the clock run down to four seconds before calling time, the ensuing kickoff would not have taken place since the clock would have run out on the field goal. But Elway was under instruction from Coach Paul Wiggin to call timeout at the 8 second mark to allow time for a second field goal try in case Stanford drew a penalty on the first attempt. Harmon's 35-yard kick was good, putting Stanford ahead 20–19. However, the team's celebrations drew a 15-yard unsportsmanlike conduct penalty, enforced on the ensuing kickoff. This was crucial, as Stanford was now kicking off from their 25 instead of the 40. At that point, Cal announcer Joe Starkey praised Stanford and Elway for their efforts, and added, "Only a miracle can save the Bears now!" With 4 seconds left, Stanford special teams coach Fred von Appen called for a squib kick on the kickoff. Due to confusion, Cal took the field with only 10 men, one short of the regulation eleven, but still legal in American football. What happened next became one of the most debated and dissected plays in college football history.

- Harmon squibbed the kick and Cal's Kevin Moen received the ball inside the Cal 45 near the left hash mark. After some ineffective scrambling, Moen lateraled the ball leftward to Richard Rodgers.
- Rodgers was very quickly surrounded, gaining only one yard before looking behind him for Dwight Garner, who caught the ball around the Cal 45.
- Garner ran straight ahead for five yards, but was swallowed up by five Stanford players. While Garner was being tackled, however, he managed to pitch the ball back to Rodgers. It was at this moment, believing that Garner had been tackled and the game was over, that several Stanford players on the sideline and the entire Stanford band (which had been waiting behind the south end zone) ran onto the field in celebration.
- Rodgers dodged another Stanford player and took the ball to his right, toward the middle of the field, where at least four other Cal players were ready for the next pitch. Around the Stanford 45, Rodgers pitched the ball to Mariet Ford, who caught it in stride. Meanwhile, the Stanford band, all 144 members, had run out past the south end zone—the one the Cal players were trying to get to—and had advanced as far as twenty yards downfield. The scrum of players was moving towards them.
- Ford avoided a Stanford player and sprinted up field while moving to the right of the right hash mark, and into the band, which was scattered all over the south end of the field. Around the Stanford 27, three Stanford players smothered Ford, but while falling forward he threw a blind lateral over his right shoulder.
- Moen caught it at about the 25 and charged toward the end zone. One Stanford player missed him, and another could not catch him from behind. Moen ran through the scattering Stanford

Band members for the touchdown, which he famously completed by running into unaware trombone player Gary Tyrrell.

Kevin Moen of California amongst the Stanford band

The Cal players celebrated wildly—but the officials had not signaled the touchdown. Stanford coach Paul Wiggin and his players argued to the officials that Dwight Garner's knee had been down, rendering what had happened during the rest of the play moot. Meanwhile, the officials huddled. The chaos at the end of The Play made the officials' task very challenging. In particular, the questionable fifth lateral took place in the midst of the Stanford band, greatly reducing visibility. After determining that Cal had scored and no one had ruled any of the laterals illegal, Moffett signaled the touchdown, rendering the illegal participation penalty on Stanford irrelevant and ending the game. The final score was Cal 25, Stanford 20. The California Golden Bears win the Stanford Axe.

1982 - "Bo over the top"

Alabama vs Auburn - Legion Field - Birmingham, Alabama {Auburn 23 Alabama 22}

Bo Over the Top was an iconic collegiate football play in the 1982 Iron Bowl. The play involved famous Heisman Trophy winner Bo Jackson and proved to be the deciding factor in the game between the Auburn Tigers and Alabama Crimson Tide. The "Over the Top" refers to the nature of the play. Jackson, a state champion high jumper in high school, jumped over the Alabama defensive line on a critical 4th down play from the 1-yard line.

QB Jason Campbell began the winning drive by hitting Chris Woods for 12 yards on first down. Three plays later, Auburn faced a fourth and 1 from the Alabama 46, but Jackson got the first down easily to the 43. After a sack, Campbell faced a 3rd and 13 and coolly hit Mike Edwards for 15 yards to the 31 with 3:30 left. On 2nd and 10, Campbell's pass was intercepted by Jeremiah Castille, but Castille was flagged for pass interference. Auburn now had the ball first and goal at the Alabama 9. A false-start penalty by Ed West set them back to the 14. After an incomplete pass and a 4-yard run by Jackson, Auburn faced 3rd and goal. Campbell then hit Jackson on a crossing route, and he was stopped 18 inches from the goal line by Castille and Tommy Wilcox with 2:30 left. In the huddle with Coach Dye, Jackson suggested a play. "Coach, I was a 7 foot high jumper in high school. Why don't we go over the top?" Dye complied with his running back and Auburn went with the play. Lead blockers on the play were running back Lionel James and fullback Ron O'Neal. Jackson plunged over the line and barely eclipsed the goal line, giving Auburn a 23-22 lead.

1982 - "End of the Bear"

1982 Liberty Bowl - Liberty Bowl Stadium - Memphis, Tennessee {Alabama 24 Illinois 15}

The 1982 Liberty Bowl was held on December 29, 1982, in Memphis, Tennessee, at Liberty Bowl Memorial Stadium. The game featured the Illinois Fighting Illini, of the Big Ten Conference, and Alabama Crimson Tide, of the SEC. Alabama won the game, 21–15. Alabama entered the game with a 7–4 record, losing their final three games. The team was led by coach Paul "Bear" Bryant, who was coaching his final game after twenty-five years with the program, announcing he would retire and hand over control of the team to Ray Perkins following the game. Bryant's retirement made the Liberty Bowl one of the most covered games that season as many news stations and newspapers sent reporters to cover the game.

In the first quarter, Ricky Moore began the scoring as he punched in a 4-yard touchdown run to give Alabama an early lead. Illinois scored their own touchdown in the second quarter as Joe Curtis scored on a 1-yard touchdown run, but kicker Mike Bass missed the extra point which gave Alabama a 7–6 halftime lead. Wide receiver Jesse Bendross extended Alabama's lead when he scored on an 8-yard touchdown run off a reverse. Illinois rallied behind quarterback Tony Eason following a touchdown pass to Oliver Williams and a 23-yard field goal from Mike Bass. Craig "Touchdown" Turner scored the final points in the fourth quarter for Alabama from a 1-yard touchdown run. Defensive back Jeremiah Castille was named the game's MVP after intercepting three passes from Tony Eason. Despite giving up 444 total offensive yards from Illinois, 423 passing yards by Eason, Alabama won the game 21–15. The Tide intercepted seven passes in this game, four from Eason and three from backup quarterback Kris Jenner. Jenner was in the game for only three plays, all of which came after Eason had to leave the game after taking a hard hit from the Alabama defense. On all three plays, Jenner attempted a pass which was intercepted. Bear Bryant finished with a collegiate record of 323 victories, 85 losses, and 17 ties. Bryant died of a heart attack January 26, 1983— less than four weeks after the Liberty Bowl.

1983 Holiday Bowl - "To be Young again"
BYU vs Missouri - Jack Murphy Stadium - San Diego, California {BYU 21 Missouri 17}

The 1983 Holiday Bowl was played December 23, 1983 in San Diego, California. It featured the ninth ranked BYU Cougars, and the unranked Missouri Tigers. Missouri scored first with a 2-yard touchdown run from running back Eric Drain giving the Tigers an early 7-0 lead. In the second quarter, BYU quarterback Steve Young scored on a 10-yard touchdown run to tie the game at 7. Missouri's Brad Burditt kicked a 37-yard field goal, as Missouri took a 10-7 lead into halftime. In the third quarter, BYU came up on top, thanks to a 33-yard touchdown pass from Steve Young to Eddie Stinnett giving BYU a 14-10 lead. In the fourth quarter, Eric Drain scored on his second rushing touchdown of the game, a 2 yarder, for the Tigers to take a 17-14 lead.

With just 23 seconds left, Steve Young gave a handoff to Eddie Stinnett. Stinnett then turned around and passed it back to Steve Young, who caught it and ran in for a touchdown, giving BYU a 21-17 win. Young achieved a rare feat in college football: one touchdown pass, one touchdown run, and one touchdown reception all in a single game. For his efforts, he was named offensive MVP.

1984 - "Rose Bowl Scoreboard prank"
1984 Rose Bowl - Rose Bowl Stadium - Pasadena, California {UCLA 45 Illinois 9}

A prank played by students from the California Institute of Technology altered the scoreboard display, an incident reminiscent of the Great Rose Bowl Hoax of 1961. A pair of Caltech students evaded security at the Rose Bowl, gained access to the electronic system and installed a computer that could be remotely controlled to alter the display on the stadium's digital scoreboard. During the game, the students from Caltech remotely altered the scoreboard display to show the teams playing in the game as Caltech and M.I.T., in place of UCLA and Illinois. One of the prank's perpetrators had received approval from his Caltech professor for the prank, which earned him credit for the course "Experimental Projects in Electrical Circuits".

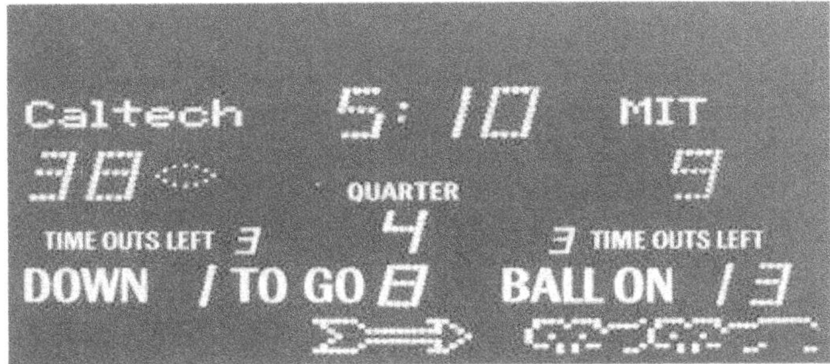

Cal Tech's scoreboard prank in the 1984 Rose Bowl

Head Coach Mike White led Illinois to a perfect 9-0 Big Ten Conference record and the first Fighting Illini visit to Pasadena in 20 years. UCLA ended fourth-ranked Illinois' hopes for a national championship with a 45-9 victory. The Bruins piled up 21 second-quarter points en route to a 28-3 halftime lead. UCLA quarterback Rick Neuheisel enjoyed the best game of his college career, completing 22 of 31 passes for 298 yards. The Bruins rushing attack ground out 232 yards to give UCLA 511 yards in total offense. Illinois ended the season with a 10-2 record, only the second Illinois team in history to win 10 or more games, and became the first and only team in conference history to defeat all nine Big Ten opponents in the same season. Trudeau's 3 interceptions tied a Rose Bowl single-game record (set in the 1963 Rose Bowl) which still stands as of 2008. Rick Neuheisel completed 22 of 31 passes for 298 yards with 4 touchdowns and no interceptions. Terry Donahue was later to state that the man-to-man pass coverage by the Illini was one of the reasons that they were able to be successful. Karl Dorrell in particular was able to beat Illinois freshman cornerback Keith Taylor. Rick Neuheisel's 4 touchdown passes tied the Rose Bowl record, set by Pete Beathard in 1963, and later tied by Chad Henne in the 2005 Rose Bowl.

1984 Orange Bowl - "Fumblerooskie"

Miami vs Nebraska - Orange Bowl - Miami, Florida {Miami 31 Nebraska 30}

Trailing 17-0 early in the second quarter, Nebraska Coach Tom Osborne reached into his bag of tricks. First, in an attempt to confuse Kosar, he switched jerseys between defensive backs Dave Burke and Mike McCashland. As a result, Burke then played in the free safety position and McCashland played in the right cornerback position. Also, Burke, wearing McCashland's jersey, intercepted a pass from Kosar at the Nebraska 26. Then, on the 12th play for a 74-yard touchdown drive, he ran a trick play known as the **fumblerooski.**

Dean Steinkuhler of Nebraska (Bottom of photo)

Facing a 3rd and 5 situation, Nebraska quarterback Gill intentionally "fumbled" the snap from center by effectively setting it on the turf, faking the ball to the fullback Mark Schellen, who, alongside Gill, Rozier and the tight end Monte Engebritson, ran right. The ball was picked up by All-American offensive guard and Outland Trophy/Lombardi Award winner Dean Steinkuhler, who ran left with the ball on a 19 yard touchdown run, cutting the Miami lead to 17-7. While it is neither the first nor the last time this play has been run, it is arguably the most famous incidence of this play, which is now illegal.

1984 Orange Bowl - "Gut Check"

Miami vs Nebraska - Orange Bowl - Miami, Florida {Miami 31 Nebraska 30}

With 48 seconds to play in the 1984 Orange Bowl, On 4th down and 8 from the Miami 24-yard line with the clock running down inside a minute, Nebraska Coach Tom Osborne called an option play, which Gill ran to his right, initially keeping the ball and running into the grasp of a Miami defender before pitching the ball at the last second to a streaking Smith, who sprinted in the rest of the way, making the score 31–30 Miami, with the extra point pending. The fourth down play was an illegal forward pass, but went unnoticed by the officials.

Turner Gill pass to Jeff Smith falls incomplete

Huskers coach Tom Osborne knew an extra point would mean his first national title. But he didn't want to win it with a tie. When Miami safety Ken Calhoun tipped away Turner Gill's two-point pass to Jeff Smith, Osborne received national praise for his guts. But he waited 11 more years to finish No. 1.

1984 - "The Butler did it"

Clemson at Georgia - Sanford Stadium - Athens, Georgia {Georgia 26 Clemson 23}

Kevin Butler kicked a 60-yard field goal with 11 seconds remaining today to give Georgia a 26-23 upset over Clemson, the nation's No. 2 ranked team. The senior from nearby Stone Mountain successfully concluded a strong comeback by the Bulldogs, who trailed the favored Tigers, 20-6, at halftime before a crowd of 82,122 in Sanford Stadium.

Kevin Butler's game winning 60 yard field goal

His kick set a Georgia record for field-goal distance and equaled the Southeastern Conference record set last week by Chris Perkins of Florida. Following Clemson's Donald Igwebuike's 48 yard field goal, Georgia took possession at its own 20 and tried to get within Butler's range. The Bulldogs got only to the Clemson 44, which normally is beyond Butler's range, but it was fourth down, and Dooley had no choice but to give Butler his big chance. He cleared the crossbar easily.

1985 - "Sooner Schooner"
Orange Bowl - Oklahoma vs Washington - Orange Bowl Stadium - Miami, Florida {Washington 28 Oklahoma 17}

The 1985 Orange Bowl, played between the Sooners and the Washington Huskies, is often called "the Sooner Schooner game" because of an incident during the game's second half. The game was tied 14–14 when the Sooners lined up for a short, 22-yard field goal which would have made the score 17–14 in Oklahoma's favor. The kick sailed through the uprights and the Oklahoma sideline thought it was good; the kickoff unit trotted out and the Schooner, as was traditional, also trotted slowly onto the Orange Bowl's wet, mushy field. However, the field goal kick was nullified due to an illegal procedure penalty on Oklahoma. A Sooner player did not report his temporary jersey number to the officials, which he was required to do before the ball was snapped.

The Schooner was already out on the field before the Oklahoma sideline and the RUF/NEKS realized the kick had been disallowed. Worse, while moving across the wet, sloppy natural turf, the Schooner's wagon wheels ended up in a sticky, muddy patch of field and got stuck – right in front of the Washington bench. The Sooners were quickly penalized an additional 15 yards for unsportsmanlike conduct. What was previously a 22-yard field goal became a 42-yard attempt after the 20 yards of penalties were marked off. The re-kick was blocked by Washington, and the game remained tied. Oklahoma ultimately lost the game 28–17.

1985 - "60 seconds of excitement"
Principia at Illinois College - Jacksonville, Illinois {Principia 26 Illinois College 22}

Illinois College led 15-6 going into the 4th quarter. Principia scored with 6:11 left on a three-yard run by QB Jon Hinds to cut the lead to 15-12. That score remained into the final minute. With 28 seconds left, Hinds hit WR Rob Guthrie on a post pattern to give Principia the lead 20-15. The jubilant Indians thought they had won the game. Dan Schone of Illinois College ran the kickoff back to the 49 yard line. QB Joe Killday then tossed a Hail Mary into a cluster of players at the 3. Four Indians knocked the ball backwards right into the hands of trailing Halfback Tim Fritzche who romped into the end zone with 2 seconds left. The jubilant Blueboys thought they had won the game. Illinois College coach Joe Brooks went by the book and ordered an onside kick. Principia WR Dan Sellars recovered at the Illinois College 48 yard line with 1 second left. Principia QB Hinds made up a play in the huddle, lining up three receivers on the same side. Sellers, one of the trio, decided his best chance would be to trail the other two and hope to catch a deflection. As Hinds took the snap, the final horn sounded. He threw a floater to the 10. Mitchell out jumped two Indians and knocked the ball away – right to Sellers. Principia wins 26-22. Two Hail Mary passes in less than 10 seconds. Three TDs in 28 seconds in a game. What a finish.

1985 - "Miracle of All Saints Day"
Kentucky at Tulane - Louisiana Superdome - New Orleans, Louisiana {Tulane 24 Kentucky 22}

Tulane's win over Kentucky was remarkable as perhaps the most dramatic and improbable finish in Tulane history. Tulane got the ball on a punt at its own 8 yard line with only 12 seconds to play in the game. Many fans had already left the Superdome. The incredible finish led Times-Picayune sports writer Brian Allee-Walsh to joke that "the Green Wave unveiled its vaunted, but never-before seen 12-second offense".

Tulane took possession of the ball at their own 8 yard line with 12 seconds left. QB Nickie Hall dropped into the end zone and threw a long "Hail Mary" toward WR Marcus Anderson. The ball fell incomplete. However, DB Chris Jacobs was called for pass interference, which was still a spot infraction at the time. First-and-ten on the Kentucky 46. After using his final timeout, Hall launched another prayer. Another incompletion but another flag. Interference on DB Venus Meaux. First-and-goal on the Kentucky 4 with 0:00 on the clock. Since a game cannot end on a defensive penalty, Green Wave kicker Vince Manalla booted a 19-yard FG to win the game for the Green Wave.

1985 - "Iron Will"
Auburn vs Alabama - Legion Field - Birmingham, Alabama {Alabama 25 Auburn 23}

Three lead changes in the fourth quarter of the 1985 Iron Bowl left Alabama behind Auburn, 23-22, at its own 12 with 57 seconds left and no timeouts. What happened next lives on in "Iron Bowl" Infamy. Earlier in the game, the Crimson Tide took a 16-10 lead into halftime thanks to the foot of Van Tiffin, who kicked three first-half field goals. After a scoreless but intense third quarter, the table was set for a fantastic finish. Alabama quarterback Mike Shula threw an interception in the end zone early in the fourth quarter, which set up a 16-play, 80-yard touchdown drive for the Tigers, culminating with a Bo Jackson touchdown plunge to take a 17-16 lead midway through the fourth quarter. Alabama running back Gene Jelks scored on a 26-yard scamper just one minute later to give the Tide the 22-17 lead. Auburn bled the clock on an 11-play, 70-yard drive that concluded with a Reggie Ware touchdown run. The Tigers would miss the 2-point conversion, but still maintained a 23-22 lead with 57 seconds to play.

In five plays, quarterback Mike Shula took Alabama to the Auburn 35 with 6 seconds to spare. On second down from the 20-yard line, Shula was sacked for an 8-yard loss with only 37 seconds remaining. A long completion set up fourth-and-short, which Alabama converted on a reverse to Al Bell, who gained 20 yards. Shula then hit Greg Richardson, who dragged defenders out of bounds on the 35-yard line to set up the game's final play. Tide kicker Van Tiffin raced on field and, without time to think, drilled the 52-yard field goal that made him a Crimson hero for all time.

1987 Fiesta Bowl - "Giftopoulos Pick"
Miami vs Penn State - Sun Devil Stadium - Tempe, Arizona {Penn State 14 Miami 10}

The 1987 Fiesta Bowl was the 16th edition of the Fiesta Bowl, played annually since 1971 at Sun Devil Stadium in Tempe, Arizona. This particular Fiesta Bowl was played on January 2, 1987 and pitted the #1 Miami Hurricanes against the #2 Penn State Nittany Lions. Since the game would determine the college football national champion for the 1986 season, the organizers of the Fiesta Bowl — which, since it established itself as a January bowl, had been played in the afternoon — decided to move the game back from New Year's Day to January 2 and play it in the early evening (Arizona time) so it could be carried in primetime in the Eastern and Central time zones by NBC, the Fiesta Bowl's then-television carrier.

Miami vastly outgained Penn State on the field, 445 yards to 162, with 22 first downs compared to the Nittany Lions' 8. However, the Hurricanes were hampered by 7 turnovers, including 5 interceptions of the Heisman-winning Testaverde. Miami's only touchdown was the result of a John Shaffer fumble that the Hurricanes recovered at the Penn State 23. Miami then took four plays to score the go-ahead touchdown. The Nittany Lions responded with their only sustained drive of the night, going 74 yards in 13 plays, culminating in Shaffer's 4-yard scamper into the end zone. The halftime score was a 7-7 tie. After Miami scored a field goal to retake the lead, Shane Conlan grabbed his second interception of the night, returning it 39 yards to the Miami 5. The first Penn State snap was fumbled, but the Nittany Lions recovered. D.J. Dozier then followed with a 6-yard run for the go-ahead touchdown. Miami still had over 8 minutes on the clock, but fumbled on their next possession. With Penn State unable to move the ball, Miami began their last drive on their own 23 with 3:07 left in the game. A 4th-down completion to Brian Blades went for 31 yards and moved Miami into Penn State territory.

With a minute left, Testaverde hit Michael Irvin at the Penn State 10. The connection put the Hurricanes inside the 5 with 45 seconds left. Even with a national championship at stake, though, Penn State linebacker Pete Giftopoulos said the Penn State defense stayed calm. On second-and-goal,

Testaverde dropped back, but Tim Johnson broke free and sacked him. On third down, Testaverde threw incomplete into the flat. On fourth-and-goal, with 18 seconds left, Testaverde threw to the end zone, but was intercepted by Giftopoulos. The interception, Giftopoulos' second of the game (and Testaverde's fifth), ensured Penn State's second national title in five years.

1987 - "48-49 Load"

West Virginia at Syracuse - Carrier Dome - Syracuse, New York {Syracuse 32 West Virginia 31}

Syracuse University's dream of an unbeaten regular season stayed alive as the 11-0, Sugar Bowl-bound Orangemen posted a miraculous come-from-behind 32-31 college football victory over stubborn West Virginia before a frenzied Carrier Dome crowd of 49,866. Syracuse University's football team trailed, 31-24, with 1:27 remaining in the game, and went on a seven-play, 74-yard drive that sealed its undefeated season.

On first down, Orange quarterback Don McPherson completed a 6-yard pass to tailback Michael Owens, then tossed a 23-yard pass to wide receiver Deval Glover to bring the ball to the West Virginia 45-yard line. McPherson threw incomplete on first down, then hit Glover again for 20 yards to the West Virginia 25-yard line. SU called a timeout with 41 seconds left in the game. McPherson went to the air again, hitting tight end Pat Kelly for eight yards to the 17-yard line, but threw incomplete on second down. On third-and-two, McPherson hit Kelly over the middle for the 17-yard touchdown pass to make it 31-30 West Virginia with 10 seconds left in the game. Syracuse went for the two-point conversion and the win on a play called 48-49 load, and they got it when McPherson rolled to his left and pitched to Owens, who ran it into in the end zone. The final: Syracuse 32, West Virginia 31. McPherson must have had a better angle that most people in the Dome. The pass looked high, and Kelly made a remarkable over-the-shoulder catch past West Virginia defender Terry White.

1988 - "Earthquake Game"

Auburn at LSU - Tiger Stadium - Baton Rouge, Louisiana {LSU 7 Auburn 6}

The **Earthquake Game** was played in front of a crowd of 79,431 at Louisiana State University's Tiger Stadium on October 8, 1988, the LSU Tigers upset No. 4 Auburn 7–6. After LSU scored the winning touchdown with under two minutes left in the game, the crowd reaction is believed to have registered on a seismograph.

Auburn led 6–0 with less than two minutes left in the 4th quarter. LSU's quarterback Tommy Hodson drove the team down the field before throwing an 11-yard touchdown pass to Eddie Fuller on 4th down. The game's name resulted from the reaction of the crowd after the final pass. According to legend, it registered as an earthquake by a seismograph located in LSU's Howe-Russell Geoscience Complex around 1,000 feet (305 m) from the stadium. The seismograph reading was discovered the morning after the game by LSU seismologist Don Stevenson and student worker Riley Milner. Word of the seismograph reading reached *The Daily Reveille* and spread to the local media. Stevenson submitted the reading to the Louisiana Geological Survey to have it preserved. Stevenson displayed a copy of the reading on his office window on the LSU campus that was later observed by an ESPN news crew, who were on campus doing a story sometime prior to when Stevenson left LSU in the summer of 1991. The news crew decided to do a piece on what they dubbed "The Earthquake Game." This news story helped to add more attention to the event.

1988 - "Puntrooskie"

Florida State at Clemson - Memorial Stadium - Clemson, South Carolina {Florida State 24 Clemson 21}

Bobby Bowden calls them barnyard plays, and none ruffled feathers like this one. The Seminoles, tied 21-21 at No. 3 Clemson, lined in punt formation at their own 21. As the punt team faked a bad snap and moved right, upback Dayne Williams put the ball between his legs. LeRoy Butler took it and sprinted left 78 yards to the Tigers 1. Florida State won, 24-21, and the puntrooskie became instant legend.

The 3rd ranked, 2-0 Clemson Tigers with coach Danny Ford hosted the 10th ranked, 1-1 Florida State Seminoles of Coach Bobby Bowden. Sanders returned a punt for a touchdown and a trick-play that goes down in college football history helped the Seminoles to a 24-21 victory over the Tigers. Clemson took a 1st quarter lead with their own trick play as WR Chip Davis threw an option pass to WR Gary Cooper for a 61-yard touchdown giving the Tigers a 7-0 lead. Florida State tied the game in the 2nd quarter with a conventional 40-yard touchdown pass from Ferguson to RB Dexter Carter but the Tigers took a 14-7 halftime lead when QB Rodney Williams scored on a 7-yard touchdown run. After Sanders returned a punt 76 yards for a touchdown and RB Dayne Williams scored on a 1-yard touchdown run Florida State appeared to have control of the game 21-14, if the defense could hold. Clemson's RB Tracy Johnson scored for the Tigers to tie the game at 21-21 with just 2:32 left in the game. Clemson readied for a final shot at scoring as Florida State prepared to punt from their own 21-yard line with just 1:33 to play. It appeared disaster had struck the Seminoles as the ball was apparently snapped over Florida State's P Tom Corlew's head but Bowden had called a play that came to be known in football lore as the "puntrooskie".

Williams, the blocking back, had intercepted the long snap and handed it between the legs of Safety LeRoy Butler who ran around the left end while 2 other Seminoles faked to the right. Clemson realized what was happening and All-American CB Donnell Woolford finally knocked Butler out of bounds 78 yards later at the Clemson 1-yard line. As brilliant as the gamble was, it still had not changed the score. After getting stopped at the goal line on 3 straight plays, the Seminoles called a timeout with 35 seconds to play and the clock stopped. Problem was that Florida State had no timeouts left but the clock was stopped anyway. Florida State scored a touchdown on the next snap but the score was called back after the confused officiating crew determined Florida State should not have been given the timeout. Strangely, no penalty was assessed but the Seminoles had to try again for the score. This time, Bowden opted to try a field goal even though his kickers had been 0 for 3 on field goal attempts in the game. Florida State's PK Richie Andrews' 19-yard field goal kick was good and the Seminoles had an improbable 24-21 win. Ferguson finished with 241 yards passing with his touchdown while Williams threw for 96 yards in the loss. The Tigers finished the season 10-2; ACC Champions, ranked 9th nationally while the Seminoles finished 11-1 and ranked 3rd nationally.

1988 - "Catholics vs Convicts"
Miami at Notre Dame - Notre Dame Stadium - South Bend, Indiana {Notre Dame 31 Miami 30}

The No. 1 ranked Hurricanes came into South Bend with the swagger of a defending national champion, and they were rolling with a thrilling comeback win over Michigan and blowouts over Florida State, Missouri, and Wisconsin by a combined score of 114 to 3. The Canes had little trouble with the Irish over the previous years, winning 24-0 in 1987 and 58-7 in 1985, but this was a new Irish team with far more talent and far more confidence from the ones that were throttled in the Irish fan-named battle between the Catholics vs. the Convicts. Tempers and emotions were high between the two, with a brawl erupting in the tunnel before the game setting the tone for a nasty, hard-hitting classic. The feisty Irish showed how charged up the players were and showed that they weren't going to be intimidated in a back-and-forth battle that was defined by two plays that ended up earning Notre Dame the national title.

Down 31-24, Steve Walsh, who finished the day with 424 yards and four scores, hit Cleveland Gary on a fourth and seven play on the Irish 11. Gary rumbled and dove into the end zone for an apparent touchdown, but he lost the football and Notre Dame recovered. The officials ruled it a fumble and not a score, even though TV replays made it look like the ball had crossed the goal line. The Hurricanes would overcome the controversy as Walsh got another chance and moved the ball down the field with little trouble. With the drive stalled, Miami had to go for it on fourth down and with the unbeaten season on the line. Walsh came through, throwing an 11-yard touchdown pass to pull the Canes to within one point with 45 seconds to play. Head coach Jimmy Johnson could've decided to kick the extra point, and Miami probably would've gone on to win the national title, but that wasn't going to happen. Miami's two-point attempt was denied when Notre Dame's Pat Terrell knocked down Walsh's desperate try, and the Hurricane 36-game winning streak was over.

1989 - "7 yards to Glory"

SW Louisiana at Northern Illinois - Huskie Stadium - Dekalb, Illinois {Northern Illinois 23 SW Louisiana 20}

Northern Illinois QB Stacey Robinson was 7 yards away from the Huskies` biggest victory since 1983. Only 3 seconds remained.  Fullback Adam Dach took out Southwestern Louisiana linebacker William Sims, and halfback Mike Strasser leveled safety Van Ray Alexander as Robinson ran left on an option play for the winning points in the Huskies` 23-20 victory. The Huskies final drive, which began on their 23 with 4:27 left. Twice, it came down to fourth down. Once, Robinson ran 4 yards and kept the drive alive by half a football. Then, on fourth and 1 at the Cajun 14 and 13 seconds left, Strasser picked up 7 yards. With 6 seconds to go, Robinson missed on a pass to Strasser in the end zone. Then came the biggest play of the season.

1990 - "Kick Gopher Kick"

Utah at Minnesota - HHH Metrodome - Minneapolis, Minnesota {Utah 35 Minnesota 29}

In another colossal meltdown, the Minnesota Golden Gophers come up with another way to lose a game. With the score tied, the Gophers appeared about to win as they lined up for a 28-yard field goal with eight seconds left. But Greg Reynolds blocked the kick, and Utah's Lavon Edwards picked up the loose ball and ran down the left sideline 91 yards for the clinching score as time expired. Utes win 35-29. Unbelievable!!

{Deseret News} Just when it looked like the University of Utah had found a half-dozen crazy ways to lose a football game Saturday night - bench a red-hot quarterback, fumble without being touched, commit a late-hit foul, miss a PAT kick, muff a punt, drop a TD pass - they up and found an equally zany way to win one. With eight seconds left, Greg Reynolds blocked a sure-thing, 29-yard field goal attempt and LaVon Edwards picked up the ball and ran 91 yards for the game-winning touchdown with no time remaining. Score it Utah 35, Minnesota 29. Bedlam ruled. The flabbergasted Utes raced onto the field and piled on top of Edwards in the end zone. Some Utah players simply fell flat onto their backs in the middle of the field and stared up in disbelief into the Metrodome ceiling. Coach Ron McBride, after breaking away from the pileup, lay prone at the seven-yard line. When he was somewhat recovered he ran sobbing to the locker room, where he was picked up by tackle Vince Lobendahn and hoisted onto a bench in the middle of a wild locker room. The team sang, prayed, hugged, high-fived and finally gave the game ball to Reynolds.

"I told you we would find a way to win!" he shouted, his voice breaking. Later, he told reporters, "Minnesota has more talent, more players, stronger players, but we just never gave up." Outside, the 32,229 fans were stunned. They filed out of the stadium as if they'd just witnessed a car accident, shaking their heads and mumbling. It was a wild end to a wild night of bloopers. In all, there were six fumbles, five interceptions, 10 penalties and one big blown lead. The Utes were up 19-0 at the end of the first quarter, and 29-14 early in the third quarter. Then the Gophers rallied. They tied the score with 4:46 left in the third quarter. Neither offense could do anything the rest of the game, but when Wayne Lammle's punt was partially blocked by Mark Keller, sailing a mere six yards and dying at the Ute 35-yard line with 1:04 left in the game, the Utes' seemed doomed. With eight seconds left, Brent Berglund settled in to try a 29-yard field goal. On the Utah sideline, McBride told special teams coach Sean McNabb, "Give us the play that has the best chance to block it." The play is called "middle block," in which the Utes stack the middle, push the line back and leap. "We're going to block it!" the Utes shouted on the sideline. Reynolds, who is 6-foot-2, bowled over the center and stuck his arm up and blocked the ball squarely. "I turned around and the ball was right there," said Edwards, "I knew I was in. I'm not the fastest guy, but I knew they weren't going to catch me." "I've been in a lot of wild games, but never anything like this," said McBride.

1990 - "Fifth down game"

Colorado at Missouri - Faurot Field - Columbia, Missouri {Colorado 33 Missouri 31}

The **Fifth Down Game** in 1990 included a play that the crew officiating the game permitted to occur in error. That play enabled the Colorado Buffaloes to defeat the Missouri Tigers by scoring a touchdown on the last play of their game on October 6, 1990. The ensuing controversy cast doubt on Colorado's claim to Division I-A's 1990 national championship, which it shares with the Georgia Tech

Yellow Jackets. It has been called one of the top memorable moments and blunders in college football history.

Colorado was ranked #12 by the Associated Press in the nation while Missouri was unranked. The lead in this game changed several times, and several big plays kept the momentum swinging. With less than three minutes to go, Colorado took possession of the ball deep in its own territory trailing 31–27. Johnson led the team on a last-ditch drive. With about 40 seconds to go, he completed a pass to Colorado tight end Jon Boman who fell down just yards short of the goal line. Boman slipped due to the poor conditions of the field, which saw the Buffaloes slip on the turf repeatedly throughout the game. This play gave the Buffaloes a first down, but it led to immediate confusion because the Buffs were running a hurry-up offense. On first down, Johnson spiked the ball to stop the clock, but the chain crew then failed to flip the down marker to note that it was now second down. On the next play, with the down marker showing it was still first down when it was really second down, a power run into the line by Eric Bieniemy was stopped just short of the goal line. Colorado then called its third and final timeout. On the next play, with the down marker showing second down when it was really third down, the Buffaloes made the same call and Bieniemy was again stopped short of the end zone. Johnson then spiked the ball (thinking it was third

down when it was really fourth) to stop the clock with two seconds left. He later claimed that he had no idea the officials had made a mistake, and believed he was spiking the ball on third down. On the following play – fourth down according to the marker, but "fifth down" in reality – Johnson kept the ball himself. Whether the ball crossed the goal line before Johnson was down remains a subject of some argument, but he was awarded a touchdown. By this time, referee J. C. Louderback and his officiating crew had realized their mistake, and conferred for nearly 20 minutes to decide their course of action. During the delay, radio and television announcers also noticed that Colorado had scored with the help of an additional play. Louderback was shown on the phone. After a lengthy consultation, the referees announced their decision: the touchdown counted, giving Colorado a 33-31 lead. They also decided that the Buffs would have to attempt the extra point. The rules do not require the extra point try if time has expired and the result will not affect the outcome of the game. However, since Colorado only led by two, Missouri could have potentially blocked the try and returned it for two points to tie the game, the try was required. Not wanting to take this chance, Johnson took the snap and went to a knee, allowing the Buffaloes to go home with a controversial win.

1990 - "The Hit – Football is a game of inches"
Mississippi at Arkansas - War Memorial Stadium - Little Rock, Arkansas {Mississippi 21 Arkansas 17}

Football is a game of inches. Twelve, to be exact. That's how close Arkansas' Ron Dickerson came to sticking the ball in the end zone on the final play of the Ole Miss-Arkansas thriller at War Memorial Stadium. Three Rebels stopped him short, and Ole Miss upset the 13th-ranked Razorbacks 21-17 before a sellout crowd of 54,890. Ole Miss, won here for the first time since 1960. Chauncey Godwin and strong safety Chris Mitchell combined Saturday to stop Dickerson on the one-foot line as the final seconds ticked away. It broke a five-game Razorback winning streak in the series, and it seemed only fitting that a goal-line stand clinched the victory.

The Hogs held a nearly unbelievable statistical edge. They ran 93 plays to Ole Miss' 43, gained 24 first downs the Ole Miss' 8, had 427 total yards to Ole Miss' 111, and had the ball 40 minutes and 30 seconds to Ole Miss' 19:30. The only thing Arkansas couldn't seem to do was find the end zone. The Razorbacks crossed Ole Miss' 10-yard line six times. On five of them they were kept out of the end zone. Arkansas had one more chance. The Razorbacks had driven from their 36 to the Ole Miss 5. With 11 seconds on the clock and both teams void of timeouts, Arkansas quarterback Quinn Grovey called a run-pass option. He took the snap and headed around left end. Grovey pitched the ball to Dickerson at about the 10-yard line, near the Arkansas sideline. Godwin met Dickerson at about the 2, then got help from Shawn Cobb. Just as Dickerson started to spin away and fall into the end zone, Chris Mitchell came over and finished the tackle.

1990 - "The Play II"
Stanford at California - Memorial Stadium - Berkeley, California {Stanford 27 California 25}

It's known simply as The Play, Cal's five-lateral kickoff return for a touchdown through the Stanford band, which gave the Golden Bears a 25-20 victory over Stanford in 1982. While Stanford's dramatic 27-25 win in Saturday's 93rd Big Game, which came on John Hopkins' 39-yard field goal as time expired, wasn't as bizarre, it was almost as absurd. Trailing 25-18, Stanford drove 87 yards to a touchdown, with quarterback Jason Palumbis hitting split end Ed McCaffrey with a 19-yard touchdown pass with 12 seconds remaining to cut the score to 25-24. Then it got strange.

The Cardinal went for a two-point conversion to win the game, but defensive back John Hardy intercepted Palumbis' pass in the end zone and Cal's fans, thinking the game was over, engulfed the Memorial Stadium field. Hardy ran through the crowd, exchanging high-fives with rooters on his way to the tunnel that leads to the locker room. But 12 seconds remained. After the crowd was cleared, Cal was assessed a 15-yard penalty for delay of game by referee Pat Flood, who had earlier threatened to award Stanford the two-point conversion unless the field was cleared of fans who had left the stands in anticipation of a victory celebration. Kicking off from the 50, instead of the 35, Hopkins dribbled a kick along the right sideline. Although several Cal players had a chance to recover, Stanford defensive back Kevin Scott covered it at the Cal 37 with nine seconds left. Scott admitted later that he was out of bounds when he recovered the kick. Palumbis, who passed for 253 yards and one touchdown, threw an incomplete pass on first down, but Cal was penalized for roughing the passer when nose guard John Belli hit Palumbis after he had released the ball, giving Stanford a first down at the Cal 22 with five seconds left. The 15-yard penalty moved Stanford into field-goal range for Hopkins, who had made kicks of 26, 29, 47 and 22 yards earlier in the game. So instead of a 53-yard field goal, Hopkins trotted onto the field and hit a 39-yarder to beat the Golden Bears.

1990 - "The Shootout"
USC at UCLA - The Rose Bowl - Pasadena, California {USC 45 UCLA 42}

It was USC's Todd Marinovich vs. UCLA's Tommy Maddox. Each team scored 21 points in the fourth quarter. UCLA scored with 1:19 left, but USC scored with 16 seconds left and won, 45-42. Marinovich won the game, but Maddox set a school record by passing for 409 yards.

Johnny Morton's game winning TD catch

The highest-scoring game in series history, the fourth quarter of this one included 42 points, three touchdowns scored in the final three minutes and four lead changes. Johnnie Morton caught a 23-yard touchdown pass from Todd Marinovich with 16 seconds left to give USC the win, only minutes after he had made a remarkable diving catch in the corner of the end zone.

1991 - "Second greatest comeback EVER!"
Weber State at Nevada - Mackey Stadium - Reno, Nevada {Nevada 55 Weber State 49}

Nevada made the second biggest comeback in NCAA football history, overcoming a 35-point deficit in the third quarter and rallying to beat Weber State, 55-49, Saturday on Eric Smith's three-yard scoring run with 1:02 left. Led by Chris Vargas, top-ranked Nevada rallied in the second-half to defeat Weber State 55-49. It remains the second biggest comeback in NCAA history.

Chris Vargas of Nevada

The comeback was accomplished in 10 minutes and 21 seconds worth possession time in the second half. Nevada, ranked No. 1 in Division I-AA, trailed 42-14 at halftime and fell behind 49-14 with 12:16 left in the third quarter. But the Wolf Pack scored the final 41 points. Vargas completed 22 of 38 passes for 346 yards and two touchdowns in a little more than two quarters, and Chris Singleton had eight receptions for 225 yards in the game. Eric Smith scored the game's final three touchdowns. His last two scores came 31 seconds apart.

1991 - "Yellowjackets spoil Presidents Homecoming"

Rochester University at Washington & Jefferson - Cameron Stadium - Washington, Pennsylvania {Rochester 20 Washington & Jefferson 14}

Jeremy Hurd ran 20 yards through left guard for a touchdown with 13 seconds remaining to help Rochester stun Washington & Jefferson in its homecoming game. The win wasn't secured until the final play when quarterback Bob Strope overthrew Larry Pitts in the left corner of the end zone with four Yellowjacket defenders around him as time expired. Washington & Jefferson entered the game ranked #2 in the South by the NCAA Division III Football Committee. The Presidents had a 31-game home field winning streak dating back to 1984. In a little over seven years (1984 through 3 home games in 1991), Washington & Jefferson was 33-1 at home in the regular season (the loss was Rochester). The Rochester defense forced eight turnovers (five fumble recoveries and three interceptions). Washington & Jefferson was averaging 419 yards per game in total offense. The Presidents finished with 373. Rochester managed 153 (88 rushing, 65 passing). In one second-half stretch, Washington & Jefferson turned the ball over on five straight possessions. One of those was a 68-yard interception return by UR's Eric Litchfield which went for a TD and a 14-7 lead. Washington & Jefferson eventually tied the score at 14-14 with 4:01 left in the game on a nine-yard pass from Strope to Chris Babirad and Scott Lautner's PAT. After an exchange of punts, Rochester took over on its own 40 with 1:12 left. After a 10-yard pass completion, Hurd carried the ball four times, gaining 15 yards. It moved the ball to the 35. Facing 4th-and-five, Rochester head coach Rich Parrinello gambled. He had quarterback Gregg Eisenberg throw deep down the left sideline for Kevin Gelabart. Washington & Jefferson was flagged for pass interference and the ball placed on the Washington & Jefferson 20. It looked like UR would run the ball into the line to straighten it out for a field goal attempt. Lined up behind – and to the left – of Eisenberg, Hurd took the handoff, took one step to his right, then saw a small hole through left guard and center. He ran through it untouched into the end zone with 0:13 left. The extra point attempt was blocked by Washington & Jefferson's Gilbert Floyd. Rochester was penalized 15 yards for unsportsmanlike conduct (celebration). It was assessed on the kickoff. Joe Caruso kicked it to Floyd at the Washington & Jefferson 32 and he returned it to the Washington & Jefferson 48 with 0:06 remaining. Strope's pass for Pitts was just a little too far over his head and Rochester escaped with a mammoth victory.

1991 - "The Pose"
Ohio State at Michigan - Michigan Stadium - Ann Arbor, Michigan {Michigan 31 Ohio State 3}

The Wolverines used Desmond Howard's Michigan-record 93-yard punt return on its way to its fourth straight victory over the Buckeyes. Howard sped away from two defenders closing on him at the 10-yard line, high-stepped out of another attempted tackle and veered to the left sideline, dodging his final pursuer at midfield and sprinting in for the touchdown that gave Michigan a 24-3 halftime lead. Howard's school-record 93-yard punt return led to his memorable Heisman Trophy pose in the end zone and boosted Michigan to its fourth straight victory over Ohio State. That Heisman pose became one of the most indelible, iconic images of the last few decades of college football.

Before Howard struck, Michigan grabbed a 17-3 lead thanks to a fake field-goal attempt on its first drive and an interception of a pass by Kent Graham in the second quarter. Facing fourth-and-2, the Wolverines lined up for a kick, but holder Ken Sollom pitched to fullback Greg McThomas on the same fake that Florida State used to score a touchdown in its 51-31 victory over the Wolverines. McThomas's first-down set up Bernie Legette's 1-yard touchdown run for a 7-0 lead. A field goal by Tim Williams of 50 yards at 12:32 of the second quarter brought the Buckeyes as close as they would get, for on OSU's next possession Graham's rollout pass was overthrown and Michigan's Lance Dotton returned the ball 18 yards to the 12. Jesse Johnson powered for first-down yardage on fourth-and-1 at the 3, then carried in from the 1 on the next play. Another Ohio State turnover, this a fumble by Carlos Snow at the Buckeyes' 21, setup J.D. Carlson's 37-yard field goal for a 17-3 margin at 6:22. Then came the punt to Howard, who broke it without benefit of a block, since 10 Wolverines rushed Williams from the line of scrimmage.

1992 - "The great Cavalier collapse"
Clemson at Virginia - Scott Stadium - Charlottesville, Virginia {Clemson 29 Virginia 28}

Clemson came back from a 28-0 deficit to shock the Cavaliers. Once again, Virginia had a big lead in an ACC game but managed to snatch defeat from the jaws of victory. After storming to a four-touchdown lead, after whipping a sellout crowd of 44,400 into a frenzy, the 10th-ranked Cavaliers fell apart. Virginia's unbeaten season collapsed in a shocking 29-28 Atlantic Coast Conference loss to the 25th-ranked Tigers. The loss was shockingly similar to a 41-38 loss to Georgia Tech here two years ago.

Terry Kirby of Virginia

The Tigers chipped away using their bruising option game and won on a 32-yard field goal by Nelson Welch with 55 seconds left to play in the greatest comeback in Clemson history.

1992 - "Goal Line Stand"
Mississippi State at Mississippi - Vaught-Hemingway Stadium - Oxford, Mississippi {Mississippi 17 Mississippi State 10}

In a defensive struggle that saw a combined 12 turnovers between the two, a goal line stand of epic proportions by the "Red Death" defense ultimately gave Ole Miss the win. Mississippi State had 11 plays in 2 different possessions inside the Rebel 10 within the last 4 minutes of the contest but failed to score. The first possession ended on a third down pass that was intercepted in the end zone by Michael

Lowery who would bring the ball out to the 2 yard line. A couple of plays later saw rebel running back Cory Philpot fumble the ball back to the Dogs, the Rebels' 7th turnover on the day. On the ensuing possession, State had fourth and goal and the pass was incomplete. However, pass interference on Orlanda Truitt kept the drive alive, moving the ball to the 2. However, the next four plays resulted in negative yardage, with the final pass falling incomplete with only 20 seconds remaining. The Rebels won 17–10.

1992 SEC Championship - "Langham Pick 6"
Alabama vs Florida - Legion Field - Birmingham, Alabama {Alabama 28 Florida 21}

The Florida Gators scored first, on a five-yard touchdown reception by Errict Rhett to take a 7–0 lead in the first quarter. The Crimson Tide responded by scoring the next 21 points. The Tide's first points came later in the first quarter on a Derrick Lassic 3-yard touchdown run to tie the game at 7–7. In the second quarter, Curtis Brown would score on a 30-yard touchdown reception from Jay Barker to take a 14–7 lead at the half. Alabama would further extend their lead to 21–7 in the third on a 15-yard Derrick Lassic touchdown run. Down by 14, the Gators would respond with a pair of touchdowns, tying the game at 21 midway through the fourth quarter. Willie Jackson would score first on a 4-yard touchdown reception on a pass from Shane Matthews late in the third, and Errict Rhett would knot the game at 21 with just over eight minutes remaining in the contest.

Antonio Langham of Alabama on his 27 yard interception return for a TD

With momentum in the favor of the Gators, with 3:16 remaining in the game, Antonio Langham would return a Matthews interception 27 -yards for a touchdown in providing the final 28–21 margin.

1993 - "Flash Gordon"
Boston College at Notre Dame - Notre Dame Stadium - South Bend, Indiana {Boston College 41 Notre Dame 39}

No. 1 Notre Dame, one week after its Game of the Century defeat of Florida State, spotted No. 17 Boston College a 38-17 fourth-quarter lead before scoring 22 points. One problem: The Irish left 1:09, enough time for Glenn Foley to drive the Eagles to the Notre Dame 24. David Gordon nailed a 41-yard field goal as time expired. The 1993 Boston College-Notre Dame (Holy War) game was played on November 20th at Notre Dame Stadium in South Bend, Indiana. Boston College came into the game ranked #12 in the country, while the Fighting Irish were ranked #1 in the country. It is the biggest upset in the history of this rivalry. The moment belonged to David Gordon, the Boston College kicker, whose career-best 41-yard field goal as time expired gave the Eagles a shocking 41-39 victory that ended Notre Dame's hope of taking a No. 1 ranking into a bowl game. Boston College's first victory over Notre Dame, the second time in four seasons that the Irish relinquished a top ranking with a loss in their final home game of the season.

David Gordon of Boston College game winning Field goal

There was 1 minute 1 second to go. On the Boston College sideline, Tom Coughlin, the head coach, remembered that their 2-minute drill in practice begins with the clock set at 1:10. On the Notre Dame sideline, McDougal looked at the clock and feared there was too much time. "Even when I'm out there with a minute and 1 second, I feel there's a chance," he said. On third-and-10 from the 25, Foley found tight end Pete Mitchell, who caught 13 passes for 132 yards and 2 touchdowns, for a 12-yard gain to the 37. Two plays later, Foley avoided the Irish rush and stepped forward for a 24-yard throw to Mitchell that brought the Eagles close to field-goal range. Foley then avoided a blitz with an incomplete pass, and on second down from the 33, threw the pass that gave Gordon his chance -- a middle screen to Ivan Boyd, who had also caught two touchdowns earlier. Boyd's 9-yard gain, to the 24 with 5 seconds to play, set up the winning kick. Gordon had missed a potential game-winning kick at Northwestern, a 40-yard attempt with 1:07 to go in a 1-point defeat. This time, Foley took a slightly high snap and put the ball in place. Gordon followed through, but did not look. Suddenly, the memory of a 47-point defeat was gone.

1994 - "The Pick that changed (Oregon) history"
Washington at Oregon - Autzen Stadium - Eugene, Oregon {Oregon 31 Washington 20}

In a game that will forever be the game and play that changed the history of Oregon Football, the Ducks and Kenny Wheaton knew they had a mighty task coming in. Washington had beaten Miami in Little Havana two weeks previous and were ranked number four in the country. Washington was led by Coach Don James and quarterback Damon Huard and were thinking national championship. Like many previous games with Washington, the Ducks played hard and took an early lead. But like always, the Ducks struggled in the second half and let the Huskies climb back into the game. With under two minutes left the Huskies were at the Oregon three yard-line. Damon Huard called for an out route and Oregon safety Kenny Wheaton remembered that in watching film he knew that Washington loved to run out routes in these situations. Wheaton stepped in front of the pass, intercepted it and headed up the sideline for a clinching touchdown, putting Oregon ahead for good 31–20.

The rest is history. Wheaton's interception created pandemonium at Autzen Stadium for both the fans and radio announcer Jerry Allen. Oregon went on to go to the Rose Bowl that year and many fans will point to that game as the beginning of success for the Ducks. They had success before that game, but the bounces and games started going more Oregon's way after Kenny Wheaton's interception.

1994 - "Comeback of the ages, almost"
Pittsburgh at West Virginia - Mountaineer Stadium - Morgantown, West Virginia {West Virginia 47 Pittsburgh 41}

In one of the most entertaining Backyard Brawls, this 100 year old rivalry didn't disappoint. There were three blocked field goals, two of which were returned for touchdowns, a blocked punt, an interception returned for a touchdown and a fumble returned for a touchdown. This might have gone down as one of the Panthers' greatest comebacks as Pitt rallied from a 31-6 deficit to take a 41-40 lead with less than 50 seconds to play. But West Virginia quarterback Chad Johnston hit Zach Abraham with a 60-yard pass with 15 seconds remaining to pull out the win. Only 23 seconds before, John Ryan's touchdown pass and quarterback sneak on a 2-point conversion apparently sealed a dramatic rally from a 31-6 deficit by Pittsburgh. Chad Johnston threw two touchdown passes in the final 1 minute 32 seconds, rallying visiting West Virginia to a 47-41 victory over Pittsburgh yesterday.

1995 - "Ty-breaking return"
Cincinnati at Miami-Ohio - Yager Stadium - Oxford, Ohio {Miami-Ohio 23 Cincinnati 16}

In the 100th meeting of the "Victory Bell" rivalry, Miami-Ohio's Ty King returned the kickoff 82 yards for a touchdown with 18 seconds left in the game to lift Miami-Ohio to a 23-16 victory over Cincinnati. The Bearcats had just tied the game on a field goal and tried a pooch kick which King caught at the 18 yard line, eluded numerous Bearcat defenders and broke free at midfield and outraced Cincinnati players into the end zone.

1996 Fiesta Bowl - "The Run"

Florida vs Nebraska - Sun Devil Stadium - Tempe, Arizona {Nebraska 62 Florida 28}

The game was billed as a classic #1 vs. #2 matchup, featuring two completely different but equally potent offenses. Odds makers had made Nebraska about a 3-point favorite going into the game. However, many experts picked Florida to win, as it was thought that Nebraska's option attack would not succeed very well on Sun Devil Stadium's grass field, and that Wuerffel's passing arm would be too deadly for Nebraska to stop.

Tommy Frazier of Nebraska

The Run - On second down from the Nebraska 25, Cornhuskers quarterback Tommie Frazier ran an option play to the right, and decided to keep the ball rather than pitch. He gained 11 yards before being met by a group of Florida defenders at the 36-yard line, which he then dragged approximately 10 yards before shrugging them off and breaking free, streaking 75 yards down the sideline to give Nebraska a 49–18 lead. Frazier had broken no less than seven tackles on the play. Frazier would finish the game with 199 yards rushing. Nebraska also set records for most rushing yards in a bowl game, with 524, and the most points in the second quarter of a bowl game, with 29.

1996 - "Punt Mountaineer Punt"

Miami at West Virginia - Mountaineer Field - Morgantown, West Virginia {Miami 10 West Virginia 7}

Tremain Mack blocked Brian West's punt with 29 seconds to play and Nathaniel Brooks returned it 20 yards for a touchdown as No. 25 Miami stunned 12th-ranked West Virginia, 10-7, in a Big East game at Morgantown.

Tremain Mack blocking West Virginia punt

To put it politely, West Virginia's punt team was not very good in 1996, the unit already having five punts blocked before the Miami Hurricanes blew into Morgantown for a meeting against the 11th-rated Mountaineers on Oct. 26, 1996. Compounding matters, Miami's speedy defensive back Tremain Mack had seven career blocked punts to his credit. His eighth against West Virginia would snatch victory out of the jaws of defeat for Miami. With only 29 seconds remaining on the clock and the Mountaineers leading 7-3, all West Virginia had to do was get off a decent punt - it didn't even have to be a good one - to win the football game. The way West Virginia's defense was playing, the Hurricanes had no chance whatsoever of getting a touchdown. But West Virginia couldn't get the ball airborne, Mack blew past West Virginia's David Saunders to literally pick the football off of punter Brian West's foot. The ball bounced into Jack Hallmon's arms at the 20, where he handed it to Nathaniel Brooks. Brooks ran the ball into the end zone to give the Hurricanes one of the unlikeliest game-winning scores in Mountaineer Field history.

1996 - "Finally"
Tennessee at Memphis - Liberty Bowl Stadium - Memphis, Tennessee {Memphis 21 Tennessee 17}

Memphis had almost no offense until it mattered, then the Tigers had enough to beat No. 6 Tennessee for the first time ever, 21-17, in a game at Memphis, Tenn. When the Tigers took over at their 30 with slightly under six minutes left, they had managed just 83 yards of offense all day. Undaunted, the Tigers marched 70 yards in 5:20, getting the winning score on Qadry Anderson's three-yard touchdown pass to Chris Powers with 34 seconds remaining. The Tigers had lost to the Volunteers in all 15 previous meetings dating back to 1968. Tennessee's running game had been stuck in neutral for weeks during the 1996 season.

Chris Powers winning touchdown catch vs Tennessee

The Volunteers gained 85 yards in 49 carries. Memphis did it despite 83 yards of total offense. On national television. In front of a record home crowd (65,885). Against a Southeastern Conference team with a 40-1 record in November since 1985. With Tennessee's running game stalled, the Tigers harassed Manning all day. A 76-yard interception set up a 1-yard touchdown run by Tigers quarterback Qadry Anderson in the second quarter to tie the game at 7-7. Tennessee appeared to take control on the opening drive of the third quarter. Manning's 11-yard touchdown pass to Jay Graham gave the Vols a 14-7 lead. That's when the game turned on another big play. Kevin Cobb returned the ensuing kickoff 95 yards for a touchdown to tie the game at 14-14. A field goal gave Tennessee a 17-14 lead with 6:01 remaining, but the offensively-challenged Tigers marched 70 yards for the winning touchdown. Anderson hit Chancy Carr for a 41-yard completion, Jeremy Scruggs rambled up the middle for 13 yards and Anderson's 3-yard touchdown pass to Chris Powers with 34 seconds remaining gave Memphis an improbable lead. Tennessee's last gasp ended with Manning on the turf and Memphis rushed the field to tear down the goal posts.

1997 - "Simply Amazing"
Michigan at Michigan State - Spartan Stadium - East Lansing, Michigan {Michigan 23 Michigan State 7}

If there was a defining moment in Charles Woodson's road to the Heisman Trophy in 1997, his one-handed interception against rival Michigan State was a big one. With time winding down in the second half of the game, Michigan State quarterback Todd Schultz tried throwing the ball away. Woodson, who had been following his receiver on the crossing route, leapt up, swiping the ball at its height and planting a foot inbounds before he tumbled over the sideline. The acrobatic, one-handed pick remains one of the most memorable plays in Michigan history. It was his second interception of the game.

1997 - "Man amongst Boys"
Marshall at Army - Michie Stadium - West Point, New York {Marshall 35 Army 25}

In a game of 135 plays, Marshall's Randy Moss had his large hands on the football just eight times today. Twice was enough. Moss, a wide receiver who is described by his coach as the best player in the country, turned his first catch into a 90-yard touchdown play, 1 yard short of the longest in the 73-year history of Army's Michie Stadium. Then, on Marshall's first play of the second half, with the Thundering Herd ahead by 2, the 6-foot-5-inch Moss jumped over the single defender, Jamar Mullen, snared an errant pass from Chad Pennington and ran for a second touchdown. This play covered 79 yards, 40 by air, and 39 by foot.

1997 - "Flea Kicker"
Nebraska at Missouri - Faurot Field - Columbia, Missouri {Nebraska 45 Missouri 38}

The Cornhuskers, who had won national championships for the 1994 and 1995 seasons, went into the game with an 8–0 record and a No. 1 ranking in the AP Poll. They had only given up seven points in their last three games and had beaten the Tigers eighteen straight times. The Tigers were unranked with a 6–3 record, and in the school's history, had never beaten a No. 1 ranked team.

In the fourth quarter, Tigers quarterback Corby Jones completed a pass to Eddie Brooks to give Missouri a 38–31 lead, giving Missouri fans hope that they would beat Nebraska for the first time since 1978 and moving coach Larry Smith to tears. The Huskers took possession from a punt after Missouri failed to convert a first down on their own 33-yard line with 1:02 left. In less than a minute, the Huskers moved the ball 55 yards. The Huskers were on the Missouri 12-yard line with only seven seconds left when Nebraska quarterback Scott Frost threw a pass intended for wingback Shevin Wiggins. The ball hit Wiggins directly in the chest near the goal line. The ball immediately shot down and hit a Missouri safety in the foot and popped back in the air. Then Missouri safety Julian Jones tackled Wiggins as time expired. As Wiggins was pulled to the ground, his leg popped up, kicking the ball into the air for a second time. Cornhusker's receiver Matt Davison leaped for the ball, his hands scraping the turf as he managed to make the catch in the end zone for a touchdown. Missouri fans stormed the field in celebration, thinking they had won.

Flea Kicker catch

The play could have resulted in a 15-yard penalty (illegal kick) if officials had considered the kick intentional. Instead, they ruled the catch a touchdown. Once fans were cleared from the field, Kris Brown kicked the extra point for Nebraska to send the game into overtime. In OT, Frost ran for a touchdown, and Jones was sacked on 4th and seven by Grant Wistrom to give Nebraska a 45–38 win.

1997 - "It's a Boilermaker Miracle"
Michigan State at Purdue - Ross-Ade Stadium - West Lafayette, Indiana {Purdue 22 Michigan State 21}

Ed Watson's two-yard touchdown run with 40 seconds to play capped off a miraculous comeback, and Michigan State's Chris Gardner missed a 43-yard field goal with three seconds left, as Purdue pulled off a stunning 22-21 victory. Michigan State clearly had the game in hand, leading 21-10, and Gardner was attempting a 39-yard field goal with just over two minutes to play. But Purdue defensive tackle Leo Perez broke through the line to block the kick and defensive end Rosevelt Colvin scooped up the loose ball and rumbled 62 yards for the touchdown. Purdue trailed 21-16 after Billy Dicken's pass fell incomplete on the conversion attempt. The ensuing onside kick was recovered by Boilermakers wide receiver Chris Daniels. Dicken completed four passes, including a 14-yarder to Gabe Cox down to the 4-yard line. Following a defensive penalty and Dicken's failed quarterback draw, Watson punched it into the end zone for the win.

1997 - "Bobcats misfire"
Montana at Montana State - Reno H. Sales Stadium - Bozeman, Montana {Montana 27 Montana State 25}

In another exciting finish of the series, Montana State fights back from a 21–7 halftime deficit to take a 25–24 lead on a three-yard run by Eric Kinnamon with 22 seconds to play. The Bobcats appeared poised to snap an 11-game losing streak to the Grizzlies, but Montana wasn't done. Thanks to a kickoff that sailed out of bounds Montana gets the ball on its own 35-yard line with no time expended off the clock. After an incomplete pass Montana quarterback Brian Ah Yat finds receiver Justin Olsen for a completion of 46 yards to the Montana State 19 with eight seconds to play. Ah Yat would recover his own muffed snap on the next play and after a Montana timeout Kris Heppner kicked a 38-yard field goal as time expired giving Montana the 27–25 win. Just as the first half ended Montana State was whistled for having too many men on the field giving Montana one extra play and the Grizzlies made the Bobcats pay scoring a touchdown on the last play of the half. The Bobcats also misfired on special teams all day. Prior to kicking the ball out of bounds they failed on three conversion attempts.

1998 - "Leap by the Lake"
Arizona at Washington - Husky Stadium - Seattle, Washington {Arizona 31 Washington 28}

Arizona had called its final timeout. There were 12 seconds left, the Wildcats down four points. Arizona was at the Washington 9-yard line. Dennis Northcutt and tight end Mike Lucky were split to the left. Malosi Leonard and Brandon Nash were to the right. Washington had 3-on-2 coverage on both sides. Jenkins took the snap, looking left for Northcutt, his top receiver. Double-covered. He looked right into the end zone. Nothing. Jenkins continued to drift back. Running back Trung Canidate swung out to the right, taking a defender with him. Also covered. Jenkins, still backpedaling, was in trouble, retreating all the way to the 20-yard line. His only choice seemed to be an incompletion to stop the clock. Well, there was one other option. All the defensive pass coverage was deep or to the outside. The middle was invitingly clear. Jenkins could run. Do or die. Score or lose. Hero or goat. With Tomey's words still echoing – "If you run, you better make it" – Jenkins planted his right foot and charged into history.

Jenkins started to run and the coaches in the press box jumped out of their chairs. "It was like, 'No . . . no . . . no!" remembered defensive coordinator Rich Ellerson, now the head coach at Cal Poly. "Actually, I was more like, 'Don't do that, you . . .' "

There's sometimes a fine line between bravery and foolishness, but Jenkins, who never lacked for confidence, had made his decision, seeking out pay dirt in the purple end zone of Husky Stadium. *"He goes," says Fox Sports Net announcer Steve Physioc.* As Jenkins reached the 10, Washington defenders Brendan Jones and Marques Hairston came up from the end zone. Linebacker Lester Towns moved in from Jenkins' right. Nash watched helplessly from the end zone; there was no one he could block.

Jenkins knew he couldn't make it if he tried to dive low. He knew he wasn't going to run over a big guy like Towns. Only one way to go. At about the 3-yard-line, Jenkins left his feet. *"He dives!" Physioc yells.* Jenkins could see the goalpost ... and then suddenly he couldn't. All three Washington defenders hit him low, flipping him heels overhead. "I remember seeing the black sky, the stars in the sky," Jenkins said. And then he saw the goalpost again. *"HE'S IN!" screams Physioc.* Jenkins landed on his feet in the end zone, tumbled to the ground and popped right back up, having somehow held onto the ball throughout the flip. "Once I realized where I was, I knew the game was over," Jenkins said. Arizona made the extra point and then needed only to kick off to end the game, winning 31-28. The Leap at the Lake turned out to be the greatest play of Jenkins career.

1998 - "Stomp, Stumble and Fumble"
Arkansas at Tennessee - Neyland Stadium - Knoxville, Tennessee {Tennessee 28 Arkansas 24}

The game matched two unbeaten teams, with the Vols sporting the No. 1 ranking while the Razorbacks were ranked No. 9. Tennessee fell behind 21–3 in the first half, stunning the Neyland Stadium crowd of 106,365 fans, but capped off a season-saving comeback with a Travis Henry touchdown run in the final seconds. Henry had 197 yards rushing and the deciding touchdown. The key play of the game and possibly the season occurred in the 4th quarter. Arkansas was nursing a 24–22 lead late in the game and was attempting to run out the clock. Tennessee Defensive

Tackle Billy Ratliff pushed Arkansas Guard Brandon Burlsworth into QB Clint Stoerner, causing him to

stumble and fumble. Ratliff recovered the ball and allowed Tennessee the chance to drive the field and score the game winning touchdown.

The 28-24 win kept Tennessee's dream season alive, which culminated with a 23-16 win over Florida State in the Fiesta Bowl to claim the BCS National Championship.

1998 - "The Wild One"

Pennsylvania at Brown - Brown Stadium - Providence, Rhode Island {Brown 58 Pennsylvania 51}

Jim Finn broke a Penn record in Providence by running for six touchdowns against the Bears, but the fourth quarter was a game all by itself. Brown outscored the Quakers 30-28 in the final period, scoring the winning touchdown with four seconds remaining, 40 seconds after Finn's 5-yard touchdown run tied it up. Finn ran for 259 yards on the day, so easily cutting through the Bears defense that the DP wrote "on one touchdown run in the fourth quarter, he would have scored even if it had been a game of two-hand touch." Finn's four touchdowns in the fourth quarter were the entirety of the Penn scoring. Just about the only thing that the '98 Bushnell Cup winner did wrong all day was a missed two-point conversion in the third quarter. The Bears, meanwhile, went through the air to win the game. James Perry threw for 470 yards and six touchdowns, four of which came in the final period.

1998 - "Desperate for Victory"

Virginia Tech at Syracuse - Carrier Dome - Syracuse, New York {Syracuse 28 Virginia Tech 26}

Donovan McNabb, The brilliant Syracuse University quarterback took the Orangemen on the magical mystery tour of all excursions, leading Syracuse to a jaw-dropping 28-26 victory over Virginia Tech in a Big East Conference thriller at the Carrier Dome.

McNabb tossed a desperation 13-yard touchdown pass to tight end Steve Brominski on the final play of the game, capping a 14-play, 83-yard drive that took all 4 minutes and 42 seconds left on the clock. On the game's final snap, the Orangemen called their beloved throwback play to the tight end. McNabb rolled to his right on third-and-goal from the 13. He looked back across the field and hung the moon for Brominski to snatch. The Syracuse tight end kept his body in front of Virginia Tech defender Michael Hawkes, who overran the play slightly. Brominski clutched the ball against his chest before falling to the turf with the winning score. Pandemonium erupted. The full Syracuse squad raced to the corner of the field and piled onto one another.

1999 - "The first one was Priceless"

1999 BCS Championship - Sun Devil Stadium - Tempe, Arizona {Tennessee 23 Florida State 16}

The 1999 Fiesta Bowl, was the BCS National Championship Game for the 1998 season, was played on January 4, 1999, in Tempe, Arizona at Sun Devil Stadium. Tennessee entered the contest undefeated and number one in the major polls. Florida State sophomore QB Chris Weinke was injured in Florida State's final ACC game of the regular season and did not participate in the championship game. Ultimately, Tennessee won their sixth National Championship after a gap of forty-seven years by beating the Seminoles by a score of 23–16. **The game was the first BCS National Championship.**

Peerless Price of Tennessee

Tennessee won the 1998 national championship, the first for the Vols since 1951, and completed the school's first-ever 13-0 season with a 23-16 win over the No. 2 Seminoles. Tee Martin completed 11 of 18 passes for 278 yards and threw TD passes to Shawn Bryson and Peerless Price, covering 4 and 79 yards respectively. For his part, Price caught four passes for 199 yards, setting a Tennessee bowl receiving record in the process. A Fiesta Bowl record crowd of 84,470 saw the game, only the second meeting between the two schools, the first meeting coming in 1958. Bryson's TD reception came in the second quarter and was followed by Dwayne Goodrich pilfering an FSU pass and returning the interception 54 yards for a score which gave the Vols a 14-0 lead. Goodrich's TD run was the third of his career. Bryson's TD came after the Vols took a Jeff Hall field goal off the board due to a roughing-the-kicker penalty. Florida State narrowed the margin to 14-9 at the half and the score remained that way until midway in the fourth quarter when Martin and Price hooked up for the pivotal 79-yard score, followed by a Seminole turnover and a Hall field goal good from 23 yards out. The Seminoles pulled to within the eventual 23-16 margin late in the game, but could get no closer. Price was named the Offensive Player of the Game and Goodrich the Defensive Player of the Game. This marked the final game for Tennessee's broadcasters John Ward and Bill Anderson, the longest-running broadcast partnership in college football.

1999 - "Blue Steele"
UNLV at Baylor - Floyd Casey Stadium - Waco, Texas {UNLV 27 Baylor 24}

Baylor had gone 4-18 in its previous two seasons, so when the Bears stood at the UNLV 8 yard line with a 24-21 lead with 28 seconds left, first-year coach Kevin Steele went for attitude and one more score. UNLV had no time outs remaining, so all Baylor had to do was kneel the ball to end the game and get Kevin Steele his first win. But Rebels corner Andre Hilliard jarred the ball loose from Darrell Bush near the goal line. UNLV's Kevin Thomas scooped it and ran 99 yards for the touchdown with no time remaining for a 27-24 victory. Baylor's loss at home against UNLV was so stunning, so unbelievable, that virtually every major sports outlet has written about it as one of the worst coaching decisions in sports history and Baylor has somehow managed to wipe every video copy of it from the face of the planet.

1999 - "Back-up Plan"
Louisiana Tech at Alabama - Legion Field - Birmingham, Alabama {Louisiana Tech 29 Alabama 28}

Brian Stallworth threw a 28-yard touchdown pass to Sean Cangelosi with two seconds to play to give Louisiana Tech an improbable 29-28 upset over No. 18 Alabama. Tech (2-2) trailed 28-22 and was facing fourth-and-26 without its quarterback, 1998 national total-offense leader Tim Rattay, who left the game two plays before with an injury. But Stallworth overcame those odds with the heave into the end zone to Cangelosi, whose leaping catch set the stage for Kevin Pond to make up for two earlier missed extra-point kicks. When he converted, Alabama (2-1), which had four turnovers and 10 penalties for 95 yards, had a loss in its final game of the century in historic Legion Field. It was also the Crimson Tide's second straight loss to Louisiana Tech, which beat Alabama 26-20 two years ago on homecoming.

Louisiana Tech got the ball back with 2:36 to play and Rattay drove the Bulldogs to the Alabama 16. Kenny King sacked him for a loss of seven yards and Rattay limped off the field during the Bulldogs' final timeout. Stallworth, a sophomore, came into the game and was sacked for 10 yards by Canary Knight. But with the clock running down, he ran back to the line, took the snap and connected with the leaping Cangelosi. Alabama's Shaun Alexander returned the ensuing kickoff about 15 yards before lateraling the ball to Santonio Beard, who ran it to the Louisiana Tech 25 before being pushed out of bounds to end the game.

1999 - "Mills kills"
Southern Miss at Louisville - Papa John's Cardinal Stadium - Louisville, Kentucky {Southern Miss 30 Louisville 27}

In a game featuring two of Conference USA's best quarterbacks, it was a punter's arm that decided Southern Mississippi's league-clinching win over Louisville. Louisville was tied 27–27 with Southern Miss with under two minutes to go with the 1999 Conference USA title on the line. Facing fourth and 5 at the Louisville 37, Southern Miss went into punt formation. Shawn Mills was leaving the field after getting into a heated discussion with head coach Jeff Bower. The punter, Jamie Purser, threw a 27-yard pass to Mills which led to a Brett Hanna field goal attempt that won the game. Southern Miss Coach Jeff Bower said he was confident when he called the trick play with time running down and overtime looming. "It was too long for a field goal," he said. "I just felt like there wasn't enough time on the clock and we weren't going to get the ball back. It was just the right opportunity." Louisville coach John L. Smith said he hated to see such a crucial game decided by trickery. "You really don't want to hear my interpretation of the fake punt," Smith said. "It's a shame to me that a league championship would come down to a play of deception. But that happens. They were smart enough to use it.

Chapter Three {2000-2017}

2000 - "The (missed) P.A.T. heard around Alabama"

2000 Orange Bowl - Pro Player Stadium - Miami Gardens, Florida {Michigan 35 Alabama 34}

In the 2000 FedEx Orange Bowl game, Michigan defeated Alabama 35–34 in an overtime battle. The 2000 Orange Bowl was the 66th edition of the Orange Bowl. The contest was televised on ABC. Quarterback Tom Brady led Michigan to the win, throwing for 369 yards and four touchdowns, while leading the team back from a pair of 14-point deficits in regulation (14-0 in the first half, and 28-14 in the second). Brady threw the game-winning score in overtime on a bootleg to tight end Shawn Thompson. The game was won by Michigan when Alabama placekicker, Ryan Pflugner, missed a PAT following their own touchdown. This was the first overtime BCS Bowl game.

QB Tom Brady of Michigan

Michigan erased a pair of 14-point deficits in winning a thrilling 35-34 overtime game against Alabama in the 2000 FedEx Orange Bowl at Pro Player Stadium. The Wolverines played in, and won, their first overtime contest in school history. With the score knotted at 28 at the end of regulation, Michigan scored on its initial play of overtime when quarterback Tom Brady found tight end Shawn Thompson on a 25-yard TD pass. Kicker Hayden Epstein hit the extra point to give U-M a 35-28 lead, its first of the contest. On Alabama's first possession of overtime, Andrew Zow hit Antonio Carter with a 21-yard TD pass on the second play of the drive. Alabama missed the Point After Try and Michigan stormed the field, celebrating their victory.

2000 - "The Pass"

Ohio State at Purdue - Ross-Ade Stadium - West Lafayette, Indiana {Purdue 31 Ohio State 27}

Drew Brees and Purdue are smelling roses. Brees threw a 64-yard touchdown pass to Seth Morales with 1:55 remaining as the 16th-ranked Boilermakers moved closer to their first Rose Bowl appearance in 34 years with a pivotal 31-27 Big Ten Conference victory over No. 13 Ohio State.

Just moments before Morales winning touchdown, Brees tossed his fourth interception and it appeared the untimely mistake would cost the Boilermakers the victory. Michael Doss returned the interception to the Purdue 2, setting up Jerry Westbrooks' two-yard touchdown run on third down that gave Ohio State a 27-24 lead with 2:16 left. But Brees shook it off, hitting Morales for the winning score just two plays later. Purdue sealed perhaps its biggest win in 34 years when linebacker Landon Johnson recovered a fumble on Ohio State's ensuing possession.

2000 - "Miracle finish #2"

Michigan at Northwestern - Ryan Field - Evanston, Illinois {Northwestern 54 Michigan 51}

Damien Anderson dropped what appeared to be a sure touchdown with under two minutes to play but Anthony Thomas' fumble on Michigan's ensuing possession allowed Zak Kustok to throw an 11-yard touchdown pass to Sam Simmons, lifting the Wildcats to an improbable 54-51 victory and sending the raucous crowd at Ryan Field into a frenzy. Coming off back-to-back shutouts, the Wolverines' defense looked helpless against a Northwestern offense that rolled up well over 600 yards in total offense.

Sam Simmons winning touchdown catch

Undaunted by Northwestern's final drive, Drew Henson moved Michigan into position for a 56-yard field goal attempt by Hayden Epstein with four seconds left. But a poor snap prevented Epstein from getting the kick away and Northwestern celebrated its second straight miraculous triumph.

2001 - "Superman can fly"

Oklahoma vs Texas - The Cotton Bowl - Dallas, Texas {Oklahoma 14 Texas 3}

The 2001 Red River Rivalry game, was a classic defensive struggle that was notable for a play made late in the 4th quarter. Both the Sooners' and the Longhorns' defenses were outstanding, holding their counterparts to less than 100 yards rushing for the entire game. When either offense could muster any momentum, they were often let down by their kicker-OU's Tim Duncan missed two field goals and UT's Dusty Mangum had one blocked. OU led 7–3 at the half on a Quentin Griffin 2-yard touchdown in the second quarter. That score held until late in the fourth quarter. The Sooners got the ball with just over eight minutes to play on their own 20-yard line, and put together a 12-play, 53-yard drive that took them all the way to the Texas 27-yard line. Facing a 4th & 16, OU sent out Tim Duncan for what appeared to be a 44-yard FG attempt. Instead, Duncan sent a pooch punt deep into the Texas zone, which caught UT's Nathan Vasher off guard. Confused, Vasher caught the ball at his own 3-yard line and was immediately downed.

Down 7–3, Texas had 2:06 to drive 97 yards on the stiff Sooner defense. On first down, Texas quarterback Chris Simms' pass was deflected by OU safety Roy Williams, who had blitzed and literally leapt over the blocker, Brett Robin, to collide with Simms at the moment he released the ball. The ball landed right in Oklahoma linebacker Teddy Lehman's hands, who walked into the end zone for a touchdown.

The play happened so fast, many fans did not know exactly what had happened. The play by Roy Williams is often called "The Superman Play" because of the way that Williams resembled Superman flying through the air with his arms stretched out at Chris Simms when he hit him. Duncan's extra point sealed the 14–3 OU victory.

2001 - "Snatch defeat from the jaws of victory"

Purdue at Minnesota - HHH Metrodome - Minneapolis, Minnesota {Purdue 35 Minnesota 28}

No team can snatch defeat from the jaws of victory better than the Minnesota Golden Gophers. Leading Purdue 28-25, the Golden Gophers chewed up the clock and then a punt put Purdue at its own 6 with 19 seconds left. Only the Golden Gophers find a way to lose a game like this. Purdue's Brandon Hance threw a 27-yard pass to John Standeford and a 39-yarder to Taylor Stubblefield. With the officials frantically trying to spot the ball and move the chains, the Boilermakers set up for Travis Dorsch's 48-yard kick just before time ran out. The Gophers didn't think it should've counted. Hance, who caught a touchdown pass and threw for three more, including the go-ahead score to John Standeford in overtime, rallied the Boilermakers from an 11-point fourth-quarter deficit to beat Minnesota 35-28 on Saturday.

2001 - "Clockgate"

Michigan at Michigan State - Spartan Stadium - East Lansing, Michigan {Michigan State 26 Michigan 24}

While the game was closely played throughout, it is the game's conclusion that is most remembered. On fourth-and-goal, Michigan State quarterback Jeff Smoker threw a touchdown pass to running back T. J. Duckett as time expired to win 26–24. Smoker had spiked the ball with one second showing on the clock to allow the Spartans to have one last play. Debates on the last remaining second continue to this day. Some contend that clock operator Bob Stehlin, known colloquially as "Spartan Bob," stopped the clock before the spike play had actually concluded, to give the Spartans one more chance. Stehlin subsequently received threatening phone calls. Stehlin has stated that seven different media outlets timed the play and concluded that hundredths of a second remained.

With 2:28 left in the fourth quarter, Michigan was forced to punt from deep in its own zone. Hayden Epstein's kick was his shortest of the day, a 28-yarder that gave the Spartans excellent field position at the Wolverines' 44 yard line. On first and second down, Smoker was sacked for two of the Wolverines' school-record 12 sacks. Following an incompletion, the Spartans faced 4th and 16 from midfield. On fourth down, Smoker's pass fell incomplete, but Michigan defensive back Jeremy LeSueur was flagged for grabbing the facemask of receiver Charles Rogers, giving the Spartans fifteen yards and an automatic first down. Two plays later, wide receiver Herb Haygood caught a pass over the middle for 17 yards and another first down. On 1st and 10, Smoker was sacked again by the Wolverine defense, but Michigan was flagged for having 12 men on the field. However, referees failed to stop the clock at the time of the penalty, forcing the Spartans to use their final timeout.

Additionally, the referees incorrectly walked off the penalty from the spot of the result of the play, costing the Spartans four yards and a down, since the down should have been reset back to first and was not. After an incompletion on the resulting 2nd and 4 from the 12 yard line, LeSueur broke up a 3rd down pass intended for Duckett in the end zone to bring up 4th down. Facing 4th and 4, Smoker completed a slant up the middle to Duckett for 8 yards that resulted in a first and goal on the Michigan 3 yard line. Michigan State rushed to spike the ball on 1st down, stopping the clock with 17 seconds left. On second and goal, Smoker rolled to the right and ran the ball down to the two yard line, but was tackled inbounds, so the clock continued to run. With time running out, the Spartans frantically lined up to spike the ball; when they did so, the stadium clock showed a single second remaining. Michigan coaches, players, and the ABC broadcasters argued that the clock should have expired on the play and that the timekeeper, purposely stopped the clock  before the ball was grounded. Michigan commentator Frank Beckmann speculated that Michigan State had benefited from its home field advantage, even calling the unfolding controversy "criminal" on the air. On the ensuing play, Smoker lobbed a pass into the back of the end zone where it was caught by Duckett, giving the Spartans a 26–24 victory.

2001 - "Reed strips teammate for touchdown"

Miami at Boston College - Alumni Stadium - Chestnut Hill, Massachusetts {Miami 18 Boston College 7}

The Canes were up 12-7 in the late stages of the game, but Boston College was on the Miami 9 yard line trying to make the game winning touchdown. However, Matt Walters intercepted a ricocheted pass and Ed Reed then ripped the ball from him and ran for a touchdown to seal the close win.

Ed Reed of Miami

Boston College moved to the Miami 9 in the final minute thanks to a 21-yard pass from Brian St. Pierre to Dedric Dewalt. St. Pierre followed with a short slant pass that was deflected by cornerback Mike Rumph to tackle Matt Walters. Walters began running with the ball before the speedy Reed ripped the ball out of his hands and raced 80 yards to the end zone.

2001 - "2:46 to the Championship"

Division II Championship - Braly Municipal Stadium - Florence, Alabama {North Dakota 17 Grand Valley State 14}

North Dakota earned its first ever trip ever to the Division II championship game in Florence, Alabama, to face the Lakers of Michigan's Grand Valley State University. Though UND had a 7–3 lead at the half, the Lakers took a 14–10 lead with 2:46 to play after Ryan Brady ran 12 yards for a touchdown.

Joel Perkerewicz of North Dakota

The Sioux had the ball on their 20-yard line as the game was winding down. Klosterman's first two passes were incomplete, and on third, he ran for yardage, but the Sioux were still 2 yards short on fourth down. Klosterman gambled and ran seven yards to keep the drive alive. Three downs later, the Sioux were at their 41-yard line, and it was fourth down again. Gambling again, Klosterman completed a pass to Luke Schleusner to get the first down, but Schleusner eluded a tackler and, with the help of a block by Jesse Smith, made it to the one yard line. With 29 seconds to play, Jed Perkerewicz took the handoff for the winning touchdown, giving the Sioux the 2001 Division II national championship.

2002 - "The Wallace Run"

Texas Tech at Iowa State - Jack Trice Stadium - Ames, Iowa {Iowa State 31 Texas Tech 17}

It is known as "The Run." The unforgettable dash of Iowa State quarterback Seneca Wallace against Texas Tech in 2002 was one of the most incredible plays in Iowa State football history. At the time, it solidified Wallace as a frontrunner for the Heisman Trophy, the award given to the nation's top college football player. In No. 11 Iowa State's 31-17 win over Texas Tech on Oct. 12, 2002, with 11 minutes left to go in the third quarter, Wallace zig-zagged a total of 135 yards on an amazing 12-yard touchdown run. As he was snapped the ball on the Red Raider 12, Wallace retreated back to the 32 yard-line. He then ran towards the right sideline, stayed inbounds along the sideline as he continued looking for a receiver, then started back to his left at the 10. After cutting behind a crunching block from running back Michael Wagner on cornerback Ricky Sailor, Wallace strolled into the end-zone untouched.

Seneca Wallace of Iowa State

Here is a transcript of the play from the late Pete Taylor, the former "Voice of the Cyclones." *"Here's Wallace, pumping, looking, running to his right, looking...and he's going to be almost caught...now he's running at the 25...and runs...down the sideline back to the 10! Now he's giving ground, goes around the 10 to the left side, to the 5, touchdown! Oh my goodness, what a run by Wallace!"*

2003 - "Pass Interference (or not)"

2003 Fiesta Bowl - Miami vs Ohio State - Sun Devil Stadium - Tempe, Arizona {Ohio State 31 Miami 24}

The pass at the end of the first overtime was ruled incomplete by the side judge. A few seconds later, another official threw a flag, initially signaling holding before changing the call to a pass interference against Miami. When asked why it took him so long to make the call, official Terry Porter said he wanted to make sure that the call was correct, explaining "I replayed it in my mind. I wanted to make double sure that it was the right call." The flag wasn't for pass interference, they said, but HOLDING. It appears that Miami's Glenn Sharpe did hold Chris Gamble off the line, but that would make the call even

more ridiculous. That means that Porter threw the flag a good 10 seconds after the snap. What it meant is that Ohio State had new life and used that to tie the game on a Craig Krenzel 1 yard TD run, to send the game into a second overtime.

Miami's 34-game winning streak came to an end in as Ohio State defeated the Hurricanes 31-24 in double overtime to win the Fiesta Bowl and the BCS National Championship. Maurice Clarett scored his second touchdown on a five-yard run in the second overtime. Craig Krenzel had a pair of touchdown runs for the Buckeyes (14-0), who ended Miami's winning streak -- the sixth-longest in college football history -- in a game of high drama that was prolonged by a controversial pass interference call. It was the first-ever overtime in a BCS title game, despite Miami turning the ball over five times and losing Willis McGahee to a knee injury in the fourth quarter. On the final play of regulation, Todd Sievers kicked a 40-yard field goal to tie it at 17-17. Kellen Winslow Jr. caught a seven-yard TD pass from Ken Dorsey in the first overtime. A controversial pass interference penalty allowed Ohio State to tie the game. On 4th-and-goal from the 5, Glenn Sharpe batted away a pass intended for Chris Gamble. Miami began its celebration, but Sharpe was flagged. Krenzel then scored on a one-yard run. In the second overtime, Maurice Clarett scored on a 5 yard run for Ohio State. The Buckeye defense held Miami on 4th down and claimed its first National Championship since the 1968 season.

2003 - "First time for everything"

Florida Atlantic at Middle Tennessee - Johnny "Red" Floyd Stadium - Murfreesboro, Tennessee {Florida Atlantic 20 Middle Tennessee 19}

Florida Atlantic University stunned Middle Tennessee State University, 20-19, in the Owls' season opener in Murfreesboro, TN. Jared Allen connected with Roosevelt Bynes on a 62-yard touchdown pass as time expired to give the Division I-AA Owls the improbable victory against the Division I-A Blue Raiders. When Eugene Gross ran for an 11-yard touchdown with 6:11 remaining in the game, it seemed MTSU was poised to prevent the upset leading 19-7. That's when the FAU comeback began. The Owls put together a 12-play, 75 yard drive capped off by a 7-yard touchdown pass from Allen to Bynes. That pulled FAU within 19-14 with 2:53 to play. FAU then stopped MTSU on three plays, forcing a punt. Colby Smith promptly angled his 36-yard boot out of bounds at the two-yard line with 1:42 left in the game. What began at the point was a game-winning, eight-play, 98-yard drive. After a three-yard rush by Doug Parker, Allen hit Bynes for a 12-yard completion for a first down at the 17. On second down, the same two connected for a 20-yard pass play for a first down at the FAU 37. Three plays later, on 4th and nine from the 38, and time running out, Allen took the snap, bobbled the ball, scrambled left and hit Bynes downfield who did the rest, eluding the MTSU defender and scampering untouched the rest of the way to give the Owls the 20-19 victory. The win was Florida Atlantic's first against a Division I-A team and also marked the first time FAU picked up a victory in its season opener.

2004 - "Bush in the Fog"
USC at Oregon State - Reser Stadium - Corvallis, Oregon {USC 28 Oregon State 20}

Even the fog couldn't obscure Reggie Bush's wily punt return. Bush was virtually untouched on the 65-yard scoring return in top-ranked Southern California's 28-20 foggy victory over Oregon State.

Playing in the fog at Reser Stadium

As fog rolled into Reser Stadium, the Beavers jumped out to a surprising 13-0 lead. But the mighty Trojans adjusted to the adverse conditions and all but took over in the second half to snap a three-game Oregon State winning streak. With just a narrow 14-13 lead, Bush's punt return came early in the fourth quarter. Although the fog was thick enough at times to interfere with pass plays, USC tight end Dominique Byrd caught two touchdowns. It would be USC last win at Oregon State until 2013.

2004 - "Trust Yourself"
Edinboro at East Stroudsburg - Eiler-Martin Stadium - East Stroudsburg, PA {East Stroudsburg 36 Edinboro 32}

It all came down to trust. East Stroudsburg University put a lot of trust in a lot of places in the final minute Saturday, and that faith -- with a healthy dose of luck added in -- gave the Warriors their first-ever NCAA Division II playoff win. Two fourth-down plays -- Evan Prall's miraculous catch on his backside for a first down, and Ben Culver's 17-yard touchdown catch with 22 seconds left -- provided a wild finish to ESU's 36-32 victory over Edinboro at a damp but not-so-dreary Eiler-Martin Stadium. With ESU (10-1) trailing 32-29, Terwilliger, who had thrown his second interception with 3:07 left, got assists from the defense and Culver. First, the Warriors defense, which held Edinboro to 94 second-half yards, got the ball back in his hands 30 seconds later, and Culver gave him field position when he brought back Matt Barley's punt 36 yards to the Edinboro 40. Five plays later, the Fightin' Scots (9-3) chased Terwilliger out of the pocket on fourth-and-11 from the 29. Avoiding the sack, Terwilliger lofted what amounted to a mini-Hail Mary, but it appeared two Edinboro defenders were in position to knock it down. But, somehow, the ball was batted into the air and found its way into the arms of Prall, who pulled it in with one hand just as he was falling to the turf barely past the first-down marker at the 17 with 54 seconds left.

QB Jimmy Terwilliger of East Stroudsburg

Chased again, Terwilliger thought about running through an open field when he spotted Culver breaking free across the back of the end zone. Terwilliger hit the open Culver for the game winning 17 yard touchdown pass, to culminate the game winning 9 play, 40 yard drive.

2005 - "The Prothro Catch"

Southern Miss vs Alabama - Bryant-Denny Stadium, Tuscaloosa, Alabama {Alabama 30 Southern Miss 21}

After going down 21–17 at halftime, the Crimson Tide came-from-behind and defeated the Southern Miss Golden Eagles 30–21. Alabama took an early 10–0 lead after Brodie Croyle threw a 26-yard touchdown pass to D. J. Hall and Jamie Christensen connected on a 33-yard field goal. The Golden Eagles then rallied with a pair of first-quarter touchdowns to take a 14–10 lead at the end of the quarter.

The first came on a defensive score when Gerald McRath intercepted a Croyle pass and returned it 33-yards and the second on a 12-yard Dustin Almond pass to Anthony Perine. Early in the second quarter Southern Miss extended their lead to 21–10 after Almond threw a 37-yard touchdown pass to Perine.

On their final offensive possession of the second quarter, Tyrone Prothro made one of the most memorable receptions in Alabama history. On a fourth-and-twelve, Croyle threw a 42-yard pass that Prothro caught on the back of Golden Eagles cornerback Jasper Faulk. Prothro had to wrap his right arm around Faulk's neck and his left arm under Faulk's right armpit to catch the ball (which appeared on replays to be blocked from his view by Faulk), and then he had to maintain possession of the ball until his knee touched down at the one-yard line. Referred to as simply The Catch, the play won the 2006 Best Play ESPY Award.

The Crimson Tide then cut the lead on the following play to 21–17 just before the half after Croyle connected with Le'Ron McClain on a one-yard touchdown reception. Alabama retook the lead in the third quarter after Tim Castille scored on a two-yard touchdown run, and led 23–21 after a failed Christensen extra point. The final points of the game came early in the fourth quarter on the second two-yard Castille touchdown run of the evening to give the Crimson Tide the 30–21 victory. For his 97 yards in kickoff returns and 34 yards punt returns, Tyrone Prothro was named the SEC Special Teams Player of the Week

2005 - "Bush Push"

USC at Notre Dame - Notre Dame Stadium - South Bend, Indiana {USC 34 Notre Dame 31}

Notre Dame Fans had spilled onto the field to celebrate a 31-28 victory over No. 1 USC when the officials restored 7 seconds to the clock. The Trojans had the ball inside the Irish 1. Leinart took the snap and spun to his left. Tailback Reggie Bush had his back -- literally. The Bush Push propelled Leinart over the goal line (illegally?) for the Trojans' 28th straight victory, 34-31.

The first quarter began with neither team moving the ball on their first possession. On Notre Dame's second possession, a Brady Quinn pass was intercepted by Keith Rivers which led to a Reggie Bush 36-yard rushing touchdown during which he hurdled would-be tackler Ambrose Wooden. The next Irish drive, which included a fourth down conversion on the Irish half of the field and the help of 28 yards in penalties, culminated in a 16-yard rushing touchdown by Travis Thomas to tie the game at 7. Less than a minute later, after a 52-yard pass from Leinart to Dominique Byrd that brought the Trojans to the Irish goal-line, LenDale White ran 3 yards for their second touchdown of the day. With both teams punting on their next drives, the first quarter ended with the Trojans leading 14–7. In the second quarter, Quinn led the Irish on a 72-yard drive that culminated in his 32-yard touchdown pass to Jeff Samardzija to tie the game at 14. The Trojans were forced to punt on their next possession and Tom Zbikowski returned the ball 59 yards for a touchdown to give the Irish their first lead of the game. Leinart led the Trojans down the field on a 69-yard drive before being intercepted in the end zone by Irish defender Chinedum Ndukwe to end the drive. Both teams did not score for the rest of the half, and the Irish led at halftime 21–14.

As the second half began, the Trojans drove 53-yards before Leinart was intercepted again. This time by Mike Richardson on the Irish half of the field. Notre Dame was unable to move the ball and punted to Bush who returned it 20 yards. Then just two plays later he sprinted 45 yards for a touchdown to tie the game at 21. On the next Irish drive, Brady Quinn completed a pass to tight end Anthony Fasano who ran it well into USC territory but Darnell Bing punched the ball loose at the Trojans' 27 yard line and Keith Rivers recovered it at the 6 to end the drive. Both teams did not score again in the quarter and it ended with the game tied at 21–21. The fourth quarter scoring began with a 32 yard field goal by D.J. Fitzpatrick to give the Irish the lead of 24–21. USC didn't answer, but on Notre Dame's next drive, Fitzpatrick missed a 34 yard field goal that would have extended the lead. With five minutes left in the game, Bush finished a Leinart-led 80 yard drive, with a 9 yard touchdown to give the Trojans a 28–24 lead. On the Irish drive, Quinn completed his four passes for 53 yards, Darius Walker ran for 29 yards, and Quinn ran 5 yards for a touchdown, giving the Irish a 31–28 lead with just over two minutes remaining in the game. On the Trojans' drive, after an incomplete pass, Leinart was sacked for a loss of 10 yards with 1:44 left in the game. Leinart was able to complete an 11 yard pass to Bush to give the Trojans a fourth down and nine situation on their own 26-yard line with only 1:32 left in the game. Leinart signaled to Dwayne Jarrett at the line of scrimmage that he would be single covered. He threw a short fade to Jarrett down the sideline just over the outstretched arms of Irish cornerback Ambrose Wooden, and Jarrett slipped away to race all the way to the Irish 13-yard line. After two rushes by Bush brought the Trojans to the 2-yard line, Leinart scrambled toward the sideline, where linebacker Corey Mays caused Leinart to fumble the ball out of bounds. Replays of the play appear to show the ball was fumbled out of bounds at the 4 yard line. Replays also showed Brennan Carroll, son of head coach Pete Carroll and a Graduate Assistant at the time, attempting to call timeout despite the Trojans having none. Attempting to call a timeout without having one is a personal foul penalty and would have penalized the Trojans 15 yards and almost would have guaranteed a game-tying field goal attempt. Although the time was stopped on field with seven seconds remaining, the stadium timekeeper let the scoreboard clock run. When the time ran out, the Notre Dame Student section began to rush the field. After a brief delay to clear the field, play resumed with seven seconds shown on the clock. The officials placed the ball at the 1 yard line.

On the last play of the game for second and goal, sometimes called the "Bush Push" and named one of the greatest college football plays ever, Carroll signaled to Leinart to spike the ball and stop the game. As it would turn out, the gesture was merely a decoy. Carroll had really told Leinart to go for the touchdown and not to tie the game and cause overtime. Leinart, opting to keep the ball on the advice of Bush, tried to sneak into the end zone. When he was stopped by a large group of Irish players, Bush pushed him into the end zone for the winning score. After an excessive celebration penalty, a missed extra point, and an unsuccessful attempt at a kickoff return, the game ended with the Trojans winning 34–31.

2005 - "Punt Gopher Punt"

Wisconsin at Minnesota - HHH Metrodome - Minneapolis, Minnesota {Wisconsin 38 Minnesota 34}

The Wisconsin Badgers and Minnesota Gophers have seen just about everything in their 115-year rivalry. Well, maybe now they have. Jonathan Casillas blocked a punt and Ben Strickland recovered it in the end zone with 30 seconds left to complete a stunning rally and lift No. 23 Wisconsin to a 38-34 victory over No. 22 Minnesota. "When you think you've seen it all, you haven't seen it all," Wisconsin coach Barry Alvarez said. With the Golden Gophers leading 34-31, Justin Kucek lined up to punt at the Minnesota 5. Kucek dropped the snap, picked up the ball and tried to get the punt off, but Casillas raced through for the block. Strickland then recovered it for the winning score. The Gophers (5-2, 2-2) led 34-24 with 3:27 to play after Gary Russell's second touchdown of the day. But the Badgers came right back, driving 71 yards in 1:17 and pulling within 34-31 on John Stocco's 21-yard TD pass to Brandon Williams. After running all over Wisconsin the entire game, the Gophers couldn't get one last first down, setting up the punt block.

The play stunned the Gopher fans and whipped the legion of red-cloaked Badger fans into a frenzy. "It was a normal punt and I was going to kick it to the right side and stuff happens," Kucek said. "I feel real bad about it, but hopefully we'll bounce back. ... I just didn't catch it cleanly, and that's about it." The ball nearly trickled out of bounds for a safety, which would have kept the Gophers in front, but Strickland pounced on it just in time. The Badgers ran out the clock, touching off a wild celebration that culminated in the Badgers once again hoisting Paul Bunyan's Axe. At least 30,000 Badger fans were in attendance, and they lingered long after the game was over, soaking in one of the most amazing victories in this bitter border rivalry.

2006 - "Race for Glory"

2006 Rose Bowl - USC vs Texas - Rose Bowl Stadium - Pasadena, California {Texas 41 USC 38}

USC entered the game on a 34-game winning streak. It was the longest active streak in Division I-A. Texas brought the second-longest active streak, having won 19-straight games and entered as the defending Rose Bowl champion, after defeating Michigan in the 2005 Rose Bowl. The 2006 Rose Bowl was, in the eyes of many, the most-anticipated matchup in college-football history. Both teams were considered good enough to win the National Championship had they existed in different years instead of having to play each other. USC had been ranked No. 1 since the preseason and Texas had held the No. 2 spot that entire time.

Vince Young of Texas run for the national championship

With Texas trailing USC 38-33, Vince Young already had used 928 Sneak to score in the fourth quarter of the 2006 BCS Championship Game. On fourth down at the Trojans' 8, Young called it again. He saw no one open. When USC end Frostee Rucker moved inside, Young moved outside, eluded Rucker and raced to the pylon. Young ran for 200 yards, threw for 267 and won the national title on his last collegiate snap.

2006 - "A time for desperation"

Boston College at NC State - Carter-Finley Stadium - Raleigh, North Carolina {NC State 17 Boston College 15}

It seemed like a time for desperation. Instead -- for one game, anyway -- it was a reason for North Carolina State's frustrated fans to believe again. NC State's late comeback that ended in a 34-yard touchdown catch by John Dunlap and a 17-15 upset of No. 20 Boston College. Boston College seemed to have the game in hand after getting the ball on N.C. State's 35 following an interception with 3:08 left. But the Wolfpack defense held, stopping Brian Toal on a fourth-down run to get the ball back at its own 28 with 46 seconds to play.

John Dunlap of NC State game winning catch

Daniel Evans threw a 34-yard touchdown pass to John Dunlap with 8.5 seconds left to cap a stunning comeback and lead the Wolfpack past No. 20 Boston College, making for a memorable debut for the first-time starter.

2006 - "Tebow Jump Pass"
LSU at Florida - Ben Hill Griffin Stadium - Gainesville, Florida {Florida 23 LSU 10}

Florida Backup quarterback Tim Tebow threw two touchdown passes, including one on a play that could have come from basketball coach Billy Donovan's playbook, and ran for a score to give the fifth-ranked Gators a 23-10 win against No. 9 LSU. Tebow made it look relatively easy. The highly touted freshman, ran nine times for 35 yards, including a 1-yard plunge on fourth down that evened the score at 7 in the first quarter. Although he threw nine passes in mop-up duty against Central Florida, Tebow had rarely used his left arm since -- aside from an occasional stiff arm.

Facing a second-and-goal play with less than a minute remaining in the first half, Tebow took the snap and ran toward the line of scrimmage. He pulled up -- much like a jump-shooter would -- double clutched to allow tight end Tate Casey to get open, then kind of flipped the ball over several defenders. Casey caught it as he fell backward.

2006 - "Greatest comeback EVER!"
Michigan State at Northwestern - Ryan Field - Evanston, Illinois {Michigan State 41 Northwestern 38}

The 2006 Michigan State-Northwestern game featured the biggest comeback in NCAA Division 1-A history. The Spartans rallied to score 38 unanswered points to beat the Wildcats 41–38 after falling behind 38–3 with 9:54 left in the 3rd quarter. Michigan State began the comeback with a nine play, 65 yard drive that was capped off with an 18-yard touchdown pass from quarterback Stanton to running back Jehuu Caulcrick. Following a Northwestern punt, Michigan State scored again, finishing an eight play, 53-yard drive with a 4-yard touchdown run from A.J. Jimmerson. On the ensuing drive, the Wildcats had gained 69 yards in only 5 plays when Bachér was intercepted at the goal line by Michigan State middle linebacker Kaleb Thornhill. The quarter ended with the Spartans down 38–17.

Michigan State's chances of completing the comeback appeared to be finished early in the fourth quarter when backup quarterback Brian Hoyer had his 6th pass of the drive intercepted by Northwestern a minute in. However, after failing to convert a short third down at midfield, the Wildcats had their punt blocked by Devin Thomas and returned for a touchdown by Ashton Henderson. Northwestern's next two drives also ended in punts, and each ensuing Spartan drive resulted in a touchdown. With the score tied at 38, the Wildcats had the ball on their own 15 yard line with 3:32 left in regulation. On the first play of the series, Bachér was intercepted by the Spartans' Travis Key at the Northwestern 40. The interception was returned to the 30 yard line. The Spartans ran the ball for the duration of the drive, advancing the ball to Northwestern's 11 yard line with 18 seconds left. MSU kicker Swenson hit a 28-yard field goal to give the Spartans the lead. The Wildcats would get the ball one more time, returning the ensuing kickoff to their own 37 yard line. Following an offsides penalty which moved the ball to the 42 yard line, Northwestern's final play for the end zone was unsuccessful and the Spartans had pulled off an incredible comeback victory.

2007 - "Tricks of the Trade"
2007 Fiesta Bowl - Boise State vs Oklahoma - University of Phoenix Stadium - Glendale, Arizona {Boise State 43 Oklahoma 42}

Years later, the discussion continues: Which was your favorite trick play in Boise State's stunning, BCS-facial, David-beats-Goliath, 43-42 overtime victory over Oklahoma in the Fiesta Bowl. Some like the Statue of Liberty handoff that Ian Johnson took in for the winning two-point conversion. How about the 50-yard hook-and-ladder from Jared Zabransky to Drisan James to Jerard Rabb that set up the OT with 7 seconds in regulation.

Boise State pulled more rabbits out of its underdog helmet than Houdini. The old hook-and-ladder. A touchdown pass from a wide receiver. And don't forget the Broncos' version of the Statue of

Liberty play. It all added up to an improbable 43-42 overtime victory against Oklahoma in one of the wildest finishes in the 36-year history of the Tostitos Fiesta Bowl. The boys from Boise, champs of the Western Athletic Conference, their presence in this game questioned because of their schedule, turned into BCS-busting men, but only after blowing a 28-10 lead built in the first 3½ quarters of their first Bowl Championship Series game. That lead turned into a 35-28 deficit when the No. 8 Sooners (11-3) roared back, taking command with 25 unanswered points — 15 in the final 1:26 of regulation.

But the No. 9 Broncos answered with a miracle of their own — three, in fact — to cap a 13-0 season. The first was a 50-yard hook-and-ladder play with seven seconds left in regulation to tie the score at 35. Quarterback Jared Zabransky threw 15 yards to Drisan James, who lateraled to Jerard Rabb for the final 35 yards.

Jerard Rabb of Boise State scoring at the end of the Hook and Lateral play

The second, after Oklahoma took a 42-35 lead in overtime, was a 5-yard touchdown pass on fourth-and-2 — from wide receiver Vinny Perretta to Derek Schouman. The third was the Statue of Liberty play involving Zabransky and running back Ian Johnson on the winning two-point conversion. Broncos coach Chris Petersen rolled the dice, electing not to go for the tie, and came up with the biggest win in school history.

Ian Johnson of Boise State game winning 2 point conversion

2007 - "Block Party"

Appalachian State at Michigan - Michigan Stadium - Ann Arbor, Michigan {Appalachian State 34 Michigan 32}

Michigan was expected to handily defeat Appalachian State, who entered the game as considerable underdogs. Las Vegas sports books did not offer a betting line because they believed that it would be a mismatch. The day before the game, an Associated Press article said that the Mountaineers were "almost certain to lose badly" and "aren't expected to be anything more than sacrificial lambs."

The game was the first to be broadcast on the then-new Big Ten Network and began with a strong first half for Appalachian State, who held a 28–17 lead at the end of the half. Michigan regained the lead at 32–31 in the fourth quarter. With no timeouts left, the Mountaineers drove 69 yards down the field in just over a minute in game time, setting up a Rauch field goal from 24 yards out with 26 seconds left. The attempt was good, giving Appalachian State a 34–32 lead. Michigan regained control of the ball on the ensuing kickoff, and a 46-yard pass from

Henne to Mario Manningham gave the Wolverines a 37-yard field goal attempt with six seconds left on the clock. The attempt was blocked by Corey Lynch, securing a 34–32 win by the Mountaineers. Immediately hailed as one of the greatest upsets in college football history, the game served as the lead story of SportsCenter and was the cover story for the following week's edition of Sports Illustrated. Appalachian State became the second FCS team to defeat a ranked FBS team, and as a result of the game Michigan dropped out of the top 25 of the AP Poll entirely, marking the first time a team had fallen from the top five to out of the poll entirely as the result of a single game.

2007 - "Fake Statue of Liberty"

Oregon at Michigan - Michigan Stadium - Ann Arbor, Michigan {Oregon 39 Michigan 7}

A week after getting stunned by Appalachian State, the Wolverines were handed their worst beating since before Bo Schembechler worked the sideline at the Big House. Dennis Dixon accounted for 368 yards and a career-high four touchdowns, helping the Ducks build a 25-point lead at halftime and cruise to an easy victory. Unlike the stunning loss to the second-tier Mountaineers, the Wolverines didn't even keep it close against Oregon. The 32-point setback was Michigan's worst since losing 50-14 at Ohio State in 1968, the season before Schembechler's coaching debut in Ann Arbor. Dixon led the way with his arm and feet, throwing for 292 yards and tying a career high with three passing TDs -- to three receivers -- and running for 76 yards and a score. He connected perfectly on 85-, 61- and 46-yard touchdown passes.

The Ducks made the Wolverines look silly lighting them up and embarrassing them with two statue of liberty plays, one of which Dennis Dixon strolled in for a touchdown after the entire defense ran with Johnathan Stewart.

2007 - "Miracle at Michie"

Tulane at Army - Michie Stadium - West Point, New York {Army 20 Tulane 17}

Army trailed Tulane 17-7 with less than 2 minutes to play and was down to third string walk-on senior QB Kevin Dunn, who had thrown one pass in his whole career... He connected on a Hail Mary with no time left to tie the game and Army won in OT. Dunn, a senior, is Army's second-string quarterback. He had thrown one pass in his career before playing Tulane. It was Kevin Dunn's first 2-minute drill at Army. It was also his first touchdown pass. Dunn completed a deflected 36-yard pass to Mike Wright as time expired to send the game into overtime, and Owen Tolson kicked a 25-yard field goal from the left hash to complete a 20-17 comeback over Tulane on Saturday night.

Army team celebrates with the Corp of Cadets

Trailing 17-10 and starting from the Army 20-yard line with 29 seconds remaining, Dunn completed passes of 27 and 17 yards to get to the Tulane 36 before spiking the ball with 4 seconds remaining. On the next snap, Dunn lofted a high pass to the back of the end zone. As the West Point cannon sounded signifying the clock reaching 0:00, the ball was deflected by two defenders and Wright came racing in to make a diving catch, dragging his feet just inside the end line. It was Wright's first career TD reception and only his second catch of the game. The Corps of Cadets rushed the field to join the celebration of Army's second overtime win this season.

2007 - "The Hat and his bag of tricks"
South Carolina at LSU - Tiger Stadium - Baton Rouge, Louisiana {LSU 28 South Carolina 16}

#14 South Carolina, coached by Steve Spurrier, came into Tiger Stadium on a rainy Saturday afternoon. The game, broadcast nationally by CBS, was messy due to the wet conditions, and South Carolina took an early 7–0 lead. LSU responded by scoring two unanswered touchdowns to make it 14–7. LSU again drove down into South Carolina territory but the drive stalled and the Tigers lined up to kick a field goal.

Colt David of LSU scoring a touchdown on fake field goal

The kick was a fake, perfectly executed by QB Matt Flynn and K Colt David, which saw David take an over-the-head no look toss from Flynn into the end zone for a touchdown. The play would go on to be selected as the ESPN/Pontiac Game Changing Performance for week 4 of the 2007 season. South Carolina would score again late in the fourth quarter but it wasn't enough and the Tigers won the game 28–16.

2007 - "Game of Inch(es)"
Concordia (Moorhead) at St. Olaf - Manitou Field - Northfield, Minnesota {St. Olaf 52 Concordia (Moorhead) 51}

In a game that featured 994 total offensive yards, the game was determined by a single inch with just 32 seconds remaining. The Cobbers were denied a chance at taking a lead in the final minute of play when their two-point conversion fell an inch short. The failed conversion left Concordia one point short as they fell 52-51 to 17th-ranked St. Olaf in Northfield. Cobber quarterback Jesse Nelson was ruled to have come up just short of the goal line on the play that determined the high-scoring affair between Concordia and the Oles. That play came just after Nelson had hooked up with sophomore receiver Jake Krause on a 10-yard touchdown pass on a fourth and seven. For Krause it was his third TD reception of the game. Despite coming up short in the officials' eyes on the point after, Nelson had the best game of his career as he ran for 104 yards and was 18-of-26 for 225 yards through the air. He also had a hand in five of the team's seven scores. He ran for two highlight reel TD's and threw for three more. The two teams marched up and down the field with little resistance from either defense. The two teams only punted four times on the day and they combined to go 15-for-15 in situations inside the red zone. Throughout the entire game, neither team was able to gain a clear-cut advantage. The lead was never more than seven points throughout the entire contest.

2007 - "Upset of the Century"
Stanford at USC - L.A. Memorial Coliseum - Los Angeles, California {Stanford 24 USC 23}

In a remarkable upset, the visiting Stanford Cardinal won 24–23 despite USC having been favored by 41 points entering the game. This result was the biggest point spread upset of all time in college football. USC entered the game with a 35-game home game winning streak (its previous home game loss also happened to be to Stanford, in 2001) which included a 24-game home game winning streak in Pac-10 play.

Mark Bradford caught a 10 yard touchdown pass from Travis Pritchard on fourth and goal with 49 seconds remaining in the game. A leaping Bradford caught the ball over cornerback Mozique McCurtis in the corner of the end zone, leaving the crowd of 85,125 at the Los Angeles Coliseum in stunned silence. Bo McNally's interception thwarted USC's final chance.

2007 - "One second to spare"
Auburn at LSU - Tiger Stadium - Baton Rouge, Louisiana {LSU 30 Auburn 24}

With a second to spare, Demetrius Byrd hauled in Matt Flynn's 22-yard fade to the back of the end zone, lifting fifth-ranked LSU to a 30-24 victory over No. 18 Auburn. Just another chapter in a long history of tight, thrilling contests between these two teams, with big hits, controversial calls and dramatic endings. Flynn scrambled for 19 yards during the final drive, then took one more shot at the end zone instead of getting the ball in the middle of the field to set a field goal attempt. He floated a pass perfectly to the back of the end zone, where Byrd emerged from behind defensive back Jarraud Powers and made a sliding catch, sending Tiger Stadium into a frenzy.

Demetrius Byrd of LSU game winning catch vs Auburn

2007 - "Shootout at Memorial I (Oxy vs Whittier)"
Occidental College at Whittier College - Memorial Stadium - Whittier, California {Whittier 67 Occidental 61}

Josh Scurlock ended his Whittier College career throwing for seven touchdowns and running for another to lead the Poets to a 67-61 victory over SCIAC rival, nationally ranked #24 Occidental College, at Memorial Field. The win marks the first time the Poets have beaten Occidental since 2000. Scurlock finished with 443 yards on 25-of-40 passing with seven touchdowns and two interceptions. He set Whittier College single-game records with the seven touchdown passes and 443 passing yards. He also rushed for 105 yards and another score. He finishes 2007 with a single-season record 2,650 yards of total offense. He was just two completions short of setting the record for completions in a season and three touchdown passes short of the season record. He leaves Whittier with career passing records in yards (6,439) and touchdowns (50).

Josh Scurlock of Whittier

Whittier 61-35 led with 12:49 left. The Poets were able to score once more with six minutes left in the game when Scurlock and Briggs connected for an 18-yard touchdown pass for what appeared to be a comfortable 67-48 lead. The Poets defense did their job again, forcing a turnover on downs from the

Tiger offense. Three plays later, however, a Whittier fumble gave Occidental great field position with 3:12 left in the game. They capitalized on their next play as backup quarterback Danny Southwick found Jason Lehman for a 25-yard touchdown pass. Their two-point conversion failed leaving the score at 67-48. On the ensuing kick-off, the Tigers recovered an onside kick to get the ball back with three minutes left. Fiorito ran the ball in from five yards out just over a minute later. Another two-point conversion failed and the score remained 67-54. The Poets offense went three-and-out on their next possession, giving the ball back to Occidental after a punt. Three plays later, a 50-yard touchdown pass from Southwick to Coverson, followed by the extra point made the score 67-61 with 23 seconds left in the game. Once again, the Tigers recovered the onside kick, giving them a chance to win the game in the closing seconds. Southwick completed a pass to Coverson to put the Tigers into Whittier territory with ten seconds left in the game. Twice, Occidental threw deep passes for the end-zone, and both times the Poet defense was able to keep the ball out of the hands of Tiger receivers. The final whistle blew three hours and forty minutes after kick-off, with the Poets on top 67-61 and in possession of the **"Myron Claxton Shoes trophy"** for the first time since 2000. The Poets 695 yards of total offense was just 13 yards short of the single game record set in 1959 against Pomona.

2008 - "Sudden Victory"
Texas at Texas Tech - Jones AT&T Stadium - Lubbock, Texas {Texas Tech 39 Texas 33}

The game was played on November 1 and was one of the most memorable games in the two team's rivalry. Heading into the game, both teams were undefeated at 8-0. However, a big difference between the teams was their rankings in the AP poll. Texas came into this game as #1, led by Coach Mack Brown. The Red Raiders, unlike their rivals, were not in the top 3. Instead, they were #6 in the country. In the game, the Red Raiders stunned the Longhorns 39-33 on a last second touchdown pass. The game appeared over on the previous play, but Texas dropped an interception. The game has gone down as one of the greatest upsets in the history of the Texas-Texas Tech rivalry (Chancellor's Spurs) and was crucial in a 3-way tie that happened in the Big 12 at the end of the season.

Texas had gone ahead 33-32 with 1:29 remaining in the game. The Red Raiders returned the kickoff to their 38-yard line, where Harrell went to work, completing passes of 8, 5, 11, and 10 yards to get a first down at the Texas 28-yard line with 15 seconds remaining. Harrell's next pass was deflected to Texas safety Blake Gideon, but Gideon was unable to catch what would have been a game-clinching interception, giving Harrell another chance with 8 seconds to go.

Michael Crabtree of Texas Tech

Harrell's pass went to Crabtree, who caught it near the sideline at the 6-yard line, broke a tackle, and went in for the touchdown with one second remaining. Thousands of Texas Tech fans rushed the field and had to be shooed off as officials reviewed the play to make sure Crabtree had stayed in bounds. As a result, the Red Raiders were charged with two excessive celebration penalties and had to kick off from their own 7-yard line following the extra point. However, Texas was unable to convert the kickoff for a touchdown, Texas Tech recovering an errant backwards pass attempt to ice the 39-33 win.

2009 – "The Greatest Game Never Seen"
Tarleton State at Texas A&M-Kingsville – Javelina Stadium - Kingsville, Texas {Tarleton 57, Kingsville 56 2OT}

In the first round of the NCAA playoffs between longtime conference rivals, one of the most dramatic games in school and NCAA history, the No. 12 Tarleton Texans needed a come-from-behind victory and double overtime to advance to the second round of the NCAA Division II playoffs with a 57-56 win at No. 13 Texas A&M-Kingsville Saturday in front of a crowd of over 13,000 people. The Javelinas scored the go-ahead touchdown to put the score at 46-43 with 45 seconds left on the clock. Tarleton started at its own 26 with a false start penalty. Facing fourth and 18, Scott Grantham hit a diving Arthur Buckingham on a 35-yard pass for a first down. Then, facing a third and 10 from the Kingsville 47, Garrett Lindholm hit the kick that tied the game at 46 from 64 yards out as time expired. Lindholm's field goal was an NCAA Division II Playoff record. Tarleton lost the coin toss in overtime and had the ball first. The Texans got to the eight, but Lindholm was forced to kick a 27-yard field goal after a delay of game penalty to go ahead 49-46. TAMUK then drove to the Tarleton two, but the Javelinas also had to kick, Christian Brom's field goal was good from 19 yards to tie the game 49-49. The Javelinas then got the ball first in the second overtime, and TAMUK scored on a two-yard run from Fred Winborn. The kick by Brom made it 56-49 and forced the Texans to do the same. Evan Robertson started from the 25 and gained five yards before two incomplete passes forced the Texans into a fourth and five from the 20. Grantham scrambled to the right and saw an opening, and after breaking several tackles and spinning into the end zone, the Texans trailed by just one point. The Tarleton coaches called for the two-point conversion, and Grantham again went to the right side on a keeper and found the winning two-point conversion to give the Texans the 57-56 double overtime victory. {Courtesy Tarleton State University}

2009 - "4 seconds to spare"

Humanitarian Bowl - Bowling Green vs Idaho - Bronco Stadium - Boise Stadium {Idaho 43 Bowling Green 42}

Max Komar cradled a sliding 16-yard touchdown catch with 4 seconds left and Nathan Enderle found Preston Davis alone in the back of the end zone for the 2-point conversion, lifting the Vandals to a dramatic 43-42 victory over Bowling Green in the Roady's Humanitarian Bowl. The score capped a wild final four minutes where Bowling Green scored twice to take the lead, then watched Idaho go 66 yards in 28 seconds to pull off the win.

Preston Davis game winning 2 point conversion catch

The Falcons took a 42-35 lead with 32 seconds left on a 51-yard pass from Tyler Sheehan to Freddie Barnes, who slipped behind the Idaho secondary for his 17th catch of the game and No. 155 in his record-setting season. But Idaho answered with a 50-yard heave from Enderle to Davis that got the ball to the Bowling Green 16. After an incompletion with 8 seconds left, Enderle found Komar -- the Vandals' leading receiver who dropped a number of passes -- sliding across the goal line to snag the low throw. It was Komar's only catch of the game. The Vandals had three wins in the previous two years, but turned it around in 2009 starting out 6-1 and closing the year with the second bowl victory in school history. For Bowling Green, it was the 14th consecutive bowl loss for Mid-American Conference teams.

2010 - "Gamble for two pays off"

Widener at Delaware Valley - James Work Memorial Stadium - Doylestown, Pennsylvania {Widener 28 Delaware Valley 27}

Widener University quarterback Chris Haupt threw an 11-yard touchdown pass to tight end Michael Penna with no time remaining and then hooked up with wideout Cedric Clayton on the two-point conversion as the visiting Pride stunned eighth-ranked Delaware Valley College, 28-27, in a Middle Atlantic Conference (MAC) game. The Pride regained the **Keystone Cup** – the award handed out to the winner of the annual meeting of the archrivals in recognition of small college football excellence in the

Philadelphia area – for the first time since 2007. After being tied 13-13 at halftime, Delaware Valley appeared to have seized control of the game with a pair of 21-yard touchdown pass by quarterback Mark Hatty. The first went to Dan Heiland with 7:14 remaining in the third quarter to cap an eight-play, 80-yard scoring drive. The second, which was set up by a Mike Jaskowski interception, went to fellow wideout Joe Gionfriddo to end a four-play, 31-yard drive just 1:51 into the fourth. Jake Sobchak hit both extra-points as the Aggies took a 27-13 advantage. Following the Aggies Corey Heard's punt, it was caught by Pride freshman Laquan Robinson, who broke a tackle, went across the field and all the way into the end zone for a 54-yard touchdown. It was Robinson's fourth return for a touchdown on the year, including three on punt returns, and it made it a 27-20 ballgame with 7:26 remaining. Widener was facing a fourth-and-six with just 2.6 seconds remaining. Haupt rolled slowly to his left, had time and found Penna, who wrestled the ball away from an Aggie defender in the end zone for a one-point deficit. The Pride elected to go for the two-point conversion and the win and lined up in a formation that had some of their offensive lineman spread out. Haupt hit Clayton for a short pass to the left, and with blockers in front of him, he ran inside the pylon for the upset win.

2011 - "Dyer's not Down"
BCS Championship Game - University of Phoenix Stadium - Glendale, Arizona {Auburn 22 Oregon 19}
        On the game's final possession, Auburn drove 73 yards to the Oregon 1-yard line and won the game with a field goal as time expired. The drive included a run by Michael Dyer in which he appeared to be tackled after 6-7 yards, but fell on top of defender Eddie Pleasant with neither his knees nor the ball touching the ground. The Auburn sideline urged Dyer to continue after getting back up, and the Oregon defense finally tackled him after a 37-yard gain.

Michael Dyer of Auburn

        The play was reviewed and the ruling on the field was upheld. Dyer then rushed for a touchdown, but a subsequent review showed that Dyer's knee went down before crossing the goal line. The touchdown was reversed and the ball placed at the Oregon 1-yard line. From there, Auburn ran the clock down to 2 seconds, and Wes Byrum kicked a game-winning 19-yard field goal as time expired, giving Auburn the national championship.

2011 - "Block party for the win"
Dickinson at Gettysburg - Shirk Field at Musselman Stadium - Gettysburg, Pennsylvania {Dickinson 21 Gettysburg 20}
        The Dickinson College football team rallied from a 14-0 deficit to overtake Gettysburg 21-20 and regain possession of the **Little Brown Bucket**. The Devils scored 21 unanswered points and blocked the Bullets' extra-point attempt in the final minute to hold on for the win. The Bullets drove 80 yards on 10 plays, scoring on a pass from Kyle Whitmoyer to John Pesce to take a 7-0 lead. Pesce scored on the Bullets' next drive as well, breaking free around the right side for a 16 yard touchdown run with 5:47 remaining in the first quarter. The Red Devils were moving once again before Peter Hak stepped in to intercept a pass at the Bullets' 15 yard line to give Gettysburg possession to start the second quarter with a 14-0 lead. The Red Devils put together a strong drive at the end of the first half, capped by a 38 yard touchdown run from sophomore fullback Kyle Smith with less than a minute to play. Gettysburg looked to add to its 14-7 lead before the end of the half. They moved the ball to the Devils' 25 yard line with the help of a Dickinson penalty. Ross Johnson stripped the ball and sacked Kody Smith to push the Bullets back. A desperation pass into the end zone was intercepted by first-year Mitch Helmandollar with five seconds to play in the half. The Devils took a knee, heading into the break trailing, 14-7. Senior linebacker

Julian Rosen picked-off a pass to give the Devils possession early in the third quarter. The Devils put together another strong drive. Senior Mike Shimkin broke free for a 46 yard run, taking the ball to Bullet six yard line. First-year quarterback Cole Ahnell dove in from the one to pull the Devils even at 14-14 with just over 11 minutes remaining in the third quarter. The Devils put together one of its best drives of the afternoon to open the fourth quarter of play. Ahnell led the Devils on a 93-yard drive, scoring on a four yard pass to tight-end Matt McDonald with a little over seven minutes remaining in the game. Whitmoyer choreographed a great drive, connecting with Aden Twer on a 43-yard bomb to the Dickinson four-yard line. Whitmoyer scrambled in for the touchdown with just 46 seconds remaining. The extra-point was blocked by the senior Corwyn Gordon, keeping the score, 21-20. The Bullets had one more card to play, attempting an on-sides kick, but senior wide receiver Cam DiFede fell on the ball and the Devils would then run out the clock for the win.

2011 - "Dreams come true"

Susquehanna University at Juniata College - Knox Stadium - Huntingdon, Pennsylvania {Juniata 17 Susquehanna 16}

Junior Scott Andrews' 18-yard field goal with 2.9 seconds remaining in the game lifted Juniata College to a 17-16 Centennial Conference football win over Susquehanna University, Saturday afternoon at Knox Stadium. That's the nuts-and-bolts of a win that Juniata's Tim Launtz had been dreaming about since he was named the Eagles' head coach on March 2, and his seniors had been striving after for four years. A victory over the archrival Crusaders, and the return of **The Goalpost** – a chunk of the upright from Stagg Field in Selinsgrove brought back to Huntingdon after Juniata's 1952 win over Susquehanna, and the 58-year symbol of the rivalry between the Eagles and the Crusaders. But as Andrews' kick split the uprights at the east end zone of Knox Stadium, there was greater significance than just a win for Launtz and his Eagles. Juniata rallied from a 13-0 halftime deficit, outscoring Susquehanna 17-3 in the second half through some grit and gutsy play calls, in a come-from-behind victory that ended the Eagles' 21-game winless streak and marked Juniata's first win over its rival since 2006. Juniata's game-winning drive answered Susquehanna's field goal with 2:05 showing on the game clock, which saw the Crusaders briefly grab a 16-14 lead. Freshman quarterback Ward Udinski and junior receiver De'Sean Popley set the table for Andrews' game-winning field goal. With a 4th-and-10 at the Susquehanna 42, Udinski connected with Popley on a 39-yard pass play to give the Eagles a 1st-and-goal. The Eagles ran three rushing plays, getting the ball down to the one-yard line, before letting Andrews kick the field goal for the victory.

2012 - "House of Horrors"

Lake Erie College at Gannon University - McConnell Family Stadium - Erie, Pennsylvania {Gannon 36 Lake Erie 33}

Once again the Lake Erie College football team and Gannon University staged a thriller in the season opener, but for the visiting Storm, Gannon University Field continued to be a house of horrors as the host Golden Knights rallied for a 36-33 victory in "The Battle of Lake Erie." The back-and-forth affair had the Storm up 33-29 and first-and-goal inside the Gannon five- yard line, but Lake Erie failed to punch it in and senior Sam Marcotte, who up to that point had kicked a school record four field goals, missed a 20-yard attempt and gave the Knights the ball back with 3:29 to play. A 60-catch and run off a deflection by Justin Caliste set Gannon up at the Storm 20-yard line. Three plays later, faced with a fourth-and-two from the 12, Liam Nadler connected with Abraham Ocasio who carried two defenders into the end zone for the go-ahead score with 1:05 to play. Lake Erie was unable to gain a first down on its final possession and after two kneel downs, the Knights secured their third straight series home win and claimed the **Ship's Wheel trophy**.

Action in the Lake Erie College-Gannon University game

Late in the third quarter, Nicely was picked off deep in his own end by Will Giles, setting up the Knights at the Lake Erie six. Three plays later, Jansen Jones plunged in from two yards out and Matt Jones added the two-point conversion to put the Knights up 29-26. After the Storm retook the lead on Phenix's big run with 14:12 to play, the teams traded punts and then the Storm came up with a big fumble recovery on a sack by redshirt freshman Austin Hoeflich at the Gannon 30 with 7:18 left. A pass from Nicely to Lindgren covered 24-yards to set the Storm up at the four. Lake Erie made it to the one on the next play, but two subsequent plays resulted in a loss of four yards and an incomplete pass. The missed field goal followed, setting up the Knights at the 20.

2012 - "10 points in a minute"
Central Arkansas at McNeese State - Cowboy Stadium - Lake Charles, Louisiana {Central Arkansas 27 McNeese State 26}

Eddie Camara kicked a 47-yard field goal with 23 seconds to play for Central Arkansas, capping a 10-point rally in the game's final 1:10 as the Bears stunned McNeese State 27-26 for possession of the **"Red Beans and Rice Trophy"**. Marcus Wiltz had a 29-yard rushing touchdown to push McNeese State's lead to 26-17 with 3:28 to play in the game. That's when things got interesting. On the ensuing possession, the Bears drove 72 yards in 2:18 and capped the march with a 19-yard touchdown connection between quarterback Wynrick Smothers and Dezmin Lewis to pull within 26-24. Central Arkansas then successfully converted an onside kick, taking over for another offensive possession at the 38-yard line of McNeese State with just over a minute left. The Bears rushed three straight times, setting up Camara's game-winning kick. Smothers finished with 254 passing yards with three touchdowns and two interceptions.

2012 - "Kicking for the Coal Bowl (trophy)"
Indiana (PA) at California (PA) - Adamson Stadium - California, Pennsylvania {California (PA) 26 Indiana (PA) 24}

In what may go down as probably the best game in the storied rivalry, 14th-ranked Indiana (PA) lost to sixth-ranked California (PA) 26-24 in a back-and-forth game that saw Vulcans kicker Cody Nuzzo connect on a 30-yard field goal with 3.5 seconds remaining to wrap up the win and the **Coal Bowl trophy**. The field goal came on the end of a six-play, 31-yard drive that began after Cal recovered an onside kick with 51 seconds remaining. The Vulcans recovery came after an 80-yard touchdown pass from Peter Lalich to Nadir Brown made it 24-23 Indiana (PA), however Nuzzo hooked the extra point to the left, preserving the Crimson Hawks one-point lead. This epic game produced two ties and four lead changes, with a combined 887 yards of total offense and seven turnovers between the two teams.

The Vulcans scored the game's first touchdown, going 10 plays and 75 yards on the opening drive. Indiana (PA) knotted the score at the beginning of the second quarter when Tuck went nearly untouched up the middle for a 14-yard touchdown. Cal scored with six minutes to go in the half, with Lalich finding RJ Thomas for a 20-yard scoring play. Ullman answered less than three minutes later with a 41-yard field goal to make it a 14-10 game. Cal then drove down the field and as time expired in the half, Nuzzo chipped a field goal in from 20 yards out to give the Vulcans the seven-point halftime lead. Indiana (PA) came out of the half down 17-10 as both teams went scoreless in the third quarter. That is when Box would enter the game for the Crimson Hawks, completing his second pass of the game to Anthony Meriwether for 20 yards and later hit Pat Brewer in the numbers for an 11-yard pickup down to the Cal two yard line. Two plays later Tuck banged it in from three yards out and Ullman's extra point would tie the game at 17-17 with 10:14 to go. With the offense still rolling, Box found Brewer again, this time in the end zone for an eight-yard touchdown. The extra point by Ullman gave Indiana (PA) its first lead of the game at 24-17 with 6:58 left in the game. The Crimson Hawks then embarked on a time consuming drive with 6:11 left on the clock, running 10 plays and getting all the way down to the Cal 13-yard line to set up a field goal attempt with just over one minute remaining. However Ullman would just barely miss it to the left, turning the ball over to the Vulcans with 1:03 remaining. The 80-yard scoring toss from Lalich to Brown would follow, setting up the final heartbreaking minute of action.

2012 - "Manziel magic"
Texas A&M at Alabama - Bryant-Denny Stadium - Tuscaloosa, Alabama {Texas A&M 29 Alabama 24}

This was the game where Texas A&M freshman quarterback and eventual Heisman Trophy winner Johnny Manziel completed 24 of 31 passes, had 253 passing yards, and two passing touchdowns with 92 rushing yards to help No. 15 Texas A&M upset No. 1 Alabama 29–24, which led him to being the first freshman to win the Heisman Trophy.

"Johnny Football" of Texas A&M

Alabama couldn't beat Johnny Football. The Crimson Tide fell behind early and couldn't catch up to freshman quarterback Johnny Manziel and upstart Texas A&M, which joined the Southeastern Conference just in time to knock off the nation's No. 1 team 29-24 in the program's first trip to Bryant-Denny Stadium. Texas A&M scored three touchdowns on its first three drives for a 20-0 lead, and although the Crimson Tide charged back, Manziel and the Aggies always stayed out of reach. The Aggies had been 1-10 against top-ranked teams with the only previous win coming 30-26 over Oklahoma in 2002. The Tide struggled to slow Manziel either passing or running, as he began the game by converting seven straight third-down plays into first downs. In one of his best moments, Texas A&M faced third-and-six at its own 41, but Alabama's pass rush left an opening as it crashed down on him. He exploited it for a 32-yard run.

2013 - "The Hit"

2013 Outback Bowl - Michigan vs South Carolina - Raymond James Stadium - Tampa, Florida {South Carolina 33 Michigan 28}

"The Hit" is widely considered to mark the turning point in the game for South Carolina and it earned a "Best Play" ESPY Award for South Carolina's Jadeveon Clowney. "The Hit" refers to a play by Defensive End Jadeveon Clowney which occurred midway during the fourth quarter of play. After a Wolverines fake punt, followed by a controversial call awarding Michigan a first down during a critical time consuming drive, Clowney gained instant fame for his violent tackle of Michigan running back Vincent Smith that came with 8:21 remaining in the fourth quarter. "The Hit" dislodged Smith's helmet and forced a fumble that Clowney himself recovered, "The Hit" set up a touchdown pass to wide receiver Ace Sanders on the next play. Although "The Hit" itself did not result in the game winning touchdown, it is considered by many to have motivated a previously lethargic Gamecock offense to rally and ultimately win the game.

Jadeveon Clowney of South Carolina

Steve Spurrier's plan to use two quarterbacks in the Outback Bowl worked so well that Dylan Thompson and Connor Shaw both earned game balls. That's a first for the Head Ball Coach, who has a well-known penchant for benching struggling QBs. Except in this case, the Gamecocks' winningest coach used his talented pair of passers by design. Shaw began The Gamecock's 33-28 victory over Michigan with a 56-yard touchdown pass to Damiere Byrd. Thompson closed it out by throwing a 32-yard TD strike to Bruce Ellington in the final minute to help South Carolina match the school record for victories in a season.

2013 - "A Fordham First"
Fordham at Temple - Lincoln Financial Field - Philadelphia, Pennsylvania {Fordham 30 Temple 29}

Michael Nebrich found Sam Ajala in the end zone for a 29-yard touchdown with four seconds remaining to give Fordham a 30-29 win over Temple at Lincoln Financial Field. The win is Fordham's first over an FBS opponent since it reinstated its football program in 1970. Nebrich completed 23 of 36 attempts for 320 yards and two touchdowns. His final pass, the game-winner, was reviewed when Temple challenged that Ajala was an ineligible receiver after he went out of bounds. The touchdown was upheld when the referees ruled that Ajala was forced out and legally re-entered the field.

Sam Ajala of Fordham winning touchdown catch

2013 - "Shootout at Memorial II (Oxy vs Whittier)"
Occidental College at Whittier College - Memorial Stadium - Whittier, California {Whittier 59 Occidental 52}

In the 70th meeting for the "Shoes Trophy" and the 106th meeting overall between Whittier and Occidental the Poets came out victorious holding onto the Coveted "Shoes" Saturday afternoon with a 59-52 victory snapping their seven game losing skid. Whittier earns their second straight victory over the Tigers holding onto "The Shoes" after they had taken them last year on the road in a 61-30 victory. They also now tie the rivalry series at 35 games apiece. The game that included big plays, a record broken, and one big defensive stand by the Poet defensive unit on the Tigers final drive kept the Poet faithful on the edge of their seats.

Whittier saw Oxy have a chance to tie the game up with a 1st and goal opportunity from the three yard line with under a minute to play after they had gone 10 plays covering 77 yards. But after three straight incomplete passes to Samuel Stekol in the end zone who hauled in a 3rd and 17 reception for 50 yards during the drive, Whittier stopped quarterback Bryan Scott on a quarterback keeper, which sealed the Poet victory. The game was tied or the lead changed hands 15 different times. Whittier totaled 516 yards of total offense (314 Passing - 202 Rushing) compared to Occidental's 567 yards (312 Passing - 255 Rushing).

2013 - "Leo comes up Golden for the Rams"
West Chester at Shippensburg – Seth Grove Stadium – Shippensburg, PA {West Chester 32 Shippensburg 29}

Shawn Leo's 26-yard field goal with 1.1 seconds remaining lifted West Chester to a 32-29 victory over host Shippensburg in a pivotal PSAC East football game inside Seth Grove Stadium. Leo, a senior from Souderton High School in Harleysville, PA, kicked the first game winner of his career. Leo would go on to being the career leader in field goals made and the 2nd leading scorer in school history for West Chester.

West Chester ended a 12-game home winning streak by Shippensburg in front of 7,458 homecoming fans. Third-string quarterback Andrew Derr took West Chester on a 7-play drive that covered 52 yards over 2:26 that culminated in Leo's game-winning kick.

2013 - "Prayer at Jordan–Hare"
Georgia at Auburn - Jordan-Hare Stadium - Auburn, Alabama {Auburn 43 Georgia 38}

Auburn hosted Georgia in the 117th meeting of the **"Deep South's Oldest Rivalry"**. Down 38–37 with 36 seconds remaining in the game, Auburn faced 4th down and 18 yards to go when junior quarterback Nick Marshall threw a 73-yard touchdown pass to sophomore wide receiver Ricardo Louis. The pass was tipped by Georgia's sophomore safety Josh Harvey-Clemons. The pass would have been overthrown had Harvey-Clemons not deflected the football and Louis was unable to find the ball after the deflection until a moment before it landed in his hands. The score allowed Auburn to win the game 43–38.

As teammates sprinted to congratulate Ricardo Louis in the end zone, Auburn IMG Sports Network commentator Rod Bramblett exclaimed "A miracle in Jordan-Hare! A miracle in Jordan-Hare!" in utter jubilation, his voice carried across the nation on radio stations broadcasting the game. Within four days, T-shirts were being sold with Bramblett's words "Miracle at Jordan-Hare" printed across the top.

Ricardo Louis of Auburn

The Play - During the timeout Malzahn called a play he dubbed "Little Rock," something he had drawn up late in 1998 while coaching Shiloh Christian School in the Arkansas state playoffs. The play involved one receiver running deep on a post route while another would run a shallow dig route far enough to make the first down. Typically this play did not call for sophomore Ricardo Louis to be on the field but Malzahn said "Let's put Ricardo at five (the deep post route) and Sammie on the boundary (the shallow dig route)." The pass was designed to go to the shallow receiver, sophomore Sammie Coates, for a first down. But the planned deep receiver Louis begged quarterback Nick Marshall to throw him the ball instead. Louis dreamed of making a big play, inspired by the words of his receiver coach Dameyune Craig who frequently challenges his players with the question "What's going to be your legacy?" Both teams took the field after consecutive timeouts, Auburn facing 4th down and 18 from their own 27-yard line with 36 seconds remaining in the game. Marshall took the snap and made a five-step drop to his own 17-yard line. Sammie Coates found himself wide open near midfield, but Nick Marshall stepped up to the 20-yard line and heaved the ball 47 yards downfield to Ricardo Louis in triple coverage. Coates dropped his head, too nervous to watch the outcome. The overthrown pass sailed beyond Marshall's intended receiver as Georgia's freshman safety Tray Matthews leapt for the interception at the 23-yard line. But his teammate, sophomore defender Josh Harvey-Clemons, also jumped for the interception and tipped the ball with his right hand causing it to ricochet over Matthews' helmet. The redirection allowed the overthrown Auburn receiver to catch up to the pass. Auburn's Louis could not initially find the deflection as the football fluttered over his head, but his peripheral vision located the ball over his left shoulder just as it reached his outstretched hands. Louis juggled the ball at the 15-yard line, finally gained control at the 9, looked over his left shoulder finding no one in pursuit and bounded into the south end zone for the touchdown with 25 seconds remaining. Terrified suspension turned into roaring triumphant celebration from the stunned crowd as Louis reeled in the catch. A 7-play, 78-yard drive had just been capped off by a miraculous 73-yard score as the Tigers took the lead 43–38. Penalty flags lay on the field, but the fears of Auburn fans were alleviated when the touchdown stood, as the flags were against Georgia for a few players taking their helmets off while the play was ongoing.

2014 - "Book of Knowledge reclaimed"
Carleton at Macalester - Macalester Stadium - St. Paul, Minnesota {Macalester 17 Carleton 14}

Michael Abramson kicked a 37-yard field goal as time expired and Macalester regained the **"Book of Knowledge trophy"** with a 17-14 win over Carleton. After 11 consecutive years of seeing the Book going to the Carleton sideline, the Scots finally claimed the travelling trophy when Abramson's kick sailed through the uprights as the clock wound down to 0:00. Macalester needed just 15 seconds to move 46 yards and into field goal position after its defense forced a turnover on downs at the Scots' 34-yard line with 15 seconds to play in the game.

Michael Abramson kicking game winning 37 yard field goal for Macalester

On the first play from scrimmage after the turnover, Samson Bialostok hooked up with Hunter Johnson for a 42-yard pass play and then spiked the ball intentionally to stop the clock with 10.7 seconds to play. A handoff to Zandy Stowell allowed the ball to get to the middle of the field at the Carleton 20, where the Scots called their final timeout with 4.0 seconds to play, setting up the winning field goal. Trailing 14-7, the Knights drove 58 yards in 10 plays before QB Zach Creighton rushed for an 11-yard touchdown, tying the game at 14-14 and setting up Abramson's heroics.

2014 - "King Solomon"
California at Arizona - Arizona Stadium - Tucson, Arizona {Arizona 49 California 45}

Anu Solomon hit Austin Hill on a 47-yard Hail Mary on the game's final play, and Arizona scored 36 points in the fourth quarter to pull off an improbable 49-45 win over California. The Wildcats recovered an onside kick after Cal was called for a batting penalty and pulled within 2 after Solomon hit Cayleb Jones on a 15-yard scoring pass. Arizona got the ball back with less than a minute left and pulled off the miracle when Hill, a senior who missed last season with a torn ACL, brought the ball down between five Cal defenders. Behind Jared Goff, who threw for 380 yards and three touchdowns, Cal led 31-16 heading into the fourth quarter. That's when Arizona kicked its high-octane offense in gear, marching for one score after another. Solomon hit Hill on a 9-yard touchdown pass, then Jones on a 16-yarder after Khalfani Muhammad scored on a 50-yard touchdown run. Muhammad scored again on a 6-yard run to put Cal seemingly in good position, up 45-30 with just over 5 minutes left. But the Wildcats kept coming. Arizona marched for a 6-yard touchdown run by Terris Jones-Grigsby then recovered a second try at an onside kick after Cal's batting penalty. Jones, who had 13 catches for 186 yards, pulled down a 15-yard pass from Solomon with 2:44 left, but the Wildcats' 2-point try failed.

Austin Hill of Arizona catching game winning pass

With a chance to put the game away, Cal couldn't finish it off. James Langford hooked a 47-yard field goal left, turning the ball over to Arizona at its own 29-yard line with 52 seconds left. Solomon completed a couple of short passes before finding Hill on a 20-yard pass that moved the chains and briefly stopped the clock. Arizona raced to the line and Solomon spiked the ball to set up the final shot at the end zone. Hill came down with it, sending the Wildcats streaming from their sideline and the Bears collapsing to the turf.

2014 - "Heartbreaker"

North Central at Wheaton - McCully Stadium - Wheaton, Illinois {Wheaton College 34 North Central College 31}

A fourth-quarter comeback effort came up just short for the North Central College football team Saturday evening, as the Cardinals lost a 34-31 heartbreaker on a last-second field goal to home standing Wheaton College in the annual **Battle for the Little Brass Bell**. Playing in front of a near-capacity crowd at McCully Stadium, the 12th-ranked Cardinals wiped out a 15-point deficit with two straight scores but could not get the Thunder offense off the field on the game's final drive, as the hosts drove 56 yards in 13 plays before kicker Sam Cote won the game with a 29-yard field goal as time expired. The first seven drives of the game resulted in points, as the only punt of the contest did not occur until midway through the fourth period.

"The Little Brass Bell Trophy" being hoisted by victorious Wheaton College

The Cardinals opened the scoring by taking their first possession 81 yards in nine plays and scoring on Dylan Warden's four-yard touchdown pass to Ryan Kuhl. The extra-point attempt was unsuccessful, leaving North Central with a 6-0 advantage. Wheaton, which entered the game ranked 11th by the American Football Coaches Association (AFCA) and 17th by D3football.com, got on the board with Cote's 37-yard field goal on its initial drive. The Cardinals' Dom Zavaglia countered with a 22-yard field goal early in the second quarter, though the Thunder followed with their first touchdown drive as quarterback Johnny Peltz fired a 13-yard TD pass to Keegan Kemp, who made the catch amid heavy pressure to give the hosts their first lead at 10-9. Ulmer made two catches for 30 yards and added a 13-yard run on the next drive before Brown scored on an eight-yard run to put North Central back in front, 16-10. Kemp struck again for the Thunder with a nine-yard scoring run to restore Wheaton's lead at 17-16. Wheaton maintained possession for nearly the entire third period in its bid to put the game away. Peltz capped off a 14-play, 87-yard drive with a nine-yard TD pass to Matt Mitchell on the first drive of the second half. After an Alex Mendez interception just two plays later, the Thunder extended their lead to 31-16 as Danny Puknaitis finished a 15-play, 83-yard jaunt with a four-yard touchdown run. The Cardinals narrowed the gap to 31-24 on their next possession, as Brown scored from three yards out on fourth down. North Central elected to pursue a two-point conversion, and the initial pass attempt was unsuccessful, though a pass interference penalty gave North Central another try. Warden ran across the goal line on the subsequent attempt, leaving the visitors within a touchdown with 11:23 remaining. North Central forced the game's only punt on the next drive, taking over on its own 20 with 7:11 left. The possession threatened to stall as the Cardinals faced fourth down-and-eight at their own 41-yard line, but Warden found Ulmer on a crossing route for a 59-yard touchdown pass and the game was tied at 31-31 with 4:53 on the clock. Sticking primarily to its running game, Wheaton was able to run down the clock and move into field-goal position, converting a fourth-down attempt at the Cardinals' 32 with just under two minutes left. The game-winning field goal glanced off some North Central fingers but still had enough distance to clear the crossbar.

2014 - "Sun Devil Magic"

Arizona State at USC - L.A. Memorial Coliseum - Los Angeles, California {Arizona State 38 USC 34}

Trailing 34-32 with seven seconds remaining, Arizona State quarterback Mike Bercovici completed a 46-yard Hail Mary pass to wide receiver Jaelen Strong as time expired to defeat #16 Southern California, 38-34, in Los Angeles. This was the first time ASU had won in the Coliseum since 1999. This completed a 9-point comeback in the last 3:02 where ASU had no timeouts.

Jalen Strong of Arizona State game winning catch

USC had several defenders on the goal line, but Strong had enough space to leap for and catch the ball just in front of the end zone and then scored the touchdown before the defenders could react. Bercovici, a California native, was starting just his second game that year, having replaced an injured Taylor Kelly.

2015 - "The Owusu Catch"

UCLA at Stanford - Stanford Stadium - Palo Alto, California {Stanford 56 UCLA 35}

One jaw-dropping catch by Francis Owusu nearly overshadowed a record-setting performance from Christian McCaffrey. Owusu pinned the ball on the back of a defender in the end zone for one of the most memorable catches in recent memory and McCaffrey did most of the rest with a school-record 243 yards rushing and four touchdowns in No. 15 Stanford's 56-35 victory over No. 18 UCLA.

Francis Owusu of Stanford

It started with McCaffrey taking a direct snap in the wildcat and handing to Bryce Love on a jet sweep. Love then flipped the ball to quarterback Kevin Hogan, who had lined up as a receiver on the play. Hogan set himself in the backfield and threw deep to Owusu. Despite being interfered with by a face-guarding Jaleel Wadood in the end zone, Owusu still managed to trap the ball against Wadood's back while not even being able to see it. Owusu managed to keep his hand on the ball to maintain control as the two fell to the ground.

2015 - "Third TD is the charm"

Union (NY) at Rochester University - Edwin Fauver Stadium - Rochester, New York {Rochester 33 Union 30}

Senior quarterback Justin Redfern threw three touchdown passes in the last 7:37, including two in a 14 second span, as the University of Rochester rallied to defeat visiting Union College, 33-30 in a Division III football game at Edwin Fauver Stadium. Redfern connected on a four-yarder and an 18-yarder to Farid Adenuga to bring Rochester within 30-27, with 2:19 to play. He threw a 50-yard TD pass to Kyle Allegrini right after the Yellowjackets recovered the ensuing kickoff when it bounced off a Union player. That put Rochester up, 33-30. Cioffi helped the final drive by throwing a 21-yard pass to Baker on 4th-and-15 at the Union 47. That put the ball on Rochester's 32. He nibbled, hitting Baker for seven yards and Packy Brown for five to reach the Rochester 20. Three straight incompletions – one a breakup by Colin Woods, another by Ugwu Okeke Ewo – left the Dutchmen facing 4th-and-10 at the Rochester 20. Union quarterback Dante Cioffi completed five of 11 passes and moved the Dutchmen from their own 38 to the Rochester 20 with 50 seconds to play.

Isaiah Smith of Rochester game saving blocked Field Goal

David Pope's potential game-tying 37-yard field goal attempt was blocked by Rochester's Isaiah Smith on fourth down. The Yellowjackets took over at their own 20 and Redfern knelt twice with the snap.

2015 - "Punt Michigan Punt"

Michigan State at Michigan - Michigan Stadium - Ann Arbor, Michigan {Michigan State 27 Michigan 23}

Michigan was about to become a Top 10 team with a 23-21 win over No. 4 Michigan State. All the Wolverines had to do was punt the ball away for a victory and take the **Paul Bunyan Trophy** back to

Ann Arbor. That was until Wolverines punter Blake O'Neil fumbled a snap with 10 seconds left and Spartans' backup defensive back Jalen Watts-Jackson made the play of his life by returning it for a touchdown and a 27-23 win.

Punter Blake O'Neill of Michigan   **Jalen Watts-Jackson of Michigan State scoring game winning touchdown**

In the 10 seconds it took for the clock to tick down, Watts-Jackson went from total obscurity to pulling off one of the most unlikely endings in college football. As Watts-Jackson lay on a maize "M" in the end zone, his teammates piled above him, he dislocated his hip in the ruckus. He was later carted off the field and taken to a hospital, barely getting a glimpse of the scene he set off. No one will soon forget it. A fan at Michigan Stadium had a heart attack on the final play of the game. Paramedics told ESPN that they transported the man to the hospital in stable condition.

2015 - "Hurricane rising"

Miami at Duke - Wallace Wade Stadium - Durham, North Carolina {Miami 30 Duke 27}

Miami gave up a 24-12 fourth-quarter lead to Duke for what appeared to be a heartbreaking loss -- only to win 30-27 in the most amazing fashion imaginable. The Hurricanes received a Blue Devils kickoff on the final play of regulation and proceeded to lateral the ball eight times -- crisscrossing the field on several occasions -- before Corn Elder broke into the clear to score a 75-yard touchdown that will be replayed for as long as replays exist. The play stirred controversy amid a number of missed calls by the Atlantic Coast Conference officiating crew.

Knee down or not?   **Corn Elder of Miami**

Hurricanes won on the wildest kickoff return of the year that was initially called back by officials and ultimately should not have counted. On a play that lasted 49 seconds, Miami lateraled the ball eight times and went back to their own 3-yard line before reversing the field and racing down the sideline to score.

The play was immediately put under review, and after the Hurricanes had rushed on the field from the benches, officials called a block in the back on Miami that would have resulted in a 10-yard penalty and an untimed down — crucially wiping out the touchdown. Officials also reviewed whether a Miami played was downed during the play, but after a lengthy review the referee announced that ... the play was still under review. Eventually, officials determined that no Miami player was ever down on the play, and that the block in the back was in fact a legal block. The touchdown stood, giving the Hurricanes a 30-27 win at Wallace Wade Stadium. The extremely vague explanations of the referee left many Duke Fans fuming, and the mysterious disappearance of the block in the back foul wasn't properly accounted for.

2015 - "Hog and Lateral"

Arkansas at Mississippi - Vaught-Hemingway Stadium - Oxford, Mississippi {Arkansas 53 Mississippi 52}

The Razorbacks appeared to have lost multiple times in the first (and only) overtime period, first facing 4th-and-25 and a 52-45 deficit. But Hunter Henry's blind 15-yard lateral fell into the hands of Alex Collins, who broke free for a wild conversion. Bret Bielema chose to go for two and the win after Allen's ensuing touchdown pass, only for Allen to be sacked. But the Rebels were flagged for a facemask penalty, and on a second try Allen scored on a quarterback keeper for the win. The conversion was the icing on the cake for Allen, who went absolute supernova in the best game of his career. The senior quarterback finished 33 of 45 for 6 touchdowns and operated the Razorbacks' play-action passing game to perfection.

Hunter Henry of Arkansas desperation lateral

Brandon Allen of Arkansas game winning 2 point conversion

"FootballScoop.com reported that Arkansas' fourth-down conversion should not have counted. According to NCAA Section 2 Article 2 Rule 8-3-2-d-5, it appears Collins should have never been allowed to run with the ball after recovering Henry's fumble. The rule specifically prevents an offensive team from advancing a fumble on fourth down. Under the rule, the play should have been dead once Collins recovered the fumble, which would have resulted in a turnover on downs and given Ole Miss the victory." Henceforth, the question, was it a fumble or a backward pass? Ole Miss Fans are still grumbling to this day about the call.

2016 - "One second to spare in Fargo"

South Dakota State at North Dakota State - Fargo Dome - Fargo, North Dakota {SDSU 19 NDSU 17}

North Dakota State, the FCS team known for toppling FBS opponents, was taken down by one of its own -- at home. Taryn Christion threw a 2-yard touchdown pass to Jake Wieneke with one second left Saturday as South Dakota State rallied from 14 down and stunned the top-ranked Bison 19-17. SDSU had been inside the Bison 5-yard line three previous times only to come up empty. But on fourth down, Wieneke ran at Jalen Allen and turned in time to catch a back-shoulder pass from Christion.

Jake Wieneke of South Dakota State

Wieneke had six catches for 108 yards, while Dallas Goedert hauled in 11 passes for 150 yards and a score. The Bison made it 17-3 on a 26-yard run by Eason Stick with 10:16 left in the third quarter. But the SDSU defense took charge after that. Christion hit Goedert from 12 yards out for a touchdown that pulled the Jacks within 17-10, and a defensive stand gave SDSU the ball on its own 20 with 2:28 to play. Christion converted two third-and-long runs on the drive. He hit Goedert on third-and-10 that took the ball down to the NDSU 2 with 5 seconds left to set up the game-winner.

2016 - "Defense is not an option"

East Texas Baptist at Louisiana College - Wildcat Field - Pineville, Louisiana {East Texas Baptist 64 Louisiana College 62}

Despite record setting performances from Easton Melancon and Shedrick Davis the 2016 edition of the **"Battle for the Border Claw"** didn't finish the way the Wildcats wanted, as #18 East Texas Baptist escaped with a 64-62 victory on Saturday night. After a Wildcat punt on their first possession, it didn't take long for the nation's highest scoring team to get on the board as the Tigers scored on a 17-yard run by McNeill, taking less than a minute off the game clock, after a successful 2-point attempt, the Tigers led 8-0. East Texas Baptist would add to their lead after an interception return for a touchdown and another successful 2-point conversion and midway through the first quarter the Wildcats found themselves down 16-0. Louisiana College would bounce back with a fury over the next three possessions, taking advantage of excellent field position along the way. A 76-yard kickoff return by Lamar Carroway set up the Wildcats first score of the game, an 8-yard run by Aurren Cooksey. The next two Wildcat scores came off Tiger turnovers, a fumble recovery by Anthony Dorsey and an interception by Josh Pickett, gave the ball to the Wildcats in plus territory. The Wildcats would take lead a 21-16 lead on an impressive 36-yard touchdown run by Aurren Cooksey, his second score of the game. East Texas Baptist would regain the lead 22-21 in the second quarter after an interception gave the Tigers the ball at the Wildcats 13 yard line, and then go ahead by a touchdown on their next drive with a 60-yard touchdown pass. Down 28-21 the Wildcats would answer the Tigers score on their next drive with a 13-yard touchdown pass to Lamar Carroway to tie the game at 28. The teams would trade punches on their next drives with Louisiana College evening the score at 35 on a touchdown pass to Shedrick Davis with 2:57 remaining in the half. The Tigers would convert a 25-yards field goal with 11 seconds remaining in the explosive first half to take the 38-35 lead into the break. Louisiana College took the lead on a 51-yard touchdown pass to Lawrence Williams, but the Tigers answered and regained the lead on a 34-yard pass of their own on the next drive. Down by three, 45-42, Louisiana College regained the lead at the 3:52 mark of the third quarter on a 27-yard touchdown pass to Shedrick Davis, but once again the Tigers answered with a 40-yard pass to go back ahead 52-49 at the end of the third quarter. East Texas Baptist would score on their next two possessions to push their three point lead at the beginning of the fourth quarter up to a 15 point advantage midway through the final frame. But just as they had done all night, the Wildcats responded, Shed Davis caught his record breaking fourth touchdown pass of the game with 4:30 minutes left in the game to cut the lead to eight at 64-56. After the defense forced a punt that backed the Wildcats up to their own 14 yard line, Easton Melancon hit Lamar Carroway on a slant pass and the speedster broke two tackles and raced for an 86-yard touchdown to bring the Wildcats within two points of the Tigers. Forced to go for two with just 2:29 left in the game, the swing pass to Nick Julien to the left was stopped one yard short of tying the game. The Wildcats would be unable to recover the ensuing onside kick and a 19-yard pass on third down and 18 for the Tigers would seal the game for the visitors and send the homecoming crowd home just short of a victory.

2016 - "The Block"

Albright at Lebanon Valley - Arnold Field - Annville, Pennsylvania {Lebanon Valley 28 Albright 25}

And that's why they call it The Rivalry. When it comes to Lebanon Valley vs. Albright, you can throw out the records, the postseason implications, and the predictions. When the longtime rivals take the field, it's simply about football. Such was the case in the 96th meeting of the two programs that saw LVC stun its longtime rival 28-25 at Arnold Field on Saturday afternoon. Lebanon Valley took an early lead, the Lions roared back to take the advantage, and the Flying Dutchmen answered with a clutch game-winning drive that preceded Anthony Jenkins' block of Albright's game-tying field goal attempt as time expired. A rabid frenzy was set off as students stormed the field to celebrate with players, coaches, and alumni before the celebration culminated with a Gatorade bath for first-year head coach Joe Buehler. Kicker Kevin Goetz set up for a potential game-tying, 39-yard field goal with four seconds left to play. After Buehler burned a timeout to ice the Lions' special teams unit, Jenkins burst through the middle of the line and stuffed Goetz's kick to preserve the heart-stopping victory. Trailing 25-21 with 4:25 remaining, the Dutchmen (4-6, 4-5 MAC) marched 75 yards during a statement-making final drive that saw quarterback Tyler Sterner complete four passes for 36 yards and rush for 11 more before Tim Pirrone's three-yard quarterback sneak reclaimed the lead for LVC with 1:02 left to play.

The March - As is tradition whenever Lebanon Valley defeats Albright, the LVC student body marches up the hill to Kreiderheim, the home of President Lewis Thayne, and request the day before Thanksgiving off from school. That day is scheduled to be a half-day of classes. It's been five years since an orderly mob of Dutchmen, led by the football team and Annville police and fire personnel, marched from Arnold Field up the hill to Kreiderheim, where they were granted the day off by president emeritus Stephen MacDonald following LVC's last win over the Lions. **{Courtesy Lebanon Valley College}**

2017 - "The Drive (to the championship)"

2017 CFB Championship Game - Raymond James Stadium - Tampa, Florida {Clemson 35 Alabama 31}

Deshaun Watson took the snap, rolled right and with one of the easiest throws he had to make all night, completed Clemson's journey to the top of college football. A frantic fourth quarter and a championship rematch between Clemson and Alabama was decided with 1 second left on a 2-yard touchdown toss to Hunter Renfrow.

Clemson took possession of the ball with 2:01 on the clock and the ball on their own 36 yard line. After another long catch by Mike Williams, the drive came to a 3rd & 3 on the Alabama 32 yard line, which was converted on a pass to Renfrow to the Alabama 26 yard line with 0:19 left. The next play saw Watson find Jordan Leggett on a pass down to the Tide 9 yard line with 0:14 left. Watson threw to the end zone on 1st & Goal; the pass was overthrown and the clock stopped with 0:09. On 2nd & Goal, Watson targeted Mike Williams, who was tripped in the end zone. The resulting pass interference call gave the Tigers 1st & Goal with the ball placed on the 2-yard line with 0:06 left. On the next play, Watson threw a touchdown pass to Renfrow with 0:01 left in the game; putting Clemson back in the lead, 35–31. For the former walk-on Renfrow, it was his second TD catch of the game.

Hunter Renfrow of Clemson game winning Touchdown catch

Watson and the Tigers dethroned the defending champs and became the first team to beat Nick Saban's Alabama dynasty in a national title game, taking down the top-ranked Crimson Tide in the College Football Playoff Championship Game. A 35-year title drought for Clemson is over. The Tigers are national champions for the first time since 1981.

2017 – "Third and 93"

Mississippi State at Louisiana Tech – Joe Aillet Stadium – Ruston, Louisiana {Mississippi State 57 Louisiana Tech 21}

There's third down. Then there's third-and-long. Then there's third-and-a-mile. Then there's what Louisiana Tech faced in a game against Mississippi State in September. The Bulldogs were actually on the brink of scoring when a bad snap sailed past QB J'Mar Smith, and a Keystone Cops routine ensued, with Mississippi State players flubbing a recovery as the ball continued to bounce toward the opposite end zone. Eventually receiver Cee Jay Powell flopped on top of the ball at the 5-yard line -- setting up a historic third-and-93 for La Tech. Spoiler alert: They didn't convert.

2017 - "Finally, a Bowl Game"

2017 Arizona Bowl – New Mexico State vs Utah State - Arizona Stadium – Tucson, Arizona {New Mexico State 26 Utah State 20 overtime}

New Mexico became a state in 1912. Forty eight years later New Mexico State went to their last bowl game in 1960. Fifty seven years later they finally went to another bowl game. Their opponent in the 1960 Bowl game was Utah State. Their opponent in this year's Arizona Bowl: Utah State.

Larry Rose III scored on a 21-yard run in overtime and New Mexico State won in its first bowl game in 57 years, beating Utah State 26-20 in the Arizona Bowl on Friday night. Utah State had the ball first in overtime and Dominik Eberle hit the right upright on a 29-yard field goal attempt, sending a groan through the Utah State crowd. Eberle made 16 for 18 field goals during the regular season, but missed three in the Arizona Bowl. New Mexico State won it when Jones burst through a hole on the left side, sending the Aggies and their fans rushing onto the Arizona Stadium field. Jones finished with 142 yards on 16 carries. The third Arizona Bowl started with some early fireworks on special teams. Utah State's Savon Scarver returned a kickoff 96 yards for a touchdown in the first quarter, then New Mexico State's Jason Huntley took the ensuing kickoff 100 yards for a score. The excitement leveled off considerably until LaJuan Hunt scored on a 1-yard run in the fourth quarter, set up by a shanked punt from New Mexico State's Payton Theisler. New Mexico State's Tyler Rogers, held in check most of the game, answered by moving the Aggies on a 69-yard scoring drive, capped by his 11-yard touchdown pass to Jaleel Scott that tied it at 20. A video review overturned the initial call that Scott was out of bounds. The long-awaited rematch turned into the Special Teams Bowl in the first half. New Mexico State's Dylan Brown made two field goals, Eberle made two and missed two, and each team had a kickoff return for a touchdown. After a third quarter of defensive stops and punting, both teams found the end zone to send the game overtime -- and, later, New Mexico State's fans onto the field.

2018 – "Phone call and a Promise"

Western Michigan at USC – L.A. Memorial Coliseum – Los Angeles, California {USC 49 Western Michigan 31}

{Detroit Free Press} It started with a phone call and a promise. With 3:13 left to play, Southern California's Marvin Tell III returned an interception for a touchdown that all but ensured the No. 4 Trojans would beat Western Michigan, 49-31, in the season opener Saturday at L.A. Memorial Coliseum in Los Angeles. Instead of sending out the regular special teams unit to attempt the extra point after Tell's TD, the Trojans brought in long snapper Jake Olson, who is blind. Olson received an escort onto the field from holder Wyatt Schmidt before the play. An official tapped Olson's left shoulder to signal to him the ball was ready for play, and then he sent a perfect snap back to Schmidt, and kicker Reid Budrovich connected for the extra point. WMU sports media director Kristin Keirns confirmed that USC coach Clay Helton called WMU coach Tim Lester earlier in the week to set up an opportunity for Olson to get in the game. Lester obliged, and the perfect moment came in the final minutes. The Broncos' special-teams unit purposely didn't rush the line when Olson was snapping, a promise the two coaches made with each other. In exchange for WMU's cooperation, USC didn't rush WMU's special-teams unit after Jamauri Bogan punched in a 4-yard TD with 6:07 left in the first quarter. Olson was greeted with a wave of hugs

and high fives when he returned to the sideline. Olson, who also long snapped at Orange (Calif.) Lutheran High School, was born with retinal cancer. He was forced to get his left eye removed when he was 10 months old and then he completely lost his vision when he was 12. The day before his right eye was removed in 2009, he attended a USC football practice, kindling his lifelong dream to play for the Trojans. Olson has co-authored two books about overcoming adversity and won the 2016 Uplifting Athletes Rare Disease Champion Award, given to a leader in college football who has realized their potential to make a positive and lasting impact on the rare disease community. Helton recognized the hard work Olson has put in both on and off the practice field the past two seasons and knew the opener against WMU was a perfect time to reward the redshirt sophomore.

2019 – "One Yard Short"

Arizona at Hawaii – Aloha Stadium – Honolulu, Hawaii {Hawaii 45 Arizona 38}

In "Week 0" of the regular season, Hawaii and Arizona played a wild affair that saw over 1,100 yards of offense and 149 plays from scrimmage. On the 149th play of the game, Arizona quarterback Khalil Tate scrambled and ran 30 yards toward the goal line but was tackled 1 yard short as time ran out. The Rainbow Warriors won, 45-38.

2019 – "Fake Knee for the Win"
Houston at Tulane – Yulman Stadium – New Orleans, Louisiana {Tulane 38 Houston 31}

One of the biggest blindsides of the year happened in a Houston-Tulane matchup. With the game tied at 31 late, Tulane kneeled down on the first and second downs and looked content to send the game into overtime. On third down, Green Wave quarterback Justin McMillan faked the kneel down and slid the ball to Amare Jones who ran 18 yards to the Tulane 47-yard line with 12 seconds remaining. On the next play, McMillan completed a pass to Jalen McCleskey to the 25-yard line and somehow split three defenders, stayed on his feet and galloped the rest of the way for the winning touchdown. One of the best endings to a football game you will ever see.

2019 - "Casey O'Brien's Wave"
Minnesota at Iowa – Kinnick Stadium – Iowa City, Iowa – {Iowa 23 Minnesota 19}

One of college football's most touching traditions is the Iowa Wave, where at the end of the first quarter, Hawkeyes fans and players wave to the kids watching the game from the university's children's hospital that overlooks Kinnick Stadium. When Iowa hosted Minnesota on Nov. 16, Golden Gopher holder and four-time cancer survivor Casey O'Brien got to participate and waved at kids he not only related to but also inspired. O'Brien has been battling cancer since he was 13, and his debut against Rutgers earlier in the season was one of the most heart-tugging moments of the year. For O'Brien to show those kids that despite their situations they can still reach their dreams was one of the best stories of 2019.

2019 – "The Piss Miss"
Mississippi at Mississippi State – Davis Wade Stadium @ Scott Field – Starkville, Mississippi {Mississippi State 21 Mississippi 20}

Ole Miss-Mississippi State is an old-fashioned, hate-filled rivalry that got a bit out of control in 2019. Rebels receiver Elijah Moore caught a touchdown with 4 seconds remaining in the game to cut the Bulldogs lead down to 21-20, with the PAT pending. Moore celebrated the TD by getting on his knees and miming a dog peeing on Mississippi State's name in the end zone. That was grounds for an unsportsmanlike penalty, which pushed the extra-point attempt back...and of course the Rebels missed. State wins the game in what is referred to in some circles as "The Piss Miss." Ole Miss Head coach Matt Luke was fired after the game, and Mississippi State's Joe Moorhead was fired a few weeks later.

2019 – "Perfection and Domination"
North Dakota State dominates

North Dakota State's dominance of the FCS continues. The Bison won their third straight national championship (and eighth in the last nine years) by beating James Madison (the team that won that title NDSU didn't) and now hold an FCS-record 37-game winning streak. Their 16-0 season is the first in college football since Yale did it back in 1894. They lost head coach Chris Klieman to Kansas State last offseason, replaced him with first-year head coach Matt Entz and didn't miss a beat.

Chapter Four – Hail Mary's and fantastic finishes

This chapter covers games that ended with "Hail Mary" passes, laterals, runs, etc. that ended in dramatic fashion with one team experiencing the thrill of victory and the other the agony of defeat.

1935 - The first "Hail Mary"

Notre Dame at Ohio State - Ohio Stadium - Columbus, Ohio {Notre Dame 18 Ohio State 13}

Notre Dame opened the season 5-0, including a 9-6 upset of Pittsburgh, which was one of the Superpower teams of the 1930's. The day before the game, Coach Elmer Layden told reporters "confidentially", that the Irish would be lucky to hold the Buckeyes to under 40 points. Obviously, this made headlines in Columbus, Ohio. Ohio State entered the game 4-0 and riding a 10 game winning streak. They were considered the favorite to capture the National Title under Head coach Francis Schmidt. The Ohio State-Notre Dame game was the most covered and most popular game of 1935. In 1969, Sport Magazine picked this game as the greatest College Football game ever. A then Ohio Stadium record crowd of 81,018 witnessed what was billed as The Game of the Century, the first ever meeting between Ohio State and Notre Dame. Tickets for this game sold for $50 each and there were widespread reports of counterfeit tickets. OSU officials said they could have sold 200,000 tickets for the game if they had room.

Action in the 1935 Notre Dame-Ohio State game

With 32 seconds left in the so-called "Game of the Century", Irish halfback Bill Shakespeare hurled a pass that traveled about 35 yards in the air to a leaping Wayne Millner for a 19-yard, game-winning touchdown. The Irish held on for a dramatic and thrilling 18-13 victory. Notre Dame Head coach Elmer Layden (who had played in the 1922 Georgia Tech game) afterwards called it a "Hail Mary" play. Henceforth, the term "Hail Mary Pass" was born and would become a part of Football jargon to this day.

1971 - "There's always time for great SIX"

Kentucky at Vanderbilt - Dudley Field - Nashville, Tennessee {Kentucky 14 Vanderbilt 7}

Kentucky defensive back Darryl Bishop intercepted Vanderbilt quarterback Steve Burger's pass with no time left on the clock and returned it 43 yards for a touchdown on the final play of the game, securing the win for the Wildcats in dramatic fashion

1978 - "Controversy at the goal line"

William & Mary at Virginia Tech - Lane Stadium - Blacksburg, Virginia {Virginia Tech 22 William & Mary 19}

A controversial 50 yard touchdown pass from David Larrie to Ron Zollcoffer as time expired gave Virginia Tech a victory and turned Lane Stadium into a madhouse. Zollcoffer made a leaping catch in the midst of three Indian defenders and fell across the goal line before he lost possession of the ball. The winning catch came one minute and 29 seconds after William & Mary had completed a long pass for a touchdown to take the lead.

1980 Holiday Bowl - "The Miracle Bowl"

BYU vs SMU - Jack Murphy Stadium - San Diego, California {BYU 46 SMU 45}

The 1980 Holiday Bowl was played December 19, 1980 in San Diego, California. The game is famous due to a furious fourth quarter rally—including a last-second "miracle" touchdown—that gave BYU a 46–45 victory over SMU. Thus, the game is known as the "Miracle Bowl", especially among BYU fans. BYU quarterback Jim McMahon threw a 41-yard touchdown pass to tight end Clay Brown with no time remaining on the clock to defeat SMU in the 1980 Holiday Bowl 46–45, which completed BYU's comeback from a 45–25 deficit which the Cougars faced with four minutes remaining.

Clay Brown of BYU game winning touchdown reception

BYU's defense couldn't handle SMU's offense, as Craig James ran for 225 yards and Eric Dickerson added 110. With just four minutes left in the game, the Mustangs scored to take a commanding 45–25 lead. Many BYU fans started leaving the stadium. McMahon screamed at them, declaring that the game wasn't over yet. He promptly threw a touchdown pass to Matt Braga, and BYU recovered an onside kick. The Cougars quickly marched down the field, ending the drive with a 1-yard touchdown run by Scott Phillips. SMU's lead had now been trimmed to 45–39. The Cougar defense forced the Mustangs to punt on the next possession, and BYU's Bill Schoepflin blocked the punt by SMU's Eric Kaifes with 13 seconds left in the game. The Cougar offense took over at the 41-yard line, with a last chance to win the game. After throwing two incomplete passes, McMahon launched a Hail Mary into the end zone as time expired. Smothered by four SMU defenders, BYU tight end Clay Brown somehow managed to leap above them and haul in the football, scoring one of the most miraculous touchdowns in college football history. With the score tied, BYU's Kurt Gunther kicked the winning extra point to give the Cougars a "miracle" 46–45 victory. BYU scored 21 points in the last 2:33.

1982 - "Hail Mary Throwback Pass"

SMU at Texas Tech - Jones Stadium - Lubbock, Texas {SMU 34 Texas Tech 27}

They had practiced the play at least 60 times, according to Bobby Leach, and it had almost never worked. Small wonder, because the play required a cross-field lateral pass by Blane Smith, following a kickoff reception, to Leach at the sideline. Smith could seldom complete such a pass. "It seemed they were always too high or too low," said Leach. But the play worked for Southern Methodist in the final seconds of the game against Texas Tech in Lubbock, Tex. And its success enabled the Mustangs to win, 34-27, to retain their perfect record, 10 victories in 10 games. The record came close to being tarnished by a tie when Texas Tech's Ricky Gann kicked a field goal that made the score 24-24 with 17 seconds left. Bobby Collins, the SMU coach, then reached back for what he calls "The Throwback Play," the flawed practice play. There was nothing to lose at that point, and the play had worked on occasion for Collins in past seasons when he coached at Southern Mississippi. The Red Raiders' kickoff was a squib that bounced, but it did carry back to Smith, who was positioned at the 8-yard line. However Smith, SMU's regular defensive safety and a former quarterback, failed to catch the football cleanly, bobbling it while the Texas Tech players converged on him. Leach was horrified. "I didn't think Blane would ever be able to get the ball to me," he said. But Smith did. In what seemed like one quick act, he gained control of the ball at the 12-yard line and whipped a lateral pass underhand ("like a shovel pass," said Leach) 15 yards to his left and back 3 yards to Leach. The receiver had lined up on the kickoff at the S.M.U. 35 and then had peeled back, faking a block. He stood at the 9, ignored and almost alone. Meanwhile, several teammates had formed a blocking wall for him up the field. Leach, a wide receiver with outstanding speed, ran 91 yards for that winning score. It was not entirely clear sailing, however. Texas Tech reserves had edged out on the field, and it occurred to Leach that one of them might tackle him illegally. There was another hazard, a spectator standing 4 yards into the playing field.

   The play took 13 seconds (Leach crossed the goal line with just four seconds showing on the clock), and not everyone knew what had happened. One SMU player, Russell Carter, even turned to a teammate and asked how Leach got the ball.

1984 - Bloomsburg "Hail Mary"

Bloomsburg vs West Chester {Bloomsburg 34 West Chester 31}

   The battle for the PSAC East inevitably comes down to **Bloomsburg** and **West Chester**. It's the same virtually every season.   In 1984, with the top spot in the PSAC East up for grabs, Jay Dedea found Curtis Still for a 50 yard Hail Mary touchdown pass as the Huskies knocked off West Chester 34-31 to ultimately advance to the 1984 PSAC State Game.

1984 - "Hail Flutie"

Boston College at Miami - Orange Bowl Stadium - Miami, Florida {Boston College 47 Miami 45}

   The **Hail Flutie** game took place between the Boston College Eagles and the University of Miami Hurricanes on November 23, 1984. It has been regarded by FOX Sports writer Kevin Hench as among the most memorable moments in sports. The game is most notable for a last-second Hail Mary pass from quarterback Doug Flutie to wide receiver Gerard Phelan to give Boston College the win. Miami was the defending national champion and entered the game ranked 12th in the nation. Boston College was ranked 10th with a record of 8–2 and had already accepted an invitation to the Cotton Bowl Classic at the end of the season. Boston College jumped out to an early 14–0 lead in the first quarter before quarterback Bernie Kosar and Miami stormed back to tie. The two quarterbacks played phenomenal games, combining for 59–84, 919 yards, and 5 touchdowns.

"55 Flood Tip play" formation   **Doug Flutie celebrates after "Hail Flutie" completion**

   With 28 seconds left, Boston College trailed 45–41. Three quick plays took the Eagles from their own 20-yard line to the Hurricanes' 48-yard line. Flutie called it the "55 Flood Tip" play, which the receivers were going to run straight routes into the end zone. Then they were to tip the football to another receiver. Flutie scrambled to his right, narrowly averting a sack. He threw the football from his own 37, requiring the 5' 9" quarterback to throw the ball at least 63 yards against 30 mph winds, after having already thrown the football 45 times during the game. The Miami defensive backs doubted his ability to throw the ball into the end zone, so they paid no attention to Phelan as he ran behind them. The ball came straight down over the mass of players untouched into Phelan's arms for the 47–45 win.

1986 - "Trips Right - Kramer to Peebles"

South Carolina at NC State - Carter-Finley Stadium - Raleigh, North Carolina {NC State 23 South Carolina 22}

   NC State jumped out to a quick 17-0 lead, turning three interceptions by South Carolina freshman sensation quarterback Todd Ellis into a pair of touchdowns and a field goal. The Wolfpack offense went dormant after that, particularly after senior quarterback Erik Kramer suffered an ankle injury early in the third quarter, giving way on one series to freshman Cam Young. The Gamecocks run and shoot offense began to click, and a one-yard run on the first play of the fourth quarter gave Coach Joe Morrison's team a 22-17 advantage. The Wolfpack had two ineffective offensive possessions after that. With 2:13 remaining, the Gamecocks seemingly secured the win by converting a third-and-12 from their own 15-yard line with a

23-yard pass from Ellis to Ryan Bethea. State was forced to use its final timeout with 2:13 remaining. But on a 2-yard loss on first down, the clock inexplicably stopped, bringing Morrison storming onto the field. After the mess was settled, Ellis took a knee on the next two plays, trying to kill the clock. But South Carolina punter Scott Bame, in the face of an 11-man Wolfpack rush, shanked his punt only 15 yards, giving State the ball on the South Carolina 39-yard line with 27 seconds to play. Kramer, playing on the gimpy ankle, couldn't complete either of his first two passes on the possession, though he did get the benefit of a first down and five yards on a South Carolina defensive holding penalty. On third down, Kramer was sacked by South Carolina defensive tackle Derek Frazier, and the Wolfpack scrambled to line up for a final play. As time expired, South Carolina linebacker Kenneth Robinson reached over center Chuck Massaro and grabbed Kramer by the jersey, but was whistled for an offsides penalty. As South Carolina players, coaches and fans stormed the field, an official signaled that South Carolina had been offside on the play and State got the benefit of one more play. While officials cleared the field, Kramer and his offense wandered over to the sidelines to get a play from the coaching staff. They called it "Trips right", with Peebles, Jeffires and running back Frank Harris running fly patterns to the right corner of the south end zone. Wide Receiver Danny Peebles became an NC State football legend, because he out-jumped and out-bumped South Carolina safety Chris Major for a game-winning touchdown pass after time had expired on the clock, for an incredulous 23-22 victory over the Gamecocks..

1987 - "Humphries to Harris Hail Mary"

NE Louisiana at Northwestern State - Harry Turpin Stadium - Natchitoches, Louisiana {NE Louisiana 33 Northwestern State 31}

Northeast Louisiana's "The Team of Destiny" needed its first miracle in Week Four with a "Hail Mary" pass from Stan Humphries to Jackie Harris to beat Northwestern State 33-31 in Natchitoches. On the game's final play, Humphries tossed a 48-yard prayer that was tipped twice before Harris snagged the ball with a diving catch near the back of the end zone.

1988 - "Holy Lateral Batman"

Holy Cross at Princeton - Palmer Stadium - Princeton, New Jersey {Holy Cross 30 Princeton 26}

Tim Donovan took a lateral and ran the last 55 yards to complete a 70-yard kickoff return on the last play of the game to give Holy Cross a 30-26 victory over Princeton. The stunning ending came just seconds after Chris Lutz kicked a 35-yard field goal to cap a frantic drive that gave Princeton a 26-24 lead with two seconds to play. Lutz dribbled the ensuing kickoff along the ground, and Daren Cromwell fielded it at the Holy Cross 30. Near the Crusader 45, Donovan took a lateral as a defender tackled Cromwell and went the rest of the way for the touchdown. Holy Cross players ran wildly onto the field; Princeton players slumped to the ground in disbelief. The lead changed hands three times in the final 73 seconds. Joe Segreti scored on a 5-yard run with 1 minute 13 seconds to play to give Holy Cross a 24-23 lead. But Jason Garrett drove Princeton 52 yards to set up Lutz's fourth field goal of the game and an apparent 2-point victory.

1989 - "68 yards for the win"

Tennessee-Chattanooga at Western Carolina - E.J. Whitmire Stadium - Cullowhee, North Carolina {Western Carolina 26 Chattanooga 20}

Terrell Wagner returned an interception 68 yards for a touchdown as time expired to break a 20-20 tie and give Western Carolina a 26-20 Southern Conference win over Tennessee-Chattanooga. Western Carolina was in a prevent defense in the final seconds when Wagner, a senior cornerback, came up with a long pass underthrown by Tennessee-Chattanooga quarterback Vince Carelli. Wagner stayed in bounds along the sideline and went the distance for the winning score with no time left on the clock. Trailing 13-2, the Mocs tied it 13-13 on Rodney Allen's 33-yard field goal with 5:20 to play in the third period following Habersham's 90-yard kickoff return for a touchdown and a two-point pass from Carelli to Cedric Smith to start the second half. The Catamounts had taken a 20-13 lead on a 20-yard touchdown strike from Todd Cottrell to Jon Reed with 13:48 remaining. Tennessee-Chattanooga, tied it 20-20 with 6:44 to go on Carelli's 54-yard pass to Shoun Habersham.

1989 - "Hail Mary, The miracle at Louisville"

Southern Miss at Louisville - Cardinal Stadium - Louisville, Kentucky {Southern Miss 16 Louisville 10}

The Southern Miss Golden Eagles played at Louisville on Oct. 14, 1989, and struck first as tailback Eddie Ray Walker scored on a five-yard run. Louisville countered with a second quarter touchdown that evened the game at 7-7. Southern Miss regained the lead early in the third quarter on a 32-yard field goal by Chuck Davis, but Louisville matched it in the fourth quarter, once again tying the game. With 23 seconds remaining, the Cardinals had the ball and attempted a 43-yard field goal. True freshman Vernard Collins, though, blocked the kick and gave USM the ball and one last opportunity to win the game.

Darryl Tillman of Southern Miss game winning touchdown

As the clock ticked down the game's final seconds, quarterback Brett Favre rolled right and fought off Louisville defensive end Ted Washington before lofting a Hail Mary pass that was tipped by wide receiver Michael Jackson and caught behind the Louisville defenders by wide receiver Darryl Tillman, who raced into the end zone to give the Eagles the 16-10 win as time expired. According to offensive coordinator Jeff Bower, the play worked exactly as it had been designed. "We put Alfred Williams, Michael Jackson and Tony Smith on the left side and Darryl (Tillman) by himself on the right. Michael is supposed to tip the ball up and hopefully one of our guys will catch it. Brett is supposed to spend a little time back there and throw it. He has to hesitate a little and throw it high." The Miracle of Louisville, is one of the greatest Games in Southern Miss Football.

1989 - "Pitt wins 31-31"

Pittsburgh at West Virginia - Mountaineer Stadium - Morgantown, West Virginia {Pittsburgh 31 West Virginia 31}

The game began with a quick exchange of big plays and touchdowns. But there was a difference: Frazier's conversion kick for Pitt was blocked by Basil Proctor and Brad Carroll's boot was true for the Mountaineers. The 7-6 score held through the first quarter. But in the second, Harris and the Mountaineers struck twice. The junior quarterback from Pittsburgh passed for two touchdowns to his favorite receiver, Reggie Rembert.

A 42-yard field goal on the game's last play capped a 22-point rally for Pittsburgh and enabled the Panthers to tie West Virginia, 31-31. Ed Frazier kicked the field goal and the Mountaineers were undone after leading, 31-9, at the end of the third quarter. Up to then the game had been a rout rather than a contest as Major Harris, the Mountaineer quarterback, had four touchdown passes. A crowd of 68,938, the largest ever at Mountaineer Field, saw the home team take advantage of a series of Pitt mistakes and appear to be in command. Turnovers by Pitt led to 17 Mountaineer points.

1990 - "Doyle to the rescue"

Alabama at Tennessee - Neyland Stadium - Knoxville, Tennessee {Alabama 9 Tennessee 6}

Philip Doyle kicked his third field goal of the game, a 48-yarder as time expired, to lift Alabama to a 9-6 victory over Tennessee in a Southeastern Conference defensive struggle. Doyle's kick was set up when Stacy Harrison blocked a 50-yard field-goal attempt by Tennessee's Greg Burke with 1 minute 35 seconds to play. Burke, whose 51-yarder tied it with 10 minutes to play, saw his potential game-winner carom off Harrison's chest and bounce downfield. Alabama took over at the Tennessee 37 and gained 7 yards in three plays before allowing the clock to run down to 4 seconds. 

The dominant force in the game was the Alabama defense, which for the second straight year disrupted Tennessee so badly the Vols changed quarterbacks in midstream. Sterling Henton, who lost his job to Andy Kelly in the Alabama game last year, took over for an ineffective Kelly early in the third quarter. Alabama held Tennessee, the S.E.C.'s leading offensive team, to just 71 yards and three first downs in the first half.

1992 - "Nedney from 60 for the win"

San Jose State at Wyoming - War Memorial Stadium - Laramie, Wyoming {San Jose State 26 Wyoming 24}

Joe Nedney kicked a school-record 60-yard field goal as time ran out to give San Jose State a startling 26-24 victory over error-prone Wyoming. Nedney, a sophomore whose previous long field goal was a 49-yarder against Utah State last season, stunned a Wyoming crowd that just seconds before had gone delirious over an 80-yard scoring drive engineered by redshirt freshman quarterback Scott Jones, who had no game experience. Jones entered the game for Wyoming with barely three minutes to play after starter Joe Hughes bruised a thigh and backup John Gustin failed to move the team. He dissected the San Jose State defense with a mixture of precision passing and a solid ground attack provided by Dwight Driver and Ryan Christopherson. With 40 seconds to play and Wyoming trailing 23-17, Jones connected with tight end Matt Swenson for a 15-yard score. Kris Mindlin`s extra point gave the Cowboys a 24-23 lead and left the Spartans with just 29 seconds to produce a miracle. Enter Joe Nedney.

1993 - "Big play Johnny"

Nevada at Arkansas State - Indiana Stadium - Jonesboro, Arkansas {Arkansas State 23 Nevada 21}

Arkansas State was in year 2 of Division 1-A existence and first year head coach John Bobo had guided them to a 1-8-1 record overall and 0-5 in Big West conference play. The last game of the season was set for an overcast November afternoon just days before Thanksgiving. Riding into Jonesboro having won 5 out of 6 and just one win from a Las Vegas Bowl berth came the Nevada Wolf Pack. This one was all about the big plays as QB Johnny Covington threw a 54 yard touchdown bomb that was tipped before being caught and kept ASU in the game. The final play of the game for the Indians found Covington again this time throwing a 35 yard strike into the back of the end zone finding Reginald Murphy for the go ahead points and leaving Indian fans besides themselves, celebrating the miraculous ending to an otherwise dismal season.

1994 - "Miracle at the Big House"

Colorado at Michigan - Michigan Stadium - Ann Arbor, Michigan {Colorado 27 Michigan 26}

The **Miracle at the Big House** refers to the final play that occurred during the Colorado-Michigan game played on September 24, 1994 at Michigan Stadium in Ann Arbor, Michigan. The game was decided on Colorado quarterback Kordell Stewart's 64-yard Hail Mary pass to Michael Westbrook, (Stewart's pass traveled 73 yards in the air from the Colorado 26 to the opposite 1 yard line, was tipped by Blake Anderson, then caught by Westbrook 4 yards deep in the end zone), the second touchdown by the Buffaloes in the last 2:16. The game was described as one of the two wildest finishes in Michigan football history.

Colorado trailed Michigan 26–21 with six seconds left when Stewart heaved the ball more than 70 yards in the air into the end zone where Westbrook caught it on a planned deflection from Blake Anderson for the game-winning touchdown. The play, which was named "Rocket Left", was called by Bill McCartney, Colorado coach and former Michigan assistant coach. Westbrook, Anderson and Rae Carruth lined up wide left and James Kidd lined up wide right. The same play was also called to end the first half, resulting in a Chuck Winters interception.

1995 - "Wolverines storm back from the dead"

Virginia at Michigan - Michigan Stadium - Ann Arbor, Michigan {Michigan 18 Virginia 17}

For the 101,444 fans in Michigan Stadium and those watching on television, the play of the century lasted less than a year, although it seemed like a lifetime to Michigan. And the Wolverines were overjoyed to replace it with their own miracle. The freshman quarterback Scott Dreisbach lofted a 15-yard scoring pass to Mercury Hayes for an 18-17 victory over Virginia as time expired today in the season-opening Pigskin Classic. It was the greatest comeback in Michigan history and gave Lloyd Carr a victorious debut as the Wolverines' head coach.

Dreisbach to Hayes winning touchdown

The Wolverines, ranked number #14 by The Associated Press, were starting a freshman quarterback for the first time since 1976. But Michigan, which trailed by 17-0 today, rallied to beat the Cavaliers, ranked Number #17 by the Associated Press. The Wolverines, who scored on their final three possessions, got the ball back with 2 minutes 35 seconds remaining. And they needed it all as they drove 80 yards in 16 plays. Michigan had just 12 seconds left when Dreisbach dived for a first down at the Virginia 15-yard line. Three incompletions later, there were only four seconds left when Dreisbach took the fourth-down snap and looked left. Dreisbach lofted a high pass that was hauled in by Mercury Hayes between the defenders Paul London and Ronde Barber in the back corner of the end zone. Hayes barely kept one foot in bounds as he caught the ball. The crowd roared after the field judge Collin McDermott pointed his finger emphatically inside the line, and then raised both arms to signal a touchdown.

1998 - Yale at Brown "Hail Mary Pass"
Yale at Brown - Brown Stadium - Providence, Rhode Island {Yale 30 Brown 28}

The 1998 Yale-Brown game was played September 19th at Brown Stadium in Providence, Rhode Island. Brown was coming off the 1997 season which they finished 6-4. They were one of the preseason favorites to contend for the Ivy League title. Yale was coming off a season in which they 1-9. It was the season opener for both teams. The game was a seesaw battle with Brown holding a 28-23 lead. Yale was down to its last play. Yale quarterback Joe Walland dropped back and threw a miraculous 27-yard, Hail Mary pass to Jake Borden. Yale wins 30-28!! According to Brown Coach Phil Estes, after the miracle finish for Yale, Todd Tomich [Yale's defensive back] came over and let us know it right in front of our bench. A picture of Borden's 27-yard touchdown catch on Joe Walland's pass in 1998 was on the cover of the Yale program for the Brown game in 1999. That same photo still sits in the trophy case in the Yale football office.

1999 - Brown at Yale "Hail Mary Run"
Brown at Yale - Yale Bowl - New Haven, Connecticut {Brown 25 Yale 24}

The 1999 Brown-Yale game was played on September 19th at the Yale Bowl in New Haven, Connecticut. Brown was coming a 7-3 season in 1998. Yale was coming off a 6-4 season in 1998. Brown was looking for revenge after last year's dramatic conclusion, in which the Eli's scored a touchdown on a 27-yard hail-Mary pass from Joe Walland to Jake Borden with six seconds remaining to win 30-28.

In a match-up of the two teams who would enter the final weekend tied for first in the Ivy, Yale appeared to have this game wrapped up, leading 24-10. But Yale quickly discovered that no lead would be safe with quarterback James Perry at Brown's helm. Perry went to work and found Campbell for a 17-yard score to cut the lead in half. Perry led the Bears on consecutive scoring drives in the fourth quarter, cutting the Bulldog lead to 24-23. It appeared that Brown would kick the routine extra point to send the game into overtime, but then Yale safety Ben Blake blocked the extra point, apparently sealing the victory for the Elis. The ball, however, bounced right into the hands of Brown's Mike Powell, who pitched it to Rob Scholl, who strolled in for the two points, giving Brown a 25-24 lead. With 12 seconds left, Yale still managed to drive into position for a 47-yard field goal, but Mike Murawczyk's kick fell short. Both Brown and Yale would finish the season as Ivy League Co-Champions. After the game, Estes was quoted as saying "We stole one, and our center went over and let them know it right in front of their bench."

1999 - "Miracle at Beaver Stadium"
Minnesota at Penn State - Beaver Stadium - State College, Pennsylvania {Minnesota 24 Penn State 23}

With one miracle play, Minnesota tipped over No. 2 Penn State's national championship hopes. The Gophers completed a 27-yard tipped pass on fourth-and-16 with 1:22 left, setting up Dan Nystrom's 32-yard field goal as time ran out to beat the Nittany Lions 24-23.

Dan Nystrom winning field goal vs Penn State

With his team trailing 17-9 in the third quarter, Cockerham hit Alex Hass for a 49-yard gain to set up his 3-yard touchdown run. Then he threw a 49-yard touchdown to Hamner, who was wide open after slipped behind the defense. That put the Gophers ahead 21-20 -- even though they had missed two 2-point conversions. Minnesota's game-winning drive started at the 20 with 1:50 left. First, Cockerham connected with Johnson on a 46-yarder to Penn State's 34-yard line. After Arrington's sack and two incomplete passes made it fourth-and-16, the Gophers' miracle pass kept the drive alive. Billy Cockerham's pass bounced off receiver Ron Johnson's hands and Arland Bruce dived to scoop it up at the 13-yard line. Three plays later, Nystrom split the uprights to spoil Joe Paterno's bid for a third national title. The Gophers' sixth win clinched their first winning season since 1990 and made them eligible for a bowl for the first time since 1986. It was Minnesota's first win over Penn State in five tries, and the Gophers' first victory over a Top 5 team since beating No. 2 Michigan 20-17 in 1986.

2000 - "Victory Right – Miracle finish #1"
Northwestern at Minnesota - HHH Metrodome - Minneapolis, Minnesota {Northwestern 41 Minnesota 35}

Zak Kustok's 45-yard "Hail Mary" pass to Sam Simmons as time expired gave Northwestern a 41-35 comeback victory over Minnesota. On the final play of regulation, Kustok heaved a long pass into a crowd in the end zone. The ball deflected sharply to Simmons, who tucked his feet just inside the goal line before stepping onto the field. The play called was Victory Right. The miracle touchdown stunned the Metrodome crowd and completed the Wildcats' rally from a 21-point deficit over the final 17:05. The Wildcats, fell behind 35-14 before turning things around when the Golden Gophers went to a prevent defense that Kustok was able to pick apart.

2000 - "Miracle in the mud"
Central College (Iowa) at Linfield College (Oregon) - Maxwell Field - McMinnville, Oregon {Central College 20 Linfield College 17}

Linfield had taken a 17-14 lead to open the overtime session on Scott Cannon's 34-yard field goal. Central College Fullback Joe Ritzert just wanted to atone for a mistake from the previous play. He ended up being a part of perhaps the wildest finish in Central College's storied football history, as the Dutch stunned previously unbeaten Linfield College (Ore.), 20-17, in overtime in a second-round NCAA Div. III playoff game. Trailing 17-14 in overtime, Ritzert was flagged for a false start penalty on third down, and Central faced fourth and six from its own 21. Dutch kicker Tim O'Neil, filling in for the injured Marc Kroloff, attempted a game-tying 38-yard field goal. But the field was a sea of mud as the result of a typical afternoon of steady Oregon rain. O'Neil slipped as he kicked the ball, and it bounced off the leg of an offensive lineman. The Linfield crowd erupted because of the apparent Wildcat victory, and players and fans alike began storming onto the field. But long snapper Reid Evans, who said he heard the thud of the ball striking another player, took a step back, saw the ball and picked it up. A rugby scrum ensued. Ritzert saw Evans with the ball and tried to help push the pile forward far enough for a first down. But Evans was in the grasp of a couple of Linfield defenders. He glanced at Ritzert, who grabbed the ball and raced untouched 21 yards to the end zone. "The only people in the way were some of their fans," Ritzert said. The officials watched the play the entire way and quickly signalled touchdown. They then conferred as coaches, fans and players stood on the field waiting anxiously, then affirmed the decision and Central went from loser to winner in a matter of seconds. **{Courtesy of Central College (IA)}**

2001 - "Big Ben"

Akron at Miami - Yager Stadium - Oxford, Ohio {Miami 30 Akron 27}

Looking for a fourth straight victory, Miami (Ohio) needed a miracle, trailing Akron 27-24 after blowing an 18-point halftime lead. With the ball at the Miami 30-yard line, Ben Roethlisberger took the snap and stepped up in a collapsing pocket. His pass went more than 60 yards downfield, and Akron defenders tipped the ball up near the 5-yard line. While on the run, Eddie Tillit corralled the catch after bobbling it once to win the game.

2002 - "Bluegrass Miracle"

LSU at Kentucky - Commonwealth Stadium - Lexington, Kentucky {LSU 33 Kentucky 30}

November 9, 2002: LSU quarterback Marcus Randall threw a 74-yard touchdown pass to wide receiver Devery Henderson with no time left on the clock in the game to defeat Kentucky 33–30. The ball was tipped by a Kentucky player before being caught at the 15-yard line by Devery Henderson of LSU, who ran it in for the score. On the final play of the game, LSU called the play "Dash Right 93 Berlin". Tigers quarterback Marcus Randall took the ball and threw it from his own 18 yard line as far as he could downfield. Soon after Randall released the ball, triumphant Kentucky fans stormed the field around Randall. The pass was 25 yards short of the end zone. However, the ball was deflected off the hand of a Kentucky player between the Kentucky 30 and 25 yard lines and fell into the hands of LSU wide receiver Devery Henderson just short of the 15-yard line. Henderson broke the shoestring tackle of the last Kentucky defender, and ran into the end zone for the game-winning touchdown.

Devery Henderson of LSU scoring winning touchdown

On the first play of the final series, the Tigers quickly got the ball to their own 26-yard line on a pass from quarterback Marcus Randall to wide receiver Michael Clayton. An LSU timeout stopped the clock with 2 seconds left, and set up a desperation Hail Mary pass. The chances for success were considered slim because Randall's arm was not strong enough to reach the opponent's end zone from 70+ yards away. Kentucky players were so confident that they had won the game that they gave head coach Guy Morriss a Gatorade bath before the final play had taken place. Fireworks spewed out of the Commonwealth Stadium suites to herald the apparent Kentucky win when the game clock read "0:00", even prior to the Hail Mary pass. Kentucky fans were up on the goal posts celebrating, only to be stunned by the "Bluegrass Miracle".

2005 - "Capital Gains"

2005 Capital One Bowl - Iowa vs LSU - Florida Citrus Bowl - Orlando, Florida {Iowa 30 LSU 25}

What a farewell gift to lame-duck LSU coach Nick Saban. LSU and Iowa had played a low-scoring game through three quarters with the Hawkeyes holding a 17-12 lead heading into the fourth. The Tigers overcame a 12-point deficit to go ahead of Iowa, 25-24, with 46 seconds to play in the 2005 Capital One Bowl.

Warren Holloway of Iowa game winning catch

But with 9 seconds remaining, LSU safety Ronnie Prude played zone instead of man. Hawkeyes quarterback Drew Tate threw a 56-yard pass to the uncovered Warren Holloway. On the last play of his career, the senior caught his first touchdown pass as time expired, giving the Hawkeyes a miraculous 30-25 victory.

2006 - "Hail Mary Left"
Arkansas State at Memphis - Liberty Bowl Stadium - Memphis, Tennessee {Arkansas State 26 Memphis 23}

Facing third-and-10 at his own 47 with only seconds left in the game, Arkansas State quarterback Corey Leonard threw a 53-yard touchdown pass to Patrick Higgins, giving the Indians a 26-23 win over Memphis. The play is called Hail Mary Left and it worked to perfection. Leonard took the snap with six seconds left, rolled left and heaved the ball into a crowd in the end zone as time expired. Higgins came out with the ball, sending the Indian squad onto the field in celebration. Officials reviewed the play and confirmed the touchdown reception, snapping Arkansas State's 10-game losing streak in the series.

Patrick Higgins of Arkansas State

The Indians had not defeated Memphis since 1989. It was Higgins' second touchdown reception, his only two catches of the game.

2007 - "Hail Mary Lateral Pass"
Akron at Western Michigan - Waldo Stadium - Kalamazoo, Michigan {Akron 39 Western Michigan 38}

Andre Jones and Alphonso Owen combined on an 89-yard kick return on the game's final play, giving Akron a 39-38 victory over Western Michigan on Saturday night. Western Michigan led 38-31 with 15 seconds left when Jamarko Simmons ran out of the end zone on a fourth-down designed safety, cutting the Broncos' lead to 38-33. On the ensuing free kick, Owen grabbed the ball, headed toward the left sideline, and then tossed it to Jones near the 25-yard line. Jones, who plays mostly at defensive back, followed a blocking wedge to the end zone for the winning score and his first career TD.

Akron scored the last 15 points of the game in the final five minutes. Zips receiver Jabari Arthur caught a school-record 15 passes for 223 yards and three TDs, including a 51-yard scoring pass from Chris Jacquemain with 4:54 left.

2007 - "Lateralpalooza - Miracle in Mississippi"

Trinity at Millsaps - Harper Davis Field - Jackson, Mississippi {Trinity 28 Millsaps 24}

This game is best known for the memorable play that occurred in the game's last two seconds. On October 27, 2007, the NCAA Division III 19th-ranked Trinity University Tigers threw 15 lateral passes and scored a 61-yard touchdown to win a game against the 24th-ranked Millsaps College Majors as time expired in the game. The Tigers had time for only one snap so there was no time to move into field goal range. They needed to score a touchdown in one play, working from their own 40-yard line. Believing that 60 yards was too far away to complete a Hail Mary pass, Trinity Coach Steve Mohr called for a 10-15 yard underneath route. The play they ran involved seven players and 15 laterals.

One of the 15 laterals by Trinity

In the video, it is clear that several Millsaps defenders stopped playing before the play was over. On the thirteenth lateral, Tomlin was taken down but tossed a no-look pitch over his shoulder to Hooten just before his knee hit the ground. Many Millsaps fans believed the play to be over and fireworks were shot off from behind the end zone in celebration. Maddux's final lateral hit the ground and bounced into Curry's hands. It appeared as though two defenders near Curry believed the play was over at that point, and Curry scampered into the end zone untouched. Millsaps safety Michael Sims, the closest player to Curry when Curry caught the last lateral, later admitted that he turned around and started walking away, believing the game to be over.

2008 - "Miracle at Murfreesboro"

Florida Atlantic at Middle Tennessee - Johnny "Red" Floyd Stadium - Murfreesboro, Tennessee {Middle Tennessee 14 Florida Atlantic 13}

Middle Tennessee put together a remarkable comeback when Joe Craddock marched the Blue Raiders 65 yards with no timeouts to rally them to a dramatic 14-13 win against Florida Atlantic in front of 25,766 and an espn2 national television audience at Floyd Stadium. Craddock did his best John Elway impersonation by leading the game-winning drive under extreme circumstances and Middle Tennessee demonstrated its tremendous character when all seemed to be lost on a festive evening in Murfreesboro. However, the miracle men would not be denied. Trailing 13-7 Middle Tennessee began its final drive at its 35 with 1:15 remaining and no timeouts. Craddock completed 4-of-6 passes for 65 yards on the game-winning drive, including the striking 32-yard aerial to Malcolm Beyah who rose above three defenders and secured the ball with no time on the clock for one of the most remarkable finishes in Floyd Stadium history. Beyah, who had two catches for 59 yards on the final drive, tied the game 13-13 with his breathtaking grab and freshman Alan Gendreau, who was frozen twice by consecutive Florida Atlantic timeouts, nailed the extra point to send the remaining Blue Raider faithful into a frenzy as the students stormed the field.

2008 - "Bedlam at UB Stadium"

Temple at Buffalo - UB Stadium - Buffalo, New York {Buffalo 30 Temple 28}

Flanker Naaman Roosevelt hauled in a 35-yard Hail Mary pass from quarterback Drew Willy to stun Temple and turn UB Stadium on its ear with bedlam. The play capped a remarkable final three minutes that saw the lead change hands three times. The Bulls won with a final score of 30–28. Willy, who completed 29-of-42 passes for a career-high 348 yards and three touchdowns, engineered the improbable comeback by marching the Bulls down the field on a five-play, 60-yard drive in just 38 seconds following a Temple touchdown. With five seconds remaining, Willy dropped back and launched his pass. Roosevelt, surrounded by Temple defenders, went up for the ball and came down with the game-winner.

2008 - "Hail Mary Denham to Grant"

Northern Colorado at California-Davis - Aggie Stadium - Davis, California {Cal-Davis 34 Northern Colorado 30}

Bakari Grant caught a 38-yard touchdown pass from Greg Denham on the game's final play as Cal-Davis rallied to beat Northern Colorado 34-30 in a thrilling nonconference football game before 9,675 fans at Aggie Stadium. Cal-Davis picked up the improbable touchdown two plays after a false start erased a try for a potential game-winning 50-yard field goal attempt by Sean Kelley. An incomplete pass led to the final throw in which Grant hauled in Denham's pass in between four defenders just past the goal line. Northern Colorado appeared in good position for its first win after taking a 30-28 lead with 1 minute, 18 seconds left on a 26-yard field goal from Michael York. However, without the benefit of any remaining timeouts, Denham drove the Aggies to the Northern Colorado 33 by completing three passes for 28 yards, two of them to Brandon Tucker for 20 yards. Cal-Davis spiked the ball with nine seconds to go in order to set up for a 50-yard field goal try. However, a crucial five-yard penalty resulted in the offense coming back onto the field. An incomplete pass left three seconds on the clock and the game's exciting finish.

2010 - "Hail Mary Davis to Jones"

Tulsa at East Carolina - Dowdy-Ficklen Stadium - Greenville, North Carolina {East Carolina 51 Tulsa 49}

In his first start at East Carolina, quarterback Dominique Davis provided one of the greatest finishes in the history of the program. Davis heaved a 33-yard touchdown pass to a leaping Justin Jones as time expired to give the Pirates a wild 51-49 win against Tulsa in coach Ruffin McNeill's debut at his alma mater. Davis whisked the Pirates downfield in nine plays.

Justin Jones of East Carolina game winning touchdown

On the final snap, he launched the ball high toward a handful of players in the end zone. The 6-foot-8 Jones out jumped everyone for it, setting off a massive celebration. A brief review upheld the call and the Pirates, who were flagged for an excessive celebration, skipped the extra point and instead took a knee.

2010 - "Hail Mary Ellis to Williams"

Troy at Alabama-Birmingham - Legion Field - Birmingham, Alabama {Alabama-Birmingham 34 Troy 33}

With just 69 seconds left at Legion Field, UAB needed go 99 yards to score a winning touchdown against a staggering Troy defense. The Blazers covered the final 44 of those yards on a "Hail Mary" pass as time expired, with Jackie Williams wrestling the ball away from a trio of Troy defenders just outside the goal line. He was rewarded for his efforts with a touchdown call, which was upheld by replay. After forcing bad throws from junior quarterback Bryan Ellis on the first two plays of the final drive, the Trojans flushed him from the pocket on third down, but he was able to connect with Pat Shed for a 20-yard gain. Ellis, who came on in relief of starter David Isabelle in the second quarter, hooked up with senior Frantrell Forrest for consecutive gains of nine and 16 yards to get to the 46. Consecutive incomplete passes left the Blazers facing another third down pass, which Ellis was again able to convert, hitting Williams for 10 yards to the Troy 44. On the final play, a trio of Trojans surrounded Williams near the goal line. Juniors Xavier Lamb, Jimmie Anderson and Ladarrius Madden had Williams surrounded, but he went up between them and came down with the ball. Replay appeared to show Williams was just short of the end zone, but officials upheld the call of touchdown called on the field.

2010 - "Little Giants fake Field Goal"

Notre Dame at Michigan State - Spartan Stadium - East Lansing, Michigan {Michigan State 34 Notre Dame 31}

The prospect of his kicker facing a 46-yard field goal to tie the game in overtime was enough to convince Michigan State coach Mark Dantonio to take a monumental gamble. Instead of having Don Conroy kick, Dantonio called for a fake field goal on 4th-and-13 from the Notre Dame 29. The plays known as "Little Giants" has holder Aaron Bates, former high school quarterback, look to hit Le'Veon Bell. The Irish were not fooled on the play and Bell was covered. But Bates waited until tight end Charles Gantt broke free and hit him with a game-winning touchdown pass on the last play of the game.

Charles Gantt of Michigan State

2011 - "Rocket"

Wisconsin at Michigan State - Spartan Stadium - East Lansing, Michigan {Michigan State 37 Wisconsin 31}

A heave. A carom. A desperate struggle for the last few inches. And after further review, a miraculous win by Michigan State. Keith Nichol caught a 44-yard pass from Kirk Cousins on the game's final play for a tiebreaking touchdown, giving the Spartans a 37-31 victory against Wisconsin.

Keith Nichol of Michigan State

With four seconds left, Cousins rolled out to his right and threw it about as far as he could. The ball went into the end zone but caromed off Michigan State receiver B.J. Cunningham's facemask back to Nichol, who caught it just outside the end zone and struggled for the goal line, fighting two Wisconsin defenders and just barely breaking the plane. The former backup quarterback was initially ruled short of the end zone, but officials overturned the call after a review, giving the Spartans the win and knocking the

Badgers from the ranks of the unbeaten. Cousins was able to buy enough time for receivers to get down the field. Cunningham was in the end zone, and the ball bounced off his helmet and into Nichol's arms. After Nichol caught the pass, Michigan State players immediately started spilling onto the field, even though officials ruled that Wisconsin's Mike Taylor had stopped him short. When the call was reversed and a touchdown was awarded, the celebration began again.

2012 - "Unbelievable"

Concordia at Bethel - Royal Stadium - Arden Hills, Minnesota {Bethel 15 Concordia 14}

An unbelievable finish at Royal Stadium allowed the Bethel University Royals, who celebrated its homecoming game Saturday, to comeback from a 14-7 deficit with 1:24 remaining in the fourth quarter to defeat Concordia College 15-14 in a MIAC classic. Trailing by seven, Bethel drove 71 yards down the field to score the game winning touchdown – but it didn't come without drama. Facing a 3rd-and-10 from the Cobber 17-yard-line with 0:01 on the clock quarterback Erik Peterson was stripped, which induced a parade of Concordia personnel onto the field, however, no one had gained possession and by the time a Cobber picked up the ball and ran 71 yards for a Concordia score, penalty flags littered the field. The Cobbers had been penalized with unsportsmanlike conduct – its only penalty of the game – for coming onto the field while no one had possession, which gave the Royals one more opportunity to score from the nine-yard-line.

With one final play Peterson found Jay Hilbrands on the far corner of the end zone for the score. Instead of kicking the extra point, Bethel decided to attempt a two-point conversion, which was successful via a Peterson to Mitch Hallstrom toss—ending the game victoriously for the Royals. Bethel fans embedded within the crowd of 5,124 people stormed the field after witnessing one of the most bizarre endings to a game in Royal Stadium history. **{Courtesy Bethel University}**

2013 - "Miracle at Lincoln"

Northwestern at Nebraska - Memorial Stadium - Lincoln, Nebraska {Nebraska 27 Northwestern 24}

Jordan Westerkamp caught Ron Kellogg III's tipped desperation heave to the end zone with no time left, giving Nebraska a 27-24 victory over Northwestern. The Cornhuskers looked like they were finished after Northwestern took a three-point lead with 1:20 left.

Jordan Westerkamp of Nebraska

They started their final drive at their 17 with no timeouts. Ameer Abdullah caught a short pass and stretched to convert a fourth-and-15. Then, with four seconds on the clock, Kellogg dropped back for a final play. The strong-armed Kellogg let fly a ball that was deflected into Westerkamp's hands in the end zone. Westerkamp held on, bringing the entire Nebraska bench running onto the field in celebration. The play was confirmed on video review.

2013 - "Kick Six"

Alabama at Auburn - Jordan-Hare Stadium - Auburn, Alabama {Auburn 34 Alabama 28}

With 32 seconds remaining, the Tigers scored on a 39-yard touchdown pass from Marshall to Sammie Coates. On the ensuing possession, with seven seconds left in the game, Alabama ran to Auburn's 38-yard line as T. J. Yeldon was knocked out of bounds by Chris Davis while the game clock expired. But Saban argued that Yeldon had stepped out of bounds with one second left in regulation. Saban's argument was validated by the instant replay officials, who put one second back on the clock. Rather than take a knee and go to overtime, Alabama attempted to win the game with a 57-yard field goal and Auburn took a timeout. Auburn's defensive coordinator, Ellis Johnson, doubted Alabama would make the long field goal and suggested that a defensive back stand in the end zone with the potential to return a missed field goal. Malzahn then put punt returner Chris Davis in the end zone for the return. As the field goal attempt fell short, Davis fielded the ball nine yards deep in the end zone and ran down the sideline. With Alabama's field goal unit being made up mostly of offensive linemen, Davis ran all the way to the end zone to win the game 34–28.

Commentator Rod Bramblett call of the last play on radio for the Auburn IMG Sports Network:

"Chris Davis is going to drop back into the end zone in single safety. Well, I guess if this thing comes up short he can field it and run it out. Alright, here we go. 56-yarder, it's got—no, it does not have the leg. And Chris Davis takes it in the back of the end zone. He'll run it out to the 10, 15, 20, 25, 30, 35, 40, 45, 50, 45—there goes Davis! (White shouts "Oh my God!") Davis is going to run it all the way back! Auburn's going to win the football game! Auburn's going to win the football game! He ran the missed field goal back! He ran it back 109 yards! [Fans streaming onto the field] They're not going to keep them off the field tonight! Holy Cow! Oh, my God! Auburn wins! Auburn has won the Iron Bowl! Auburn has won the Iron Bowl in the most unbelievable fashion you will ever see! I cannot believe it! 34–28! And we thought 'A Miracle in Jordan-Hare' was amazing! Oh, my Lord in Heaven!' Chris Davis just ran it 109 yards and Auburn is going to the championship game!"

2014 - "Hail Mary Ivy to McKenzie"

Florida A&M at Jackson State - Mississippi Veterans Memorial Stadium - Jackson, Mississippi {Jackson State 22 Florida A&M 16}

DeSean McKenzie hauled in the winning touchdown in the final seconds to lift Jackson State to a 22-17 win over Florida A&M in the season opener for both teams. The 60-yard TD pass from LaMontiez Ivy spoiled what would have been a fourth quarter comeback win for Florida A&M, which retook the lead with just 46 seconds to go on a 1-yard touchdown pass from Damien Fleming to Gerald Hearns.

2014 - "Central Florida sinks East Carolina"

Central Florida at East Carolina - Dowdy-Ficklen Stadium - Greenville, North Carolina {Central Florida 32 East Carolina 30}

Central Florida wide receiver Breshad Perriman pulled in a 51-yard touchdown pass from Justin Holman as time expired to give the Knights a 32-30 victory over East Carolina. With five seconds left on the clock, Central Florida lined up at its own 49 and snapped the ball to Holman, who uncorked a 51-yard bomb to the 6-foot-3, 214-pound Perriman, who beat three East Carolina defenders to the ball.

The touchdown left the East Carolina sideline stunned and its fans in a state of disbelief, as only minutes earlier the Pirates had erased a 26-9 fourth-quarter deficit with a 21-0 run that put them up 30-26 with 2:17 left in the game.

2014 - "Edward Waters stuns Pikeville"

Edward Waters at Pikeville - Hambley Athletic Complex - Pikeville, Kentucky {Edward Waters 49 Pikeville 48}

  Edward Waters (Fla.) outscored the University of Pikeville football team 35-7 in the fourth quarter to complete an improbable comeback with a last-second heave into the end zone. Trailing 48-42 with 35 seconds left, the Tigers recovered an onside kick at their own 45 yard line with no timeouts. From there, Tyler Mahla completed a nine-yard pass on second down, then spiked the ball at the Pikeville 46 to bring up fourth and one with just a few ticks remaining. Instead of looking for a short completion and dash out of bounds to get closer to the end zone, Mahla put up a 46-yard bomb that Devion Laws came down with to tie the score at 48 with no time left in regulation. All of the pressure was on kicker Christopher Miglioranzi to seal the win, and his teammates made things even harder on him with a celebration penalty. But even after moving back 15 yards, he was able to guide the ball through the goalposts for the win.

2014 - "Cortland is gonna win the football game!"

Ithaca College at SUNY-Cortland - Cortland Stadium Complex - Cortland, New York {SUNY-Cortland 23 Ithaca College 20}

  Holder Luke Hinton threw a 4-yard touchdown pass to receiver Jon Mannix on the final play of the game after a botched field goal snap to lift SUNY Cortland to an improbable 23-20 win over nationally 23rd-ranked Ithaca College in the 56th Annual **Cortaca Jug** rivalry game in Cortland. Trailing 20-17, Cortland started its final drive on its own 49-yard line with 1:35 remaining and no timeouts left. The Red Dragons used all of their second-half timeouts while forcing an Ithaca three-and-out. On 2nd-and-5 at the Ithaca 46-yard line, John Grassi completed a 35-yard pass to Jack Delahunty to the Ithaca 11. Dylan Peebles carried the ball three straight times – the first two for gains of three and four yards and the third for no gain. With time winding down, Cortland raced out its field goal unit for a potential game-tying 20-yard field goal.

Luke Hinton of Cortland throwing the winning touchdown pass to...

Jon Mannix of Cortland winning touchdown catch

Hinton, however, was late getting out on the field, and then was looking back at the kicker during the snap with five seconds left. He recovered to grab the ball and briefly considered trying to place the ball for the kick, but decided against it and rolled out to the left. Mannix – one of the wings on the play – broke free on the left side of the end zone and Hinton threw his first collegiate pass for the game-winning score. **{Courtesy of SUNY-Cortland}**

2014 - "39 yard Field Goal, free. Miner's Cup, Priceless!"
Michigan Tech at Northern Michigan - Superior Dome - Marquette, Michigan {Michigan Tech 34 Northern Michigan 31}

For the second time this season, Garrett Mead was the hero. The senior kicker split the uprights on a 39-yard field goal as time expired to give Michigan Tech a 34-31 win at Northern Michigan. The Huskies keep the **Miner's Cup** for the fifth consecutive year. Northern Michigan drove 50 yards in seven plays to tie the score with 1:47 remaining. Quarterback Shaye Brown hit Marcus Tucker in the back corner of the end zone to pull his squad within 31-29. The Wildcats then used a reverse pass to Brown as a receiver for the conversion to tie it. Tyler Scarlett needed nine plays to get Mead into position for the game winner. Brandon Cowie's ninth catch of the game converted a third-and-10 to keep the drive alive. Mead hit his second 39-yarder of the game for the winner. Tech held a comfortable first-half lead at 21-7 after receiving touchdowns from Andrew Clark and Cowie to go with Charlie Leffingwell's first rushing TD of the season. Northern Michigan came back with a score just 13 seconds before halftime to climb within 21-14 at the break.

Garrett Mead game winning Field Goal

A muffed punt gave the Wildcats the ball at the Tech 11 early in the third quarter. It also put the momentum on the Northern Michigan sideline. The hosts scored on the next play, then took the lead 23-21 on a safety after Tech's center-to-punter snap went awry near the goal line. The ensuing free kick saw Kollin Long make a critical open field tackle to keep Northern Michigan at their own 30. The Huskies' defense forced a three-and-out, and Tech marched 68 yards to reclaim the lead. Leffingwell had a brilliant 31-yard run to cap the drive, going the final 15 yards after contact. Mead added to the lead with his first 39-yard field goal, leaving the score 31-23 with 11:34 to play. Northern Michigan missed a 35-yard field goal on its next possession, but got the ball back with five minutes to go and scored to pull even. Scarlett rushed four times and threw four times on the game-winning drive, the key play being a 23-yard completion to Cowie on third-and-10 at midfield.

2015 - "Miracle at Memorial"
BYU at Nebraska - Memorial Stadium - Lincoln, Nebraska {BYU 33 Nebraska 28}

In arguably the most exciting season-opening game in Nebraska football history, BYU quarterback Tanner Mangum's 42-yard Hail Mary pass to Mitch Mathews as time expired gave the Cougars a 33-28 win. Playing in front of the NCAA-record 341st consecutive sellout with 89,959 fans at Memorial Stadium, Nebraska built a 28-24 lead heading into the fourth quarter of Mike Riley's debut as the Big Red's head coach.

This play snapped a string of 29 consecutive home opener victories for the Cornhuskers. Mangum, a freshman just two months removed from a mission for The Church of Jesus Christ of Latter-day Saints, was the backup to senior Taysom Hill, who had left the game earlier with a season-ending Lis franc injury. This game was Mangum's first organized football game in nearly four years.

2015 - "Hail Foltz"

Stonehill at LIU-Post - Bethpage Federal Credit Union Stadium - Brookville, New York {Stonehill 40 LIU-Post 37}

Talk about being at the right place at the right time. LIU Post never trailed in the entire game ... except on the final play, a 41 yard Hail Mary pass from Matt Foltz to Corey White as time expired to give Stonehill the 40-37 win over their Northeast-10 rivals. The Pioneers looked to have iced the game after Malik Pierre's third touchdown run, this one from 13 yards out, with 2:13 left to play.

Foltz drove the Skyhawks down the field, capping the drive with a 13 yard touchdown pass to Kaleb Lutton with 62 seconds left to cut the LIU Post lead to 37-27. Although LIU Post recovered the ensuing onside kick, the Pioneers drew an unsportsmanlike conduct penalty, pushing them back to their own 26. A three-and-out by the Skyhawks defense, paired with another Pioneer personal foul penalty, pushed the ball back to the LIU Post 15. The Skyhawks got strong field position, starting at the LIU Post 43. Four plays later, Foltz found Dave Harrison for an 11 yard touchdown strike with 5.9 seconds remaining to make it a 37-34 game.

Matt Foltz of Stonehill

The Skyhawks recovered the ensuing onside kick at the LIU Post 41 yard line, setting up the greatest Hail Mary pass from a Massachusetts college since Doug Flutie's Orange Bowl winner in 1984. Stonehill scored 20 points in 62 seconds to complete their amazing comeback.

2015 - "Block Six"

Florida State at Georgia Tech - Bobby Dodd Stadium - Atlanta, Georgia {Georgia Tech 22 Florida State 16}

It all started when Roberto Aguayo, perhaps the best kicker in the country, attempted a 56-yard field goal to win it for the Seminoles (6-1, 4-1 Atlantic Coast Conference) with 6 seconds remaining. But the kick had to be low to get some distance on it, and Patrick Gamble managed to get a hand on the ball.

Georgia Tech players blocking 56 yard field goal attempt

While most of the Georgia Tech players celebrated, thinking they were going to overtime tied at 16, Austin went back to retrieve the ball as it bounced inside the 25-yard line. Lance Austin ran toward the ball, rolling along at the Georgia Tech end of the field as the final seconds ticked off the clock. He hesitated, a bit confused as his coach screamed for him to leave it alone. Austin had other ideas. The sophomore scooped up the ball at his own 22 and took off the other way. He didn't stop running until he reached the end zone, his 78-yard return of a blocked field goal on the final play giving Georgia Tech a stunning 22-16 upset of the No. 9 Seminoles. After that, it was bedlam in Bobby Dodd Stadium. The white-clad Georgia Tech fans stormed the field, celebrating with the players after perhaps the most improbable win in school history.

2016 - "Hail Mary Lateral"

Central Michigan at Oklahoma State - Boone Pickens Stadium - Stillwater, Oklahoma {Central Michigan 30 Oklahoma State 27}

Central Michigan upset No. 17 Oklahoma State in stunning fashion. But should the Chippewa's even had a chance to make that play on an untimed down? Oklahoma State was penalized for intentional grounding on its final offensive play, which is a loss of down penalty. Rules state that the game cannot end on an accepted live-ball penalty. Chippewa's quarterback Cooper Rush connected with receiver Jesse Kroll, who was covered heavily by Cowboys defenders and nearly tackled. Kroll instinctively lateraled to Malik Fountain, who ran in for the game-winning touchdown. The play covered 49 yards and gave Central Michigan a thrilling 30-27 win.

Malik Fountain of Central Michigan

According to the rule book, Central Michigan should have never been awarded possession of the ball, because the penalty was on the offense and included a loss of down, an extra play should not have been added. According to Rule 3-2-3. "The period is not extended if the foul is by the team and possession and the penalty includes loss of down." Simply put, because there was no time on the clock, Central Michigan should not have gotten that extra play.

2016 - "Hail Mary - Dobbs to Jennings"

Tennessee at Georgia - Sanford Stadium - Athens, Georgia {Tennessee 34 Georgia 31}

Tennessee scored 20 points in the final quarter -- six on the final play of the game -- to upend Georgia 34-31 in yet another come-from-behind victory for the Vols. Tennessee overcame another sluggish start including two first-half turnovers for the rally. In all, three touchdowns between Tennessee and Georgia were scored in the final three minutes -- and two in the final 10 seconds.

Jauan Jennings of Tennessee game winning catch vs Georgia

It looked as though Georgia would get the win after freshman quarterback Jacob Eason hit a 47-yard, go-ahead score to Riley Ridley. However, a good return by Tennessee and a defensive offsides penalty by Georgia set up a final 43-yard attempt. That's when Joshua Dobbs completed a desperation pass to Jauan Jennings for the win on the final play of the game.

2017 – "Hail Mary – Franks to Cleveland"

Tennessee at Florida – Ben Hill Griffin Stadium – Gainesville, FL {Florida 26 Tennessee 20}

{Associated Press} Tyrie Cleveland was one of the last players to leave Florida Field. He slapped hands, posed for pictures, and just before disappearing into the locker room tunnel, he turned and waved one final time. He easily could have taken a bow. Cleveland hauled in a 63-yard touchdown pass from Feleipe Franks as time expired, and No. 24 Florida stunned 23rd-ranked Tennessee 26-20 in a wild, wacky and sometimes unwatchable rivalry game Saturday. Franks scrambled away from the rush on a first-and-10 play with 9 seconds remaining and found Cleveland behind safety Micah Abernathy for a Hail Mary that no one -- especially the Volunteers -- saw coming. The final play capped a crazy fourth

quarter in which the teams combined for 37 points and little, if any, defense. After watching Florida's offense sputter all afternoon, there surely were arm-chair quarterbacks everywhere thinking the Gators (1-1, 1-0 Southeastern Conference) should take a knee and head to overtime. Instead, they burned the Volunteers (2-1, 0-1) with a deep pass for the second time in as many visits to Gainesville. Two years ago, Will Grier found Antonio Callaway for a 63-yard touchdown on a fourth-and-12 play with 1:26 remaining that propelled Florida to a 28-27 victory. This time, the play called "Train Right Open, Big Ben In" will go down in Florida lore as one of the most memorable in school history. It gave the Gators a 12th win in the last 13 years against Tennessee and allowed them to avoid the program's first 0-2 start since 1971.

Jones surely will face more criticism for his team's questionable play-calling. Tennessee failed to get standout running back John Kelly the ball on a first-and-goal play from the 1-yard line in the third quarter and again on three first-and-goal tries from the 9 in the fourth. Tennessee also can blame three missed field goals for not being ahead late. The Gators looked as if they had the game in hand early in the final frame, but found a way to let the Volunteers get back in it. Franks made one huge mistake: An interception in Florida territory that set up Tennessee's tying field goal. The Vols failed to find the end zone and settled for three points with 50 seconds left. Overtime looked to be on tap -- and then Franks found Cleveland. Fellow receiver Brandon Powell was the first to congratulate Cleveland in the end zone. Powell slapped him so hard upside the helmet that it knocked his mouthpiece out. Teammates and coaches piled on a few seconds later. It was a surreal scene, especially for a team that didn't score an offensive touchdown in the first seven quarters of the season.

The party continued inside the locker room. There was little to remember from the first three quarters. The defenses were stout, but there were plenty of offensive blunders and head-scratching play calls. Florida led 6-3 to open the fourth and looked as if it iced the game when C.J. Henderson returned an interception 16 yards for a score. Freshman Malik Davis followed a series later with a 74-yard run. But the touchdown was overturned on review after officials realized Davis fumbled at the 2. Justin Martin caught Davis from behind and knocked the ball loose. It bounced through the end zone for a touchback.

The Vols scored five plays later, cutting it to 13-10 on Kelly's 24-yard run. But Kelly also made a huge mistake. He was flagged for unsportsmanlike conduct for doing the "Gator Chomp" in the end zone, and the penalty helped the Gators get the ball in Tennessee territory. Franks found Brandon Powell in the flat for a 5-yard score, capping a 44-yard drive that gave Florida a double-digit lead. Still, Tennessee kept coming back and figured it would end up in overtime for the second time in three games. Franks and Cleveland didn't let it happen.

2017 – "Heartbreak at Kinnick"

Penn State at Iowa – Nile Kinnick Stadium – Iowa City, Iowa {Penn State 21 Iowa 19}

{Hawkeyesports.com} One play stood between the University of Iowa football team knocking off fourth-ranked Penn State on Saturday night inside Kinnick Stadium. The Nittany Lions were down to their final play, trailing 19-15 with four seconds left in the contest. On fourth and goal from the 7, Penn State quarterback Trace McSorely connected with Juwan Johnson for the game-winning touchdown pass as time expired to send the Nittany Lions to a 21-19 victory over the upset-minded Hawkeyes. Iowa grabbed the 19-15 lead -- its first of the game -- on a 35-yard touchdown run by senior Akrum Wadley with 1:42 remaining. The Nittany Lions' final drive started from their own 20. Penn State converted a fourth-and-2 from its own 40 when McSorely hit Saeed Blacknall for a 6-yard gain and first down. After McSorely scrambled for 12 yards into Iowa territory, he completed passes of 18 and 14 yards to the 10. After a 3-yard completion on first down, Iowa forced a pair of incompletions to set up a fourth-and-goal. Following a timeout, Johnson faked to the outside before cutting in to catch the game-winning touchdown to send the Nittany Lions to a 4-0 record this season. Penn State finished with 579 yards of total offense and All-American running back Saquon Barkley was a human highlight package, finishing with 358 all-purpose yards. He had 28 rushes for 211 yards, caught 12 passes for 94 yards, and had three kick returns for 53 yards. McSorely was 31-of-48 for 284 yards and one touchdown -- the game-winner. The Hawkeye offense had 273 yards in the contest. Sophomore quarterback Nate Stanley was 13-of-22 for 191 yards and two touchdowns, and Wadley accounted for 155 yards and two touchdowns. He had 80 yards rushing on 19 attempts and four receptions for 75 yards. Following a 70-yard touchdown pass to Akrum Wadley, Penn State took over at its own 21-yard line with 10:02 left. The Nittany Lions rode Barkley down the field as the running back had 10 touches on a 16-play, 75-yard drive. After the drive stalled, Penn State sent kicker Tyler Davis in for a 31-yard field goal attempt. It came away empty when Iowa sophomore defensive end Anthony Nelson blocked the attempt to turn the momentum in Iowa's favor. The Hawkeyes followed with a quick strike attack, needing just one minute and three plays to cover 80 yards. It started with a Penn State pass interference penalty before Stanley connected with Ihmir Smith-Marsette and Matt VandeBerg for 8 and 22 yards to the Nittany Lion 35. Then Wadley broke free for a 35-yard touchdown run on a draw to give the Hawkeyes their first lead. The problem; there was still 1:42 left in the contest.

The 66,205 fans in attendance were on the edge of their seats until the 211th minute of Saturday's primetime showdown. A stop on fourth-and-goal would have sent the Hawkeyes to their second straight victory over a top-five foe and sent the Kinnick crowd into hysteria.

Instead, the stadium was stunned when Johnson broke free for the game-winning touchdown. It broke Iowa's streak of four straight night game victories in Kinnick Stadium and dropped the Hawkeyes' record to 3-1.

2017 – "It's a Buckeye Miracle"

Penn State at Ohio State – Ohio Stadium – Columbus, Ohio {Ohio State 39 Penn State 38}

{Associated Press} In the tunnel at Ohio Stadium that leads from locker room to the field, J.T. Barrett was posing for pictures with friends, receiving handshakes and hugs and thanking one older man with a scratchy voice for screaming himself hoarse. Barrett smiled and laughed. Apparently, the Ohio State quarterback even busted out some moves in the locker room celebration. The stoic fifth-year senior doesn't show much emotion on the field. And if he gained any particular gratification from playing the best game of his decorated career seven weeks after a lot of Buckeyes fans were wondering if he should be benched, he was not about to let on. This is certain: When Barrett said goodbye to his friends and left the Horseshoe on Saturday night he did so as a Heisman Trophy candidate with absolutely nothing left to prove. Barrett was near flawless against No. 2 Penn State, capping a brilliant performance with a 16-yard touchdown pass to Marcus Baugh with 1:48 left in the fourth quarter that gave No. 6 Ohio State a 39-38 victory. Buckeyes coach Urban Meyer called it one of the best games he has ever seen a quarterback play. Barrett was 33 for 39 for 328 yards and four touchdown passes, three in the fourth quarter after the Buckeyes (7-1, 5-0 Big Ten) were down 35-20. He also ran for 95 yards on 17 carries. In the fourth quarter, he was 13 for 13 for 170 yards. Terry McLaurin, who caught Barrett's first TD pass of the game, which gave the quarterback 91 in his career to break Drew Brees' Big Ten record. Penn State led 38-27 with 5:42 left and it looked as if the Nittany Lions (7-1, 4-1) were going to knock the Buckeyes out of the College Football Playoff race. Saquon Barkley scored two long touchdowns for Penn State, but it was Barrett who surged into the Heisman race in what was billed as the Big Ten game of the year and lived up to the hype.

Barrett and the Buckeyes got the ball back down five with 3:20 left. They quickly marched to the 16 and then Barrett found his big tight end Baugh for the lead.

The blackout crowd at the Horseshoe poured onto the field to celebrate after Barrett took a final knee. He calmly wandered through the mayhem. Barrett had been the target for much criticism after the Buckeyes' offense struggled in a September loss to Oklahoma. He said he just tried to get better. Barrett went 19 of 35 with no TDs and an interception against the Sooners. He looked like a different player Saturday, but he wasn't buying that. Receiver K.J. Hill said Barrett's calmness keeps the Buckeyes cool, and, yes, he does cut loose sometimes. Barkley was held to 44 yards on 21 carries, and that included a 36-yard touchdown run in the first half. And the Nittany Lions had trouble pass blocking Ohio State's talented defensive line, with Nick Bosa and Tyquan Lewis, especially after tackle Ryan Bates went out with an injury. On their final drive, quarterback Trace McSorley got pressured on each play, was sacked one and threw three incomplete passes.

2018 – "Dawgs come up smelling like Roses"

Oklahoma vs Georgia – Rose Bowl Stadium – Pasadena, California {Georgia 54 Oklahoma 48} (2 overtimes)

{Associated Press} After ending the first overtime Rose Bowl, one of the greatest Granddaddies of Them All, Sony Michel was swarmed by Georgia teammates as he broke down in tears. The senior tailback had gone from possible goat to all-time hero for Georgia, sending the Bulldogs to the national championship game with one last burst in a game full of them. Michel raced 27 yards for a touchdown in the second overtime to give No. 3 Georgia a 54-48 victory against No. 2 Oklahoma in the College Football Playoff semifinal Monday night. Michel, who had a fumble in the fourth quarter returned for a go-ahead Oklahoma touchdown, ran for 181 yards and three scores for the Bulldogs (13-1), but none bigger than the last one.

In the final game of his great career, Oklahoma's Baker Mayfield threw for 287 yards and two touchdowns, and caught a touchdown pass that gave the Sooners a 17-point lead with 6 seconds left in the first half. But the Heisman Trophy winner could not get the Sooners (12-2) into the end zone in the first overtime when a touchdown would have ended the game. The Bulldogs will play Alabama on Jan. 8 fin an all-Southeastern Conference national championship game at Mercedes-Benz Stadium in Atlanta, about 70 miles from their campus. After Georgia made its first trip to the Rose Bowl since 1943 a heart-stopping success, the Bulldogs will play for their first national title since 1980. The 104th Rose Bowl was also the highest-scoring, surpassing last year's 52-49 USC victory against Penn State. There was a lot more on the line in this one, the first CFP game to go to overtime as well. After an offside penalty on Georgia gave Oklahoma a first down on third-and-five in the second OT possession, the Sooners stalled again and Austin Seibert came out for a 27-yard field goal. Leaping through the line, Lorenzo Carter got his outstretched hand on the kick and the ball fluttered down short of the uprights. Any score would have ended it for the Bulldogs, and on the second play Michel slipped one tackle and was home free. The Bulldogs sprinted off the sideline and toward the corner of the end zone to mob Michel. Confetti rained down. Meanwhile, Mayfield stood motionless on the sideline for several seconds, bent over with his hands on his knees and head down. Mayfield battled flu-like symptoms the week leading into the game, but he played just fine. Michel and his roommate and running mate Nick Chubb were awesome for Georgia. Chubb ran for 145 yards and two touchdowns, including a 2-yarder on a direct snap with 55 seconds left in regulation to tie it. The Sooners had taken a 45-38 lead when Steven Parker returned Michel's fumble for a TD with 6:52 left in the fourth. Both teams settled for field goals in the first overtime. First, Georgia's Rodrigo Blankenship hit from 38 to make it 48-45. Then it was Mayfield's turn. A touchdown would have sent the Sooners to Atlanta, but on a third-and-2 from the 17 Georgia All-America linebacker Roquan Smith nailed Jordan Smallwood a yard short of the first down. Seibert kicked a 33-yarder and the Bulldogs and Sooners played on, but not for much longer.

2018 – "The Pass"

2018 CFP Championship Game – Mercedes-Benz Stadium – Atlanta, Georgia {Alabama 26 Georgia 23} (Overtime)

 {Associated Press} To add another championship to the greatest dynasty college football has ever seen, Alabama turned to its quarterback of the future, and Tua Tagovailoa proved that his time is now. The freshman quarterback, who had played mostly mop-up duty this season, came off the bench to spark a comeback and threw a 41-yard touchdown to DeVonta Smith that gave No. 4 Alabama a 26-23 overtime victory against No. 3 Georgia on Monday night for the College Football Playoff national championship.

 Tagovailoa entered the game at halftime, replacing a struggling Jalen Hurts, and threw three touchdown passes to give the Crimson Tide its fifth national championship since 2009 under Coach Nick Saban. The Tide might have a quarterback controversy ahead, but first Alabama will celebrate another title. For the third straight season, Alabama played a classic CFP final. The Tide split two with Clemson, losing last season on a touchdown with a second left. Smith streaked into the end zone and moments later confetti rained and even Saban seemed almost giddy after watching maybe the most improbable victory of his unmatched career. A few hours later, Alabama was voted No. 1 in the final AP college football poll for the 11th time, three more than any other program. After Alabama kicker Andy Pappanastos missed a 36-yard field goal that would have won it for the Tide (13-1) in the final seconds of regulation, Georgia (13-2) took the lead with a 51-yard field goal from Rodrigo Blankenship in overtime.

 Tagovailoa took a terrible sack on Alabama's first play, losing 16 yards. On the next he found Smith, another freshman, and hit him in stride for the national championship. Tagovailoa was brilliant at times, though he had a few freshman moments. He threw an interception when he tried to pass on a running play and all his receivers were blocking. He also darted away from pass rushers and made some impeccable throws, showing poise of a veteran. Facing fourth-and-goal from the 7, down seven, the left-hander moved to his left and zipped a pass through traffic that hit Calvin Ridley in the numbers for the tying score with 3:49 left in the fourth quarter. He finished 14 for 24 for 166 yards. The winning play was, basically, four receivers going deep. Freshmen were everywhere for the Alabama offense in the second half: Najee Harris at running back; Henry Ruggs III at receiver; Alex Leatherwood at left tackle after All-American Jonah Williams was hurt. It's a testament to the relentless machine Saban has built.

 But this game will be remembered most for his decision to change quarterbacks trailing 13-0. Saban now has six major poll national championships, including one at LSU, matching the record set by the man who led Alabama's last dynasty, coach Paul Bear Bryant. This was nothing like the others. With President Trump in attendance, the all-Southeastern Conference matchup was all Georgia in the first half before Saban pulled Hurts and the five-star recruit from Hawaii entered. The president watched the second half from Air Force One. The Tide trailed 20-7 in the third quarter after Georgia's freshman quarterback, Jake Fromm, hit Mecole Hardman for an 80-yard touchdown pass that had the Georgia fans feeling good about ending a national title drought that dates back to 1980. Fromm threw for 232 yards and for a while it looked as if he was going to be the freshman star of the game, the first to true freshman to lead his team to a national title season since Jamelle Holieway for Oklahoma in 1985.

 A little less than a year after the Atlanta Falcons blew a 25-point lead and lost in overtime to the New England Patriots in the Super Bowl, there was more pain for many of the local fans. Two years ago, Georgia brought in Smart, Saban's top lieutenant, to bring to his alma mater a dose of Alabama's Process.

Smart, who spent 11 seasons with Saban -- eight as defensive coordinator in Tuscaloosa -- quickly built `Bama East. It was Georgia that won the SEC this season. Alabama had to slip into the playoff without even winning its division.

With the title game being played 70 miles from Georgia's campus in Athens, Dawgs fans packed Mercedes-Benz Stadium, but it turned out to be sweet home for Alabama. Now Saban is 12-0 against his former assistants. But not without angst. Alabama drove into the red zone in the final minute and Saban started playing for a winning field goal to end the game. A nervous quiet gripped the crowd of 77,430 as `Bama burned the clock. With the ball spotted in the middle of the field, Pappanastos lined up for a kick to win the national championship. The snap and hold looked fine, but the kicked missed badly to the left.

For the second straight week, Georgia was going to overtime. The Bulldogs beat Oklahoma in a wild Rose Bowl in double overtime to get here, and after Jonathan Ledbetter and Davin Bellamy sacked Tagovailoa for a big loss on the first play, Alabama was in trouble -- second-and-26. Not for long. Tagovailoa looked off the safety and threw the biggest touchdown pass in the history of Alabama football.

2018 – "Will it ever End"

LSU @ Texas A&M – Kyle Field – College Station, Texas {Texas A&M 74 LSU 72} (7 overtimes)

{Associated Press} With Texas A&M's game with No. 8 LSU tied at 72-72 in the seventh overtime on Saturday night and the Aggies set to attempt a 2-point conversion, receiver Kendrick Rogers was frantically being tended to on the sideline for severe cramps in his calves. Rogers was able to get himself together just in time to get back in the game and grab Kellen Mond's 2-point conversion pass that gave A&M at 74-72 victory in a game that tied the NCAA record for most overtimes in an FBS game. Mond connected with Quartney Davis on a 17-yard throw to tie it at 72. Greedy Williams was called for pass interference on the first 2-point conversion try, giving the Aggies (8-4, 5-3, No. 22 CFP), another shot. After a false start by Texas A&M, Mond found Rogers for the conversion to end it.

Throngs of fans rushed the field to celebrate after the grab by Rogers. Joe Burrow had a 10-yard TD run to put LSU (9-3, 5-3, No. 7 CFP) up 72-66 in the seventh OT, but his 2-point conversion throw failed. The 74 points LSU allowed are the most ever given up by a ranked team, eclipsing the 73 No. 24 Fresno State gave up to Northern Illinois on Oct. 6, 1990, and the first seven overtime game involving a ranked team. The 146 combined points are the most in an FBS game in NCAA history and the second-most in college football history behind the 161 points Abilene Christian and West Texas A&M scored in Abilene Christian's 93-68 win in 2008. Mond threw for 287 yards and six touchdowns, three 2-point conversions and ran for one more TD as Texas A&M snapped a seven-game skid against LSU and got its first win over the Tigers since 1995. LSU coach Ed Orgeron's clothes might have already dried by the time this one ended after he was prematurely doused with Gatorade after the Tigers appeared to have a clinching interception in the fourth quarter. But the play was reviewed and it was ruled that Mond's knee was down before the throw, keeping the Aggies alive and setting up the wild finish. Burrow threw for three touchdowns and ran for three more as the Tigers were denied their first 10-win regular season since 2012 and likely knocked out of contention for a New Year's Day bowl game. Mond threw a 25-yard TD pass to Jace Sternberger and a 2-point conversion to Rogers in sextuple overtime before Burrow had a 4-yard touchdown run and Burrow ran for a 4-yard TD and threw for the 2-point conversion to push it to a seventh OT. Clyde Edwards-Helaire took a pitch from Burrow and launched an 11-yard TD pass to Tory Carter to put the Tigers on top in the fifth overtime, but the 2-point conversion failed. Mond answered with a 6-yard throw to Rogers, but A&M's 2-point try failed, too to send it to the sixth OT. Mond found

Davis on a 19-yard touchdown pass on the last play of regulation to send it to OT. Orgeron felt like the clock ran out before Mond spiked the ball to stop the clock with 1 second to allow for that play. Both teams kicked field goals in the fourth overtime to send it to the fifth. Burrow threw a 25-yard touchdown pass to Dee Anderson in triple overtime and Justin Jefferson grabbed the 2-point conversion. Rogers made it 49-49 and forced quadruple overtime when he grabbed a 25-yard TD pass and the 2-point conversion. Both teams settled for field goals in the first overtime. Mond had a 3-yard touchdown run in double overtime and LSU sent it to triple OT when Nick Brossette followed with a 3-yard run, too. This was a game for the ages and one that both teams will remember for a long time.

Chapter Five – Epic Failures

This chapter is dedicated to the games where teams had large leads and couldn't hold them. Defense was not a priority for these teams, obviously! These games are some of the biggest blown leads in college football history.

1984 - "Epic Fail #1" {Salisbury State-Randolph-Macon} (33 points)
Salisbury State at Randolph-Macon - Day Field - Ashland, Virginia {Salisbury State 34 Randolph-Macon 33}

Randolph-Macon raced out to a 33-0 lead in the first quarter. Yes, 33 points scored in the first quarter, but they could not hold on to the lead, as Salisbury State roared back with 34 unanswered points, to stun the Yellow Jackets in front of their home crowd.

1984 - "Epic Failure #2" {Maryland-Miami} (31 points)
Maryland at Miami - The Orange Bowl - Miami, Florida {Maryland 42 Miami 40}

Maryland backup quarterback Frank Reich threw six touchdown passes against the University of Miami in the second half of the Orange Bowl. The Terrapins, who had been losing 31-0 at the half, ended up winning the game 42-40. In the first two quarters of the game, Miami outgained the Terps 328 yards to 57 and ran up their 31-point lead–but they didn't do it graciously.

For the second half, Maryland's coach replaced first-string quarterback Stan Gelbaugh with Reich, who had a steady, consistent arm. The new QB completed 12 of 15 passes and gained 260 yards. In the third quarter, he threw two touchdown passes and ran a third in himself to cut Miami's lead to 34-21. In the fourth, he drove 55 yards in nine plays, and his teammate Tommy Neal scored a 14-yard touchdown to make the score 34-28. Then, with about nine and a half minutes left to play, Reich threw a long pass that glanced off Miami safety Darrell Fullington's hands and landed in Maryland player Greg Hill's, who ran it in for another touchdown. The score was 35-34, and the Terps had the lead. Then Miami fumbled the kickoff and Maryland's Rick Badanjek grabbed the ball and scored again. Now the Terrapins were winning 42-34. For a minute, it looked like Reich's luck had run out–Miami got the ball after a bad punt snap and scored a quick touchdown, making the score 42-40–but Terp Keeta Covington prevented the two-point conversion and preserved Maryland's miraculous victory. Maryland quarterback Frank Reich went on to play in the NFL and in a 1993 AFC playoff game, led the Buffalo Bills back from a 35 point deficit to defeat the Houston Oilers, 41-38. It was like Déjà vu all over again!

1989 - "Epic Failure #3" {Minnesota-Ohio State} (31 points)
Ohio State at Minnesota - HHH Metrodome - Minneapolis, Minnesota {Ohio State 41 Minnesota 38}

The Buckeyes came back from a 31-0 deficit to stun the Golden Gophers, 41-37. Unfortunately for Golden Gopher fans, this would not be the last game where Minnesota would "Snatch defeat from the jaws of victory".

The Buckeyes just couldn't get anything going. After a sack that resulted in a Greg Frey fumble that was recovered by the Gophers on the Ohio State 22-yard line, Minnesota extended their lead to 10-0 -- and it got worse from there. The Gophers' pass rush consistently disrupted Frey, turnovers and missed opportunities haunted Ohio State, and at the end of the first quarter Ohio State had eight yards of total offense and trailed 17-0. The Gophers piled on, taking advantage of Buckeye mistakes and extending their lead to 31-0 with 4:29 remaining in the first half. Things were looking grim for the Buckeyes. But it only takes one mental mistake to swing the momentum of a game, and Minnesota was penalized for having 12 men on the field during an Ohio State punt, giving the Buckeyes a fresh set of downs on their own 35-yard line. A pass interference call against the Gophers gave the Buckeyes another boost, and after the Gophers held them on third down, giving Ohio State a fourth and one at the Minnesota one-yard line, Carlos Snow was able to roll it into the end zone for the Buckeyes' first points of the day. A two-point conversion attempt was successful, cutting Minnesota's lead to 31-8. On their next possession the Buckeyes added a field goal, making it a three-possession game with plenty of time remaining.

The Buckeyes forced a fumble - Minnesota's first of the 1989 season -- and recovered on the Minnesota 23, but then promptly threw an interception. The defense forced a Gopher punt that was downed at the one-yard line, and the Buckeyes took it all the way down the field to score. By the end of the third quarter they had narrowed the deficit to 31-18. The game was within reach with a quarter to play.

The Gophers added a field goal and extended their lead to 16 with 11:24 remaining in the game, but the Buckeyes were undeterred. On their next possession, another Carlos Snow touchdown and a successful two-point conversion, also from Snow, made it 34-26. The Buckeyes defense, surely energized by the offensive turnaround, forced a three-and-out, but a miscommunication between center Greg Beatty and Greg Frey resulted in a fumbled snap, Ohio State's sixth turnover in that game, and the Gophers recovered. Another Minnesota field goal extended their lead to 37-26. On the Buckeyes' next drive, a holding call negated a touchdown pass and the Buckeyes found themselves in a third-and-goal situation from the 18 yard line. A 17-yard pass put the Buckeyes on the one-yard line, and head Coach John Cooper decided to go for it on fourth down. Frey scored on a quarterback keeper, and another successful two-point conversion brought the Buckeyes within three points of the Gophers. The defense forced a three-and-out on the most critical series of the game, forcing the Gophers to punt and giving the Ohio State offense a little under two minutes to secure a win. And that's precisely what the Buckeyes did. They drove down the field and added a touchdown, and with the successful PAT, established a four-point lead over the Gophers. Minnesota had 15 seconds remaining to try to get the win, but they were unable to do so. At the time, the Buckeyes erasing a 31-point deficit was tied for the biggest comeback win in college football history.

1993 - "Epic Failure #4" {California-Oregon} (30 points)
Oregon at California - Memorial Stadium - Berkeley, California {California 42 Oregon 41}

Dave Barr threw for three second-half touchdowns, including a 26-yarder to Iheanyi Uwaezuoke with 1 minute 17 seconds left as No. 17 California rallied from a 30-0 deficit to beat Oregon, 42-41. It was the biggest comeback in Cal history, surpassing a 29-28 victory against Arizona on Nov. 4, 1989, in which the Golden Bears overcame a 21-0 deficit. Uwaezuoke's catch culminated a 9-play, 85-yard drive, but Cal still trailed by 1 point. The Bears elected to go for the 2-point conversion, and Barr found Mike Caldwell in the corner of the end zone to complete the stunning second-half turnaround in which Cal outscored Oregon, 35-11.

Barr finished with 368 yards, completing 21 of 31 throws. His two other touchdown passes went to Damien Semien, who caught 7 for 182 yards. Oregon had a final chance to regain the lead, but O'Neil's pass was intercepted by Artis Houston with 29 seconds to play and Cal ran out the clock.

2001 - "Epic Failure #5" {2001 GMAC Bowl} {30 points}
East Carolina vs Marshall - Ladd-Peebles Stadium - Mobile, Alabama {Marshall 64 East Carolina 61}

This game featured what was then the biggest comeback (at the time) in NCAA Division I-A (now FBS) bowl history, as Marshall came back from a 38-8 halftime deficit to force overtime and eventually win 64-61 in double overtime. It was also the highest-scoring bowl game in history. The 2001 GMAC Bowl remains the highest-scoring bowl game ever.

Franklin Wallace of Marshall

Byron Leftwich turned a nightmarish start for 25th-ranked Marshall into one of the most memorable finishes in NCAA football history. Leftwich tossed an eight-yard touchdown pass to Josh

Davis in the second overtime as the Thundering Herd rallied from a 30-point halftime deficit to stun East Carolina, 64-61, in the GMAC Bowl. With no timeouts, Marshall drove 80 yards in the final minute of regulation and tied it at 51-51 when Leftwich threw an 11-yard TD pass to Darius Watts, who made a leaping grab in the right corner of the end zone with seven seconds left. The Thundering Herd got the first possession of overtime and took a 58-51 lead on Frank Wallace's two-yard run. The Pirates needed only one play to pull even as Travis Henry scored on a 25-yard dash. East Carolina got the ball first in the second overtime but had to settle for Kevin Miller's 37-yard field goal. Leftwich went to work again, hitting Denero Marriott for 21 yards to the 4. After a pair of running plays lost four yards, Leftwich found Davis in the middle of the end zone for the winning score.

2006 - "Epic Failure #6" {2006 Insight Bowl} (31 points)

Insight Bowl - Minnesota vs Texas Tech - Sun Devil Stadium - Tempe, Arizona {Texas Tech 44 Minnesota 41}

This game is tied for the biggest comeback in NCAA Division I FBS bowl history. The Red Raiders, after falling behind 38-7 with 7:47 remaining in the third quarter, rallied to score 31 unanswered points to send the game to overtime. The Gophers scored a field goal in overtime, but the Red Raiders responded with a touchdown to win. Two days after his team's loss in the Insight Bowl, Minnesota head coach Glen Mason was fired. This was the latest in a series of Minnesota second-half collapses under Mason, which also included one of the previous three biggest bowl collapses in Division I-A history.

The Golden Gophers jumped ahead 7-0 after Texas Tech Coach Mike Leach went for it on fourth-and-1 at his own 45. Harrell was stopped on a sneak, and six plays later Cupito found tight end Jack Simmons for a 2-yard touchdown with 9:27 to go in the first quarter. Four minutes later, Minnesota made it 14-0 after linebacker Mike Sherels intercepted Harrell at Tech's 37. Pinnix capped a six-play drive with a 2-yard run. Another Harrell turnover killed a Tech scoring drive. He fumbled on a sack by Willie VanDeSteeg, and Steve Davis recovered at the Golden Gophers' 13. Minnesota marched 87 yards -- its longest scoring drive of the year -- to take a 21-0 lead on Justin Valentine's 1-yard plunge on the first play of the second quarter. Tech had a chance to slice the deficit when cornerback Antonio Huffman picked off Cupito's pass at the Minnesota 20. But Pinnix jarred the ball loose, and it bounced into the end zone, where the Gophers recovered for a touchback. After Tech's Shannon Woods scored from 1 yard out to make it 28-7, the Gophers answered with an 81-yard drive that ended in a 3-yard touchdown pass from Cupito to Logan Payne in the final minute of the first half. Minnesota looked as if it ended any Tech hopes for a comeback by opening the third quarter with a 16-play, 78-yard drive that consumed 7:13. Joel Monroe's 20-yard field goal gave the Gophers a 38-7 lead. The Red Raiders mounted a furious comeback, scoring 31 unanswered points in less than 20 minutes. Alex Trlica's 52-yard field goal as regulation expired sent the game into overtime. Tech's comeback began with 4:58 to go in the third quarter, when Graham Harrell hit Joel Filani for a 43-yard score to cut the lead to 38-14. That touchdown started an avalanche that helped beat Minnesota. Trailing 38-35 with no timeouts, the Red Raiders took over at their own 11 with 1:06 remaining. Eight plays later, Trlica tied it.

2007 - "Epic Fail #7" {Abilene Christian-Chadron State} (29 points)

Abilene Christian at Chadron State - Elliot Field - Chadron, Nebraska {Chadron State 76 Abilene Christian 73}

Abilene Christian looked to be on their way to advancing to the quarterfinals of the 2007 NCAA Division II football playoffs over Chadron State. The Wildcats jumped out to a 49-20 lead with 2:49 left to play in the third quarter. Abilene Christian tailback Bernard Scott single-handedly carried the Wildcats in the first three quarters, rushing for 303 yards and five touchdowns on the game. In the third quarter alone, Scott broke off runs of 55 and 90 yards, which one would think would have secured the win. Alas, it was not to be.

Isaac Stockton of Chadron State

Joe McLain flipping in for the winning touchdown

Joe McLain would throw the first of his four fourth quarter touchdown passes (22 yards to Joel Schommer) two plays after the Chadron defense forced a three-and-out just one minute into the fourth quarter and the comeback was on. A Josh Knouse interception set up a McLain to Danny Woodhead 16 yard touchdown strike to cut the Abilene Christian lead to 49-34 with 13:13 left in regulation. The Wildcats would respond with a Billy Malone touchdown pass to Kendall Holloway to make it 56-34, but the Eagles would score three touchdowns and a field goal in the final 11 minutes of regulation to force overtime. The teams would trade touchdowns in the first two overtime possessions before Abilene's Matt Adams kicked a 21 yard field goal to give the Wildcats a 73-70 lead. The Eagles took advantage of the defensive stand, as Woodhead's 13 yard run setup McLain's game winning 12 yard touchdown run, completing what was, at the time, the largest comeback win in D2 football history.

2011 - "Epic Fail #8" {Bloomsburg-West Chester} (35 points)
Bloomsburg at West Chester - John Farrell Stadium - West Chester, Pennsylvania {Bloomsburg 55 West Chester 42}

Undefeated Bloomsburg spoiled West Chester's 2011 Homecoming in spectacular, though it didn't look possible after the first 20 minutes of the game. The Golden Rams scored touchdowns on each of their first five possessions, with Brian McDermott and Rondell White each scoring a pair of touchdowns to help give West Chester a 35-0 lead with 10:29 left in the second quarter. And then, Bloomsburg decided to show and, well, be Bloomsburg. Unlike most come-from-behind wins, where the trailing team is likely to pass like crazy, the Huskies went with their run game, answering West Chester's fifth touchdown with a nine play drive - six rushes, three pass attempts - capped off by Franklyn Quiteh's 11 yard touchdown run with 6:45 left in the half. Bloomsburg would score on five of their next six possessions (the sixth possession ended at halftime) to tie the game in the third quarter. West Chester forced a three-and-out and took possession with 5:41 left in the third and the ball at their 22. J.P. Patrick picked off a Matt Carroll pass three plays later and took it 31 yards for the go-ahead touchdown with 4:26 left in the third to make it 42-35 Bloomsburg. The Huskies would add a pair of field goals and an Eddie Mateo touchdown before the Golden Rams added a late fourth quarter score. But, by that time, most of the crowd of 6,502 inside Farrell Stadium - at least the fans on the home side - were in shock over West Chester's collapse.

2015 - "Epic Fail #9" {Adams State-Western State} (36 points)
Western State at Adams State - Rex Stadium - Alamoso, Colorado {Adams State 52 Western State 51}

Western State dominated the first half, leading Adams State 42-6 in the closing seconds of first half in the annual Colorado Classic rivalry game. Unfortunately for the Mountaineers, they played the second half. The Grizzlies started to pick up momentum coming into halftime after Auston Hillman's 37 yard touchdown pass to Chad Hovasse closed out the first half and cut the Mountaineers lead to 42-13. Adams State would score a pair of touchdowns in the third quarter and another two in the fourth quarter, as Hillman's 5 yard touchdown pass to James Holtrop with 30 seconds left tied the game, setting up overtime.

The teams traded field goals in the first overtime, but Hillman and Holtrop connected again in the second overtime, this time from 24 yards out, to give the Grizzlies a 52-45 lead. The Mountaineers would answer with a Brett Arrivey 3 yard touchdown pass to Kyle Adkins to make it 52-51. The Adams State defense successfully defended Arrivey's two point conversion attempt to complete the comeback.

2016 - "Epic Failure #10" {2016 Alamo Bowl} (31 points)
Alamo Bowl - Oregon vs TCU - Alamodome - San Antonio, Texas {TCU 47 Oregon 41}

The Horned Frogs trailed 31-0 at halftime, but an injury to Oregon Quarterback Vernon Adams Jr. just before the halftime break would result in a scoreless second half for the Ducks. TCU scored on all 9 possessions after halftime, completing the comeback in the second half with a late field goal. The two teams traded touchdowns in the first overtime and field goals in the second. The Horned Frogs scored in the third extra period, failed their 2 point conversion, but held the Ducks out of the end zone. The 31-point comeback tied the largest comeback in NCAA college football bowl game history with the 2006 Insight Bowl. Thrust into the starting role in place of the suspended star Quarterback, TCU's Bram Kohlhausen made the absolute most of his final chance with the Horned Frogs -- in historic

fashion. Starting in place of Trevone Boykin, who was suspended after a bar fight two days earlier, Kohlhausen led the No. 11 Horned Frogs back from 31 points down for a 47-41, triple-overtime victory over No. 15 Oregon on Saturday night in the Alamo Bowl. Kohlhausen passed for 351 yards and accounted for four touchdowns, running in for the winner in the third overtime.

Down 31-0 at halftime, TCU coach Gary Patterson changed shirts and his team changed gears, racing for 31 second-half points. It didn't look possible when Oregon (9-4) was rolling to a 28-0 lead behind standout senior Quarterback Vernon Adams Jr., and led 31-0 at halftime. Adams passed for 197 yards and a touchdown and led the Ducks on four consecutive touchdown drives, eluding sacks and throwing downfield as Oregon rolled early. But Oregon stopped in its tracks when Adams was hurt on a rare called run for him. Adams knocked heads with TCU linebacker Derrick Kindred, left the game and never returned. Jeff Lockie drove Oregon to a field goal that made it 31-0 at halftime, but the Ducks stalled there. TCU scored on all of its possessions in the second half and overtime... The Horned Frogs started their march back with 17 points in the third quarter, twice scoring touchdowns on fourth down. Kohlhausen threw a touchdown pass to Jaelen Austin, then ran 2 yards for his first score. Jaden Oberkrom's 22-yard field goal with 19 seconds left tied it, and TCU scored first in the first overtime when Kohlhausen hit Emanauel Porter for a 7-yard touchdown. Oregon answered with Royce Freeman's third touchdown run. After the teams exchanged field goals in the second overtime, Kohlhausen sneaked around the right end on an option, and seemingly disappeared behind his blockers until he was in the end zone. TCU's 2-point conversion pass attempt failed, but Oregon's final chance to tie and keep the game going ended with an incomplete pass on fourth down near the goal line.

2016 - "Epic Failure #11" {Fresno State-Tulsa} (31 points)
Tulsa at Fresno State - Bulldog Stadium - Fresno, California {Tulsa 48 Fresno State 41}

Tulsa not only overcame a 31-point first-half deficit, but also rallied to tie the game with 1:09 left to send it to overtime. The Golden Hurricane rallied in dramatic fashion, completing the largest comeback victory in program history and surpassing 20-point rallies against Oklahoma State in 1995 and

Arkansas in 1971. Fresno State led 31-0 with 10 minutes, 16 seconds left in the second quarter. Both teams failed to score in the first overtime session as Fresno State fumbled and Tulsa missed a field goal. In a thrilling 48-41 win in double overtime, Tulsa QB Dane Evans provided the winning touchdown against Fresno State. On 3rd-and-3 on the first series of the second overtime, Evans perfectly executed a fake handoff, racing 18 yards up the middle, diving into the end zone, for what proved to be the winning score.

The Tulsa defense held Fresno State on downs. After a field goal from Redford Jones had tied the game at 41 with a minute left in regulation, TU was gifted a fumble on Fresno State's possession to open the first overtime but came up empty on its series and Jones missed a long field goal. The Hurricane picked up no yards on the first play of its second-overtime drive, then lost yardage because of a false start. Evans found Justin Hobbs for a 12-yard gain, and TU faced third-and-3 when Evans scored on his 18-yard run.

2017 – "Epic Failure #12 {Texas A&M-UCLA} (34 points)
Texas A&M at UCLA – Rose Bowl Stadium – Pasadena, CA {UCLA 45 Texas A&M 44}

{Associated Press} UCLA practiced a fake spike last week, never imagining that it would cap off the biggest comeback in school history. Josh Rosen faked the spike and threw a 10-yard touchdown pass to Jordan Lasley with 43 seconds remaining and UCLA overcame a 34-point deficit to stun Texas A&M 45-44 on Sunday night. Rosen was 35 of 59 for 491 yards and four fourth-quarter touchdowns, and Jalen Starks and Soso Jamabo had scoring runs for the Bruins in the opener for both teams. UCLA overcame a deficit of more than 20 points for the first time since overcoming a 22-0 hole in the first quarter of the 2005 Sun Bowl against Northwestern. Rosen threw for 292 yards and the four scoring passes in the final 15 minutes to overcome a 27-point margin. UCLA scored touchdowns on five straight possessions after trailing 44-10 with 4:08 to play in the third quarter. Rosen threw touchdown passes of 9 and 42 yards to Darren Andrews before finding Theo Howard for a 16-yard score on a broken play with 3:08 remaining. UCLA got the ball back with 2:39 to go and drove 66 yards in 10 plays, including an 11-yard throw and catch to tight end Caleb Wilson. Rosen capped the remarkable comeback with a fade to the far corner of the end zone after faking the spike to freeze the defense. JJ Molson kicked the winning extra point. The intent of the fake was to catch Texas A&M off guard, but the Aggies were already discombobulated by a series of breakdowns that had allowed UCLA back into the game. The most memorable happened when cornerback Deshawn Capers-Smith was in position to intercept Rosen's pass, only for it to sail through his hands to Andrews for the 42-yard strike that cut it to 44-31 with 8:12 to play. Braden Mann also had a 43-yard field goal with 4:41 remaining tipped by defensive back Adarius Pickett. Rosen threw for the third-most yards in a game in school history.

Texas A&M quarterback Kellen Mond was stopped short of the first-down marker on a scramble with 20 seconds left to close out the biggest FBS comeback since 2006. Wilson had 15 receptions for 203 yards, and Andrews had 12 catches for 147 yards. Trayveon Williams rushed for 203 yards and two touchdowns, and Keith Ford added 114 yards rushing and three touchdowns for Texas A&M. The Aggies lost for only the second time in six openers under coach Kevin Sumlin. Rosen spent much of the game under constant pressure from Texas A&M for the second straight season until mounting the stunning comeback. After being sacked five times last season in a 31-24 overtime loss at College Station, Rosen was dropped three times and lost two fumbles in his return after missing the final six games last year with a shoulder injury.

Texas A&M had largely dominated the line of scrimmage on both sides of the ball before melting down, rushing for 382 yards and limiting UCLA to 70 yards on the ground. Williams had a 72-yard run where he bounced outside and raced down the UCLA sideline, which set up a 2-yard rushing touchdown by Ford, and the sophomore added a 61-yard scoring run late in the first half.

Redshirt freshman Nick Starkel got the start at quarterback for Texas A&M, and completed his first three throws during an 11-play, 75-yard drive that ended with a 5-yard touchdown run by Ford. The touted freshman Mond entered the game on the sixth possession for Texas A&M and played the entire second half after Starkel suffered an apparent left foot injury. Starkel returned to the sideline on crutches with his foot in a walking boot. Mond was 3 of 17 for 27 yards and rushed for 55 yards on 15 carries, and Starkel was 6 of 13 for 62 yards.

2018 – "Epic Failure #13" {Oregon State-Colorado} {28 points}
Oregon State at Colorado – Folsom Field – Boulder, Colorado {Oregon State 41 Colorado 34 overtime}

{Associated Press} When Travon McMillian ran 75 yards for a touchdown against Oregon State on the first play of the second half, the Colorado Buffaloes admittedly let up, as did their fans. Why not? It was 31-3. The Buffs are about to go bowling. The Beavers are getting bowled over again. Fans figured they might want to enjoy a beautiful autumn afternoon, streaming to the gates for an early exit from this blowout rather than watching any more of the Beavers' 23rd consecutive road loss.

Jack Colletto's 1-yard sneak in the extra period gave Oregon State its first lead and the Beavers' defense held on four downs inside the 7 to give first-year head coach Jonathan Smith his first league victory. It was Jake Luton who rallied the Beavers from a 28-point second-half deficit but they wouldn't have their first road win since 2014 without Colletto, who returned from an awful first half in his first career start to score twice on keepers to keep the comeback alive.

2019 – "Epic Failure #14" {UCLA-Washington State} {32 points}
UCLA at Washington State – Martin Stadium – Pullman, Washington {UCLA 67 Washington State 63}

{**Associated Press**} Coach Chip Kelly says he never lost faith in his UCLA team, even as it lost its first three games. Kelly said the Bruins played hard all 12 quarters of those losses, and that paid dividends when they fell behind at No. 19 Washington State on Saturday. Dorian Thompson-Robinson threw a 15-yard touchdown pass to Demetric Felton with 1:07 left in the game as UCLA overcame a 32-point second-half deficit to claim a wild 67-63 victory over the Cougars. The Bruins overcame a record nine TD passes by Washington State's Anthony Gordon. After Felton's TD, Gordon was sacked and fumbled -- the team's sixth turnover of the game -- on the next possession with about a minute remaining, and UCLA recovered and ran out the clock. Thompson-Robinson threw for 507 yards and five touchdowns for UCLA. Gordon threw for 570 yards and broke the school record with nine TD passes for Washington State.

Easop Winston Jr. was Gordon's favorite target. He caught four touchdown passes for Washington State. Washington State jumped to a 35-17 lead at halftime and pushed that to 49-17 early in the third quarter. But UCLA, which failed to score more than 14 points in each of its three losses, stormed back, erupting for three touchdowns in the final four minutes of the third. That was part of a run of seven touchdowns in eight possessions, many fueled by WSU turnovers. Thompson-Robinson ran for one touchdown and threw scoring passes to Chase Cota and Felton to bring the Bruins within 49-38. In the fourth, Thompson-Robinson hit Devin Asiasi with a 7-yard touchdown pass and then found Cota for a two-point conversion pass to bring UCLA within 49-46 with 14:28 left in the game. Gordon broke the WSU touchdown record with his eighth, a 33-yarder to Winston, for a 56-46 lead with 10:08 left. Thompson-Robinson ran over from the 3 to cut WSU's lead to 56-53 with 8:10 left. Washington State was forced to punt, and Kyle Philips returned it 69 yards for a touchdown, putting the Bruins ahead 60-56 with 7:31 left. But Max Borghi caught a short pass from Gordon and ran 65 yards for a touchdown and a 63-60 lead with 6:11 left. That set the stage for the winning touchdown.

On the first series of the game, UCLA linebacker Josh Woods intercepted a Gordon pass. Thompson-Robinson hit Joshua Kelley on a 14-yard touchdown pass for a 7-0 lead. Gordon replied by finding Winston with a 4-yard touchdown pass. The Bruins replied with a 31-yard field goal by JJ Molson for a 10-7 lead. Washington State scored four touchdowns in the second quarter, beginning with Gordon's 28-yard pass to Winston, to take control. Gordon found Travell Harris for a 10-yard touchdown pass and a 21-10 lead. Felton returned the ensuing kickoff 100 yards for a touchdown as the Bruins pulled within 21-17. Gordon replied with short touchdown passes to Winston and Tay Martin for a 35-17 lead that stood at halftime. In the third, Gordon hit Renard Bell and Dezmon Patmon for touchdowns and a 49-17 lead.

2019 – "Epic Failure #15" {Oklahoma-Baylor} {25 points}
Oklahoma at Baylor – Baylor Stadium – Waco, Texas {Oklahoma 34 Baylor 31}

Charlie Brewer threw two touchdown passes to Denzel Mims and ran for two more in the first half when the Bears jumped out to a 28-3 lead. Gabe Brkic kicked a 31-yard field goal with 1:45 left after Jalen Hurts threw four touchdown passes in a big comeback, where the Sooners trailed by 25 points in the first half, and No. 10 Oklahoma kept its playoff hopes alive and ended No. 12 Baylor's bid for an undefeated season, beating the Bears 34-31 on Saturday night. While the Sooners were without standout receiver CeeDee Lamb, Hurts was 30-of-42 passing for 297 yards with all of his TDs coming after Baylor took a 28-3 lead early in the second quarter. The quarterback, who had three turnovers, also ran for 114 yards. Baylor, which had its 11-game winning streak snapped, joined No. 7 Minnesota in losing their first games Saturday. The only remaining undefeated FBS teams are No. 1 LSU, No. 2 Ohio State and No. 3 Clemson. Oklahoma erased a three-touchdown halftime deficit and tied the game at 31-all on Hurts' 2-yard TD pass to Brayden Willis with 5:25 left. The Bears had run only seven plays for 35 yards in the second half until that point, and their only first down had been on a play when JaMycal Hasty fumbled, and then punted again. The Bears had one more chance after the field goal. They got to the Sooners 40 before linebacker Nik Bonitto's interception with 29 seconds left.